The Complexity of Human Thought

Robert Leve

The Complexity of Human Thought

Springer

Robert Leve
University of Hartford
West Hartford, CT, USA

ISBN 978-3-031-09103-2 ISBN 978-3-031-09104-9 (eBook)
https://doi.org/10.1007/978-3-031-09104-9

This Springer imprint is published by the registered company Springer Nature Switzerland AG
The registered company address is: Gewerbestrasse 11, 6330 Cham, Switzerland

For my Uncle, Morris Leve
A World War II fighter pilot
He died so others might live
Nuenen Holland still remembers him
For Victoria Leve
While I was writing, she learned
ancient Greek

Preface

Many people never read a book preface as they are impatient to get to the substance of the book, and I must confess that sometimes I have been among that group of readers. However, in this preface, I have included some important material that I believe will be worth the reader's time. It puts a perspective on what follows, and in that sense provides a basis to understand this interdisciplinary exploration of the complexity of human thinking.

Our universe is a delightful place and a joy to explore. It is delightful because it is complex, which means it is composed of a vast number of variables that constantly change and interact with each other. Imagine how dull our lives would be if our universe was a flat monochromatic desert of stone extending as far as our eyes could see. Thankfully, it is not! This book is my attempt to understand the complexity of the delightful universe we inhabit using the concepts of the new and growing field of complexity science.

The discoveries of astronomy in the past 200 years have told us that our universe is expanding and becoming more diverse since the emergence of time at the expansion of a singularity commonly known as the Big Bang. However, our universe is expanding in another way. The knowledge and understanding that life forms have concerning our universe has also been expanding and becoming more complex since they emerged. I'm reminded of that by the increasing number of books that I mean to read, and that pile only seems to increase. In other words, the ideas generated in those publications are increasing, and often those ideas are interconnected and create more books and more complexity.

Our early ancestors in the form of simple bacteria developed gated pores through which they could "sense" the environment outside of themselves. On some primitive level, they must have reacted to their universe, and the bacteria that had functioning gated pores may have been better able to survive than their bacterial friends without gated pores. In our universe, we are better off knowing that something is out there, especially if it's nasty, and you might even have the ability to do something about it. We humans and other higher life forms have evolved sensory-neurological systems more complex and more sophisticated than our bacterial ancestors.

Therefore, we are more likely to be aware of a greater part of that universe and how those parts continually interact with each other.

The great Irish philosopher Bishop George Berkeley advanced a theory called immaterialism, which denied the existence of any material substance, believing that objects are really only ideas perceived and created by our intellect. In other words, the exterior universe only exists in our minds. This has been simplified by the colloquial expression, "If a tree falls in the forest and no one hears it, it never happened." This philosophy may provide fodder for interesting philosophical debates; however, if the tree falls on me, I will certainly believe that the tree exists.

Berkeley's idea that there is no external universe has had more than its share of philosophical critics, but his ideas did put an emphasis on the importance of the sensory and organizational systems in life forms. However, rejecting Berkeley's idea that there is no objective reality does not mean that the study of our sensory-neurological systems is unimportant. In fact, our sensory-neurological system allows us to not only comprehend our external universe but also alters it and makes it more complex.

As evolution has resulted in increasingly sophisticated sensory and neurological structures, we seem to expand the universe because we continue to discover additional variables and properties.

In other words, there is an external universe, but life forms can only know of its existence through some sort of sensory system, be it elementary gated pores or a sophisticated physiological system of neurons, retinas, tympanic membranes, cerebral cortex, and a host of other parts of the human neurological system. If life forms did not have that sensory system, we might as well inhabit that dull featureless desert of nothingness. I don't think I am doing an injustice to bacteria by saying that we humans have a greater awareness of our universe than those bacteria. As I sit at my desk writing, I am aware of the forest outside my house, the many books on my bookshelves, the pictures on my office wall, the pleasant sound of the wind, and many other things, but I doubt a bacterium with gated pores is also aware of those things. However, the expanding knowledge of our universe creates a problem for humans that likely does not afflict the bacteria. As we expand our knowledge of the universe, it becomes more and more complex.

Perhaps the expanding complexity of our universe is an important concept of complexity science. Whether through evolution or our own intellectual efforts, we are increasing our awareness of our universe, and so we are also increasing the complexity of that universe and our cognitive universe.

I pose this idea as a question and not as a declarative statement. If it is valid, then our cognitive universe is expanding and becoming more complex. It means that our universe in the form of its many variables and their interactions is increasing, and that contributes to our knowledge and understanding. However, it also generates a serious problem, one of information overload. We humans have certain limitations in terms of how many environmental variables and their associations we are able to assimilate. If we try to assimilate too much information, we may hit a tipping point and fall into informational chaos.

Fortunately, we humans have developed a number of cognitive skills that help us cope with this problem of informational overload. First, we can try to ignore or decrease the amount of information we take in within a given time. This technique can be helpful, but it means we will be ignorant of some information that might be useful and needed.

Second, we can learn and utilize methods that focus on the associations between variables rather than among the variables themselves. The field of mathematics provides a good example. The simple equation a + b = c can be used to add any two variables together. This association can apply to pins, apples, people, or anything we can think of. Using mathematical equations allows us to understand the relationships between many different aspects of our environment without having to focus on any particular environment variable. Another simple equation $E = mc^2$ shows the relationship between all the energy and mass in our universe which encompasses lots of everything. If we know these associations, we can understand any number of environmental variables, which also helps to simplify our environment.

Third, we organize the sensory stimuli of our environment into cognitive models that allows us to understand the relationships between the different sensory stimuli and brings them together into a coherent form. Taking in various discrete forms of the outside environmental energy and creating a single integrated cognitive model makes the environment easier to understand and less confusing. Much of the text explains the role of cognitive models in thinking and how they form.

And lastly, there are properties of our universe that naturally tend to simplify its very complexity. These are a major part of the study of complexity science. Principles such as self-organization, complex adaptive systems, the development of rules, and others seem to be properties of our universe that help us simplify it. We will use these ideas of complexity science in this text to help us understand human thinking.

The ideas for this book have been enhanced by the students I have taught over many years and who have, in turn, taught me by their curious questions and insightful criticisms. I can't name them all, but I thank all of them for our shared interest in complexity science. I also want to thank Nathan Murphy, my research assistant who contributed to my ideas. He also created some of the diagrams when my computer skills were too incompetent to create them myself.

I have been fortunate, while writing this text, to have the support and friendship of a small group of active faculty at my university and who, like me, are students of complexity science. These include Jane Horvath, Ralph Zegarelli, Power Boothe, Ed Gray, Patricia Mellodge, Sundeep Muppidi, and Jennifer McLeer. We meet every other Friday, and our group makes up the faculty of the van Rooy Center for Complexity. I want to also thank Jean-Pierre and Marie-Claire van Rooy whose interest in complexity science initiated and supported the van Rooy Center at the University of Hartford. Their generous grant enabled the creation of the Center and established a program of studies in complexity for our students.

The production and editorial staff at Springer were very gracious and made the publication of this book a pleasant experience. I want to especially acknowledge my editor Megan McManus, Pradheepa Vijay, Brian Halm, and Lavanya Devgun. Thank you for your help in providing light to my ideas on complexity and cognition.

Canton, CT, USA Robert Leve

Contents

Chapter 1
Origins of Complexity

Abstract This introductory chapter introduces the purpose of human thinking and how the concepts of complexity science establish order and predictability in an ever-changing complex environment. Humans and all life forms inhabit a universe that is very diverse and must be simplified in order to escape overload and cognitive chaos. The concepts of complexity science explain how life forms organize the environmental diversity that surrounds them and develop functional cognitive processes that enable them to correctly react to that environment. The establishment of interconnected networks, inherent self-organization, and complex adaptive systems are part of this complex process. Lastly, the reciprocal relationship between diversity, cognition, and complexity is discussed as a means of establishing a bounded stability that allows life forms to survive.

Keywords Complexity science · Self-organization · Emergence · Complex adaptive systems · Flocking · Complex networks

What is the purpose of thinking? I suppose there are many different ways to answer this question, but perhaps we higher life forms had no choice in the matter. For better or for worse, we live in an environment that contains a multitude of stimuli (variables) that are all interacting with one another such that a change in one usually will cause changes in others and to complicate things further, that environment never stays the same, but is in constant motion, which is a rather confusing and overwhelming place to be. So how do we manage to exist and even thrive in such a complicated place? The answer is cognition. The basic purpose of cognition is to allow an organism to cope with that confusing and overwhelming place by collapsing the environmental complexity into a series of manageable and relevant concepts that provide a sense of emotional and intellectual stability. Seen from that perspective, the major purpose of cognition is simplifying the overwhelming world we inhabit. Most of the time, we never notice the complicated, ever-changing environment surrounding us because our cognitive abilities are so efficient. In a way we live in a local bubble ignorant of what is outside and protected from the unpleasant emotion of being overwhelmed, drowned in the very universe surrounding us. This

R. Leve, *The Complexity of Human Thought*,
https://doi.org/10.1007/978-3-031-09104-9_1

text is an attempt to understand the process of cognition and how it protects us from being overwhelmed by the constantly changing confusion of our world.

Intellectual behavior in humans is a process that is highly complex in that it is difficult to analyze and very difficult to predict. This is likely true for not only humans but also for other life forms ranging from insects to fish to birds to mammals. Although this has been obvious to many keen observers throughout human history recent advances in the study of complexity science have shown that a host of phenomenon in our world is complex in nature and therefore does not follow logical and predictable laws. In spite of the validity and utility of scientific laws and theories, the universe is too complex for our attempts to accurately control and predict the multitude of phenomenon going on about us. Since the beginnings of the earliest proto-scientific inquiry, through the development of mathematics, and especially after the scientific revolution in 1700, a central goal of science is the attempt to find stability and predictability in our complex universe. Science and mathematics have made great strides in that endeavor; however, the universe is far too multitudinous, complicated, and complex for science to achieve perfect predictability in many situations. A simple algebraic equation yields a solution that describes one part of our universe, but it describes an abstract universe where we have exact knowledge of all the variables in that equation. In our real universe, things change and even the most exact measurement contains some error which means that perfect predictability and perfectly stable descriptions are only achievable in very few situations. The polar opposite of stability and perfect predictability is chaos and randomness. The actual universe we inhabit lies somewhere between chaos and stability and predictability and randomness.

Complexity science is the emerging field that attempts to identify and study the area between complete randomness and perfect scientific predictability and stability. Complexity science dictates that we live in a world of bounded predictability in that most phenomenon of our universe can be predicted, but depending on the particular event or area of study, there are limits to this predictability. The utility of complexity science is that it not only identifies the principles and phenomena that describe the unpredictability and chaos in our universe, but it also describes those principles that indicate predictability. If this description seems somewhat abstract, it is because complexity science applies to a wide range of intellectual studies and is almost universal in its application. A short description of these principles illustrated by examples will help explain the advantages and utility of complexity science.

One of the most important principles of complexity science is the principle of emergence which is also referred to as sensitivity to initial conditions. Emergence describes situations in which a seemingly small and insignificant change in a complex interactive environment can cause a cascade of unexpected and unpredictable changes. The large effect of these changes on the environment will seem out of proportion to the insignificance of the initial event. In more technical terms, this is called nonlinearity, a phase transition, or in simpler terms, a given result is greater than the sum of its parts. The classic example of emergence (though I find it rather far-fetched) is the butterfly effect in which a butterfly flapping its wings in the Amazon jungle interacts with wind patterns, moisture, and temperature gradients such that it forms a category five hurricane that devastates the islands of the Caribbean. History is replete with examples of emergence. For example, the preachings of an obscure Jewish man in Judea, a minor part of the Roman Empire, resulted in the adoption of Christianity as the state religion in the Roman Empire and eventually as the predominant religion of Western civilization. These examples demonstrate that predicting the effect of such emergent agents is at best very difficult and more likely, rather impossible. Attempting to analyze the causal path of such emergent phenomena might be a useful post hoc task for historians and meteorologists, but I doubt that anyone living in ancient Judea would have predicted the words of that young man would have such profound implications for the lives and deaths of many millions of people. Similarly, I would challenge any meteorologist to identify the particular butterfly that caused the emergent hurricane either before, during, or after the effects of that hurricane were realized. By their very nature, emergent agents are unpredictable as are the phenomena they create, and they are a demonstration of universal unpredictability.

Another principle of complexity science is self-organization sometimes called spontaneous order. Self-organization occurs when spontaneous order seems to arise from interactions between agents without the influence of any external communication or control. In other words, the spontaneous order arises without the demands of any administrative authority. An example in biology is the construction of huge termite mounds in the area of North East Brazil. These structures are up to 4 meters in height and contain a vast network of underground tunnels connected to a large central tunnel. There are over 200 million of these in an area the size of the United Kingdom and seen from the air they are spaced in a regular pattern (Fig. 1.1).

This multitudinous series of complex structures are the work of individual termites going about their work without any external control. Amazingly, the decentralized work of all these individual termites has produced these regularly spaced

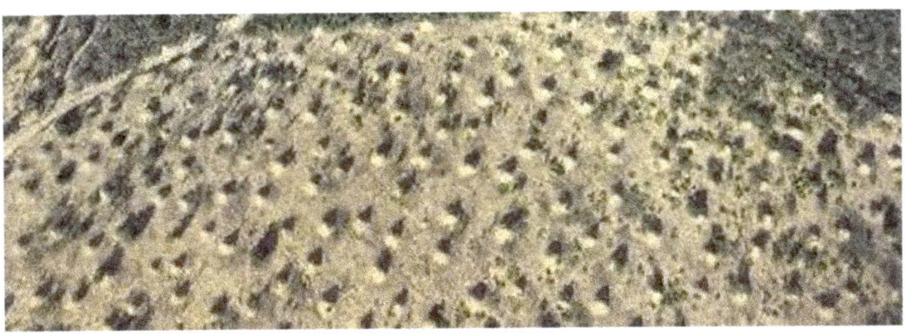

Fig. 1.1 Brazilian termite mounds seen from an aerial photograph. (Google earth satellite image, *current biology*)

mounds, and they are 4000 years old (Martin et al. (2018)). The beautiful and regular hexagonal shape of a honeycomb in a beehive is another example of self-organization. The regular pattern of the honeycomb is created by individual bees without the guidance of a master bee telling each individual where and how to deposit the wax and honey (Fig. 1.2).

Interestingly, this principle of complexity science demonstrates the relationship between predictability and randomness. In respect to the termite mounds, we can certainly predict that large termite mounds are going to be created in that area of Brazil and the mounds will be regularly spaced; however, we are not able to predict location of each individual mound, and we can only make a reasonable estimate in predicting the distance of each mound from every other mound. This seems to reflect our description of bounded predictability. In respect to the myriad number of termites engaged in building the mound, we would not be able to predict the location of any particular termite at any given moment. In that situation, our predictive ability would be rather close to randomness. The same description seems to apply to the honeycomb (Pirk et al., 2004), and although we can certainly predict the hexagonal shape of each honeycomb cell, there would certainly be slight fluctuations in the exact size and shape of each cell. Here, our bounded predictability might be quite a bit better than with the termite mounds, but as with trying to predict the position of individual termites, we would have great difficulty identifying the location of any particular honeybee that helped create this beautiful self-organized structure. In these two situations, the utility of complexity science helps us to realize the bounded predictability of our cognitive powers.

Fig. 1.2 Regularity in the honeycomb pattern of beehives. (Photograph by seagul)

Another important concept in complexity science is flocking. In flocking, individual agents create well-organized groups by following a few simple rules and without any outside direction. Flocking is commonly seen by watching the migratory flight of wildfowl and the schooling of fish. There are two simple rules of flocking behaviors. Agents must be separated by a certain distance that is not too close or too distant, and they must be in relative alignment with the other agents around them (Figs. 1.3 and 1.4). By flocking together, wildfowl or fish create distinctive patterns such as the familiar V created by geese and the somewhat round-shaped ball of a school of herring, (Lissaman & Shollenberger, 1970).

I think my favorite example of flocking is the tightly knit crowds of penguins who band together as a way of dealing with the bitter cold winds of the Antarctic winter. The penguins at the head of the group facing the wind are subject to the most heat depleting position, so they peel off from the head of the crowd and walk to the rear where they are sheltered from the bitter wind by the mass of other penguins. The flocking behavior of the entire group of penguins forms an elongated oval which is in constant forward motion toward the head of the group although the group stays in the same space. In this case, the rules are to stay close to the penguins surrounding you, keep moving forward at a slow pace until you reach the head of the oval, then peel off to the back of the group. Once again, there is no boss penguin directing everyone, but by flocking in this way all the penguins can stay warm, huddled in their group, and only face the heat depriving

Fig. 1.3 Flight pattern of migratory geese. (Image by Manfred Antraias Zimmer)

Fig. 1.4 A school of fish forming a revolving ball. (Photograph by Isabel Fowler)

wind for a short period of time. In this situation, we have an enhanced predictive ability. We can predict reasonably well the area occupied by the huddling penguins, and we might be able to predict the position of individual penguins with some accuracy. However, trying to predict the exact position of an individual penguin at any given moment is difficult in that they are unlikely to move in a straight line and we might have a hard time predicting their position at the end of the huddled oval after they have peeled off from the front of the group. In this situation to, complexity science shows us the bounded predictability of our flocking phenomenon.

Complexity science identifies another principal of constant change within a bounded system. This is known as a complex adaptive system. We humans live surrounded among a myriad of complex adaptive systems. Basically, a complex adaptive system describes a system in which the individual parts of the system are constantly adapting to changes such that the larger system remains remarkably stable and predictable within certain limits. Complex adaptive systems are entities such as large cities, national and local economies, power grids, traffic flows, and even the military. For example, large cities such as New York require the constant inflow of goods, services, and people, and the constant outflow of the same. This is maintained by the action of individual agents responding to the needs and changes of other agents without any knowledge of the overall status of the city. A local grocery may find that it is short of apples so that agent places a larger order with the local apple supplier agent who tells the local trucking agent to deliver the larger order of apples to the grocery. Perhaps, the larger sales of apples were due to the result of a lecture on healthy nutrition at the local PTA meeting, or a television program on the health benefits of apples on a local station, but whatever the cause the cities need for additional apples was taken care of.

Another example is the increase in temporary postal employees, Amazon shipments, and UPS trucks around the Christmas holidays. This adaptation to the increase in gift packages is anticipated by and taking care of by the individual postal, Amazon, and UPS agents adapting to a change in the nation's gift-giving behavior. These are just some examples of how a large and complex system such as New York City remains stable because of the many individual agents responding to each other without any overall administrative direction.

Certainly, all the many agents are not responding to directions of New York's Mayor. They just adapt to changes in demand of food, garbage, and gifts without the overall guidance of the Mayor of New York or any other single leader. In fact, the occupant of the Mayor's office is in constant change due to the real and perceived political needs of the city. Thankfully, we humans live in a world of complex adaptive systems some of which we have created and others have simply emerged as a result of our thinking and behaviors responding to changes in our environment. Of course, we humans are not the only ones who are fortunate enough to exhibit complex adaptive systems as they exist in many other life forms. Wolf packs, lion prides, and chimp bands are also stable complex adaptive systems maintained by the different and changing behaviors of each member.

Complexity theory emphasizes another phenomenon concerning networks which are composed of nodes and hubs. Nodes are the discrete elements in an environment which make up the network, and hubs are a central node location connected to a large number of nodes. Perhaps this simple description is best illustrated by the example of airline patterns in the United States and around the world. Although airlines fly to many cities in the United States which are nodes, certain cities are hubs in that airlines are likely to fly through that airport hub while flying to another city. For example, if I wanted to fly from the Raleigh-Durham airport in North Carolina to Sarasota Florida on Delta Airline, there is a good chance that rather than flying directly to Sarasota I would fly to Atlanta which is a major hub for Delta Air Lines and then take another flight to Sarasota. There are many examples of networks with n nodes and hubs an important one being the Internet (Fig. 1.5).

An important property of networks is that hubs increase the accuracy of prediction in a network. We can use common airline hubs as an example. If we boarded a plane in San Antonio, Texas to Portland, Oregon, not knowing our next airport stop, the probability that we would pass through Billings, Montana, is quite small because it is not a hub airport, whereas the probability we would pass through Denver, Colorado, is much higher because that is an airline hub. This observation that hubs increase our accuracy of prediction will be important in later chapters because

Fig. 1.5 Pattern of network with hubs

strong personal beliefs and prejudices seem to act as cognitive hubs in a network of nodes composed of bits of environmental information.

I suppose that adaptation to any environment simple or complex is a rather obvious function of all life forms. Certainly, the biological evolution of life forms developing different structures (legs, fins, wings, brains, etc.) and separating into different species as a result of their adaptation to the many and varied earth environments is just one example of the many ways in which life forms adapt to their environments. Organic life forms possess this ability we call adaptation, whereas inorganic forms are not really capable of changing themselves in response to their environment. Perhaps, I might argue this point with myself in that I might point out that a grain of sand moved by the wind might be considered to be adapting to its windy environment; however, this might be more of a philosophical exercise above my level of understanding. However, the movement of a grain of sand certainly seems different than the multitude of ways in which organic forms can change their structure and behavior in response to the effects of their environment, so I prefer to hold onto the notion that the evolution of earth's many varied life forms is a different phenomenon than a grain of sand bouncing off other grains of sand driven by the wind.

Just as life forms are a complex adaptive system, so too the cognitive behavior emitted by higher life forms is also a complex adaptive system that is in constant change. We are always adapting to the many stimuli of the complex environment we live in, and we are constantly trying to make sense of that environment so that our adaptive behaviors bring us advantages in survival, stability, and pleasure. As we shall see in succeeding chapters, this process of cognition is a very complicated affair which involves the development of cognitive models that allow us to understand and adapt to our exterior environment. In that sense, the remaining parts of this book are an attempt to analyze how we use this gift of complex cognition.

Chapter 2
Diversity and Complexity

Abstract As diversity increased in our universe from the beginning of its singular expansion, it created increased complexity in the form of subatomic particles, atoms, various astronomical structures, organic life forms, and ultimately the organization and complex neurology of the human brain. Through interactions with the energy inputs of the exterior environment and cognition, a complex adaptive system formed and became organized. This complex adaptive system formed cognitive representations of the exterior environment which allowed living organisms to react to that environment and even predict environmental changes crucial to human functioning and allowing individual and species survival. Complexity cannot exist without diversity and in that sense complexity is an organized form of diversity. If diversity is a grouping of independent environmental variables, then complexity is a dependent grouping of environmental variables that interact with each other so that a change in one will bring about changes in one or all of the others. In our universe, interactions between variables are so pervasive that we inhabit a vast universe of complexity.

Keywords Organoids · Singularity · Reductionism · Cognitive interactions · Diversity and complexity

To understand this process of complex cognition, we need first to understand complexity. Where did the complexity of our universe come from? This seems like a very simple question and in a sense perhaps such complexity and unpredictability should not be surprising because it is and has been an integral principal of our universe that emerged from its very inception. Our universe began from a singularity, a single point of high intensity and infinite energy. In that state, the future universe was simple enough that it had no complexity because it was singular without any variation or at least no variation that we can discern since such a singularity is unknowable at this point in our present state of scientific understanding. However, when that singularity began to expand 13.7 billion years ago (explode is the vernacular term used in the common description of the "Big Bang Theory"), its expansion became more diverse as time went on and that diversity created complexity.

R. Leve, *The Complexity of Human Thought*,
https://doi.org/10.1007/978-3-031-09104-9_2

That is to say that the expansion did not occur in a perfectly uniform way. It separated into diverse parts in its expansion, and as soon as this variation occurred, complexity became a principal factor in the new universe. As a general rule, there is a relationship between diversity and complexity such that **the greater the diversity of a phenomenon, the more opportunities it has to become complex.** Complexity is a word with many meanings in common usage, but in this text "complexity" will refer to entities or agents that interact in such a way as to make the outcome completely or relatively unpredictable.

Complexity seemed to emerge early in our universe in that three minutes after its formation the universe cooled into subatomic particles and these began to coalesce into atoms. After the coalescence of atoms, gravity emerged and formed them into gas clouds, stars, and galaxies. Astronomical observation suggests that the first quasars formed about a billion years, and since then, larger structures such as galaxies and superclusters have been forming. One of the first processes of this inflation is that the many different types of subatomic particles, atoms, stars, and galaxies began to interact with each other to form and reform into a diversity of different structures. Though we have developed laws to understand this process, the individual creations of such a process are too complex to predict in terms of how each of these structures took its individual form. Thus, the particular form that clouds of hydrogen atoms took as they formed into stars, galaxies, and superclusters is individual to each particular hydrogen cloud and was likely unpredictable. By definition, the differentiation and interaction of the structures created by the expansion of the singularity are complex, and thus, complexity as a process is an integral part of the creation of our universe.

Other emergent properties of the singularity expansion are motion and time. Originally, the expansion of the singularity created space as space did not exist when the singularity was only a point of infinite energy. However, as the expansion continued motion was imparted to the movement of released energy and to the newly created particles, and they moved about often colliding with one another. As gravity emerged it caused particles, atoms, stars, and galaxies to collide and interact with each other. Time was created through this process since time and movement are intimately connected. If nothing moves, then there is no way to measure time, and for practical purposes, it does not exist. Conversely, if there is movement, then it must occur within a period of time. Thus, time and motion are two aspects of the same thing, and the existence of one implies the existence of the other. The creation of motion and time is very important in an understanding of complexity at every level whether ranging from simple subatomic particles to the complexity of human intellectual behavior because the essence of complexity is the interaction of energy and matter in our universe. Complexity is a study of change and how change occurs through interactions. If there were no interactions between particles of matter and forms of energy, then there would be no change and we would live in a rather dull, simple, and unchanging universe. As we have already discussed, interactions occur through motion between things, and it occurs over some period of time.

As the universe continued to age, the matter became more diverse and complicated. Subatomic matter joined together to form atomic elements which joined together to form simple molecules and then larger molecules. Each of these steps produced greater complexity. There is little diversity in the formation of subatomic particles into atoms but greater diversity in the formation of atoms into simple molecules and yet even greater diversity in the formation of larger molecules such as proteins. As we continue on this scale of chemical diversity, the proteins form living cells, organic structures, and complete living organisms. Since there is greater diversity in these scales of matter, there is more opportunity (more degrees of freedom) for each to form unpredictable and complex structures. If we travel from the scale of subatomic particles to the intricacies of the human body, then each step along this path allows for more diversity and more complexity. For example, the interaction of atoms in the physical world is understandable with even a simple knowledge of chemistry. A water molecule is composed of two atoms of hydrogen and one atom of oxygen that have interacted to form a chemical bond. However, which of the many diverse hydrogen and oxygen atoms will bond to form water is relatively unpredictable.

Over time, more complex atoms were created in the explosions of stars, and many of these atoms such as calcium, carbon, nitrogen, and phosphorus make up the structure of life forms including the human body. As these and other atoms came together, they formed protein molecules which are more complicated than atomic elements. As higher forms of molecules formed, they created the first cells and these cells formed even more complex internal and external structures such as a backbone, intestines, kidneys, fins, arms, eyes, and fingers. The development of cells into such structures is a form of self-organization in that such specialization allowed for a better reaction to the vicissitudes of the external environment and allowed for the exploitation of new environmental niches. An organism with increased structural sophistication is able to better interact with its environment which provides many advantages including increased survival. That kind of self-organization resulted in the development of many types of advantageous structures, and these structures formed differentiated physiological systems. Such systems need to be accurately integrated with one another, and so these organisms developed complex adaptive systems. For example, the advantage of having fingers is enhanced if they are coordinated with eyes and each must adapt to input and changes from the other. Trying to grasp a needed object by randomly moving our fingers about the environment is quite inefficient compared to letting our eyes move our fingers directly to that object. As organisms developed other useful structures, these became increasingly complex and the adaptation between their functions became more adaptive.

Perhaps, a basic principle of life forms is that life will self-organize through interactions with its environment and will increasingly develop complex adaptive systems.

All life forms will react in some fashion to stimuli in their environment, but in higher life forms, neural structures such as nerves and a brain were generated which allowed physiological structures a faster and more accurate reaction to the exterior environment. This culminated in neurons, synapses, and glial cells which formed the human brain, likely the most complex structure in our universe. Depending on an individual's age, there may be plus or minus 100 billion neurons each with over

10,000 synaptic connections and many times that amount of glial cells which tend to the oxygenation and maintenance of the neurons. These physically complex neural structures gave rise to simple and complex forms of intelligence such as learning, insight, motivated behavior, and, in some creatures, language.

Just as the inherent process of complexity is crucial to understanding the many forms and changes in inorganic and organic matter, the complexity inherent in our universe is also crucial to understanding the thinking and behavior that has emerged from the organic structure of simple and complex life forms.

Recent studies on neural organoids have shown that behavior seems to emerge from neural tissue and begin to self-organize (Muotri, Cell Stem Cell, 2019). Organoids are an artificial group of neurons created and kept alive in laboratories. Interestingly, after 6 to 9 months, the cells begin to generate electrical activity in the form of micro-circuitries, and these patterns seem to resemble the electrical activity of a six-month preterm infant. In this instance, neurons seem to interact with each other in an attempt to self-organize. Of course, such organoids do not have sense or response organs and thus cannot interact with their external environment, so their behavior is limited. However, even these elementary forms of a brain seem to create the beginnings of cognition in that the neural cells are attempting to communicate by generating electrical circuits.

Behavior of life forms and especially the intellectual behavior of higher life forms may have emerged from neural cells, but it has a complexity that is separate from our physical neurological structures in that the complexity of intellectual activity cannot be reduced to a study of only biological, molecular, or atomic matter. Trying to understand intellectual behavior in that way minimizes our understanding of these processes. Intellectual functions, their changes and interactions, and the social institutions they create (politics, governments, economies, etc.) are very complex and need to be analyzed and understood through a complexity science of their own. If we look at the fact that humans and other neurologically sophisticated organisms are a combination of nothing more than carbon, oxygen, hydrogen, and other atoms, we can see that cognition is an emergent phenomenon in that we can hardly expect that such a simple accretion of chemical elements could have produced a process such as complex thinking. I am always amazed thinking that out of a combination of atoms and molecules can emerge the beauty and complexity of Beethoven's Fifth Symphony or the New Hebrides Overture of Felix Mendelssohn. This unlikely emergence of beautiful interacting sounds is a complex adaptive system of complex thinking, and understanding the interactions and complexities of intelligence will be the task of the following chapters.

As mentioned in the preface of this text, there is evidence that over time our universe is becoming increasingly complex. Arising from a singularity that had no complexity, the diversity of our universe increased as did the interactions between its many parts. Life forms and their neurological systems which may be the most complex things in our universe were created out of that diversity. In addition, to the increasing complexity of our universe, our life forms have also increased that complexity through the evolutionary sophistication of our sensory–neurological systems. As our sensory neurological systems expanded in their sophistication, we were able to become aware of more of our universe and with increased precision. We not only became aware of many more variables in our universe, but also of the many interactions between them. In other words, over time, the complexity that we life forms try to understand and predict is going to continue. That means, we are never going to run out of new discoveries, and we need to expect that and take joy in our increasingly complex world.

Reductionism

Reductionism is a concept in science that attempts to explain complex phenomenon by reducing them to more elementary levels. For example, a reductionist view states that human intellectual behavior can be reduced to the brain which is composed of cells, so we can explain the brain by understanding cells. Further, cells are composed of molecules, so we can understand cells by studying molecules. Of course, molecules are composed of atoms, so we can best understand molecules by studying atoms. We can continue this process of reduction through subatomic particles, and if taken to absurdity, it arrives at the original singularity that created the universe, thus indicating that we can best understand intellectual behavior by studying the expansion of the singularity. One problem with reductionism is that if it attempts to explain something, then it ought to also predict.

While many scientists view reductionism as a useful concept in the linear view of science, the introduction of complexity science which is nonlinear seems to make the concept of reductionism untenable as a useful enterprise in understanding cognition. Complexity has been shown to exist at all levels of science, and so in order to gain a valid description of a phenomenon, we need to understand that phenomenon within its individual level of complexity. The extent and type of complexity at each level of scale are likely different. Most, though not all, chemical reactions are regular and predictable, whereas much of human intellectual behavior is complex, unpredictable, and often chaotic. A reductionist approach to understanding human behavior is likely to be inadequate and simplistic as it would ignore much of the higher level of complexity at the scale of human behavior.

If we try to understand human behavior from a scale of atoms, we would be adding the complexity from the subatomic scale, then the atomic scale, the molecular scale, and through the complexity of additional higher levels, and thus, we would increase the amount of complexity rather than decrease it (Miller, 2009). Another problem is that human behavior is generated by experiences, and trying to explain human behavior solely through understanding our organic particles does not include such experiences. Even a perfectly cloned individual cannot live in the same environment as its original form and so is likely to exhibit different behavioral patterns as the result of our clone existing in different environments. To generate a perfectly behaviorally identical human, we would need the clone to live in an identical developmental environment such that the sequence of experiences would be the same for every second of existence from birth to death. Such a situation certainly seems highly improbable and practically impossible. The problem with such a reductionistic approach to explain cognition is that even at an atomic level we would have to arrange all the atoms everywhere in the clone's universe to duplicate the original and have them do exactly the same things at exactly the same time. The ultimate problem with such a reductionist approach is that it includes neither the environmental experience nor the complexity that would arise from such a situation. Thus, the interaction of experiences and human organic structures is very complex, is a nonlinear process, and cannot be adequately explained by linear reduction.

Chapter 3
Cognitive Models

Representations of Environments

Abstract Cognitive models emerged to react to and arrange the huge number of environmental stimuli that make up our exterior environment. These cognitive models serve to organize the associations between seemingly vast amount of random environmental stimuli in the form of light and acoustic waves, tactile sensations, and other energy inputs. In that way, life entities and especially intelligent forms are able to create stable internal representations of their environment. These stable internal representations allow life forms to coordinate the release of organic energy congruent with demands of their exterior environment. Due to the complexity and constantly changing aspects of our environment, cognitive models must organize many and ever-changing variables of that environment to provide some level of either rudimentary or sophisticated level of comprehension. These cognitive models must also prevent life forms from becoming overloaded by the vast complexity of the surrounding stimuli and falling into cognitive chaos.

Keywords Cognitive representation · Functional relationships · Association · Representational models · Principles of life · Life space

The most basic function of intelligence is to form an internal representation of the organism's environment, so it can learn and react to that environment. Almost all life forms have developed processes and structures that enable the acquisition of information about the environment they inhabit whether that environment is localized, relatively slow-moving, and simplistic as in lower life forms or complex, rapid, and extensive as with humans. Simpler life forms have developed rudimentary information gathering structures such as diffusion across pores, gated channels, and electrogenic pumps which are chemically based and relatively slow. In higher life forms, the basic structure, the neuron, is electrochemical and characterized by a rapid rate of transmission. The evolutionary advantages of neurological structures that provide rapid information flow are confirmed by the fact that all humans have so many neurons and interconnected synapses (Basar, 1990; Freeman, 1991). The vast number of connections indicates the complexity of the life space that a human

R. Leve, *The Complexity of Human Thought*,
https://doi.org/10.1007/978-3-031-09104-9_3

must inhabit, and to be useful, this informational complexity must then be organized into a form that is functional for the individual and species.

Biological and biochemical investigations of neurological structures have provided a compendium of knowledge about our system of information acquisition; however, there are functional relationships inherent in our universe that likely determine the interactions between neurological structures and the exterior universe (Cassier, 1950). These functional relationships may have arisen from the interaction of an organism with its environment. They are related to, but independent of physical structures, and they impose limitations and constraints on the process by which information is exchanged. Analyzing the functional requirements of the interaction between neurological structures and the outside universe is likely to provide fruitful insights toward understanding how we gain, integrate, and organize information (Goudsmit, 1989). There is certainly a survival and evolutionary advantage to the acquisition of environmental information since that can provide an organism, simple or complex, with behaviors that are advantageous in coping with the dangers of an environment and providing a benefit in the competition for resources.

A number of investigators, (Prigogine & Stangers, 1984) postulate that life forms are structures that take in and store energy which is released in a controlled fashion at a future time. Obviously, such energy releases cannot be random and disorganized, but must be in concordance with the structure and demands of the organism's universe if a life form is to survive as an individual and continue as a species.

The central task of cognition for complex life forms is to coordinate the release of energy with the demands of the outside environment. To do this, the life form must have an inner representation or model of the outside universe and the central task of any cognitive process is to create a congruence between the environment and the cognitive model (Vandervert, 1995).

Life forms cannot **"know"** their environment directly. An environment is known through inputs that affect our sense organs, for example, our eyes receive photons, our ears receive sound waves, and our free nerve endings sense pressure as touch, and similar processes occur with other sense organs. Without going into a lengthy explanation of sensation and perception, these sensory inputs are coordinated to form a representative model of the outside environment to which any organism with sensory apparatuses can then respond.

To be functional, there must be a congruence between the model and the environment and life forms have developed many different methods of achieving this congruence ranging from representations that are rigid and genetically based to flexible representations or models that are learned and characteristic of more complex life forms. Instinctual behaviors may be useful to life forms that need to respond to stable environments having slow and limited rates of change; however, more complex life forms such as humans have developed a wide repertoire of models that can be instinctual or non-instinctual and capable of responding to great environmental complexity and rapid environmental changes.

Any effective system of information acquisition must possess methods of organizing environmental information (Inchingolo, 1994). A single neuron, a simplistic binary (basically an off–on signaling device), hardly seems a good candidate to represent the complexity of the outside universe, however, through combinations and arrangements of vast numbers of neurons and their synaptic connections, humans gain the necessary information for species survival and individual adjustment. In order for so many neurons to function as effective information-providing entities, they must be organized according to certain rules and subject to certain limitations (Vandervert, 1995), and there is little doubt that such organizational rules exist. To assume the opposite would mean that each neuronal connection functions in isolation and such a simplistic system with so many neurons would quickly lead to overload and chaos, (Kincanon & Powel, 1995).

A valid question is "what is the process through which the simple and complex personal models of the universe are created." In other words, is there a basic process that underlies the process of higher cognitive thinking in a complex species such as humans? As long ago as 300 BC, Aristotle entertained this question and in his text *De Anima* reflected on the role of association as the central process in cognition. Association is a term that implies that a connection exists between two or more phenomenon in our universe and by knowing one phenomenon allows us to have at least some information about the other. That is true whether we are in physical contact with actual objects or have developed mental images or concepts that are related to each other. However, one of the basic properties of the universe that underlies the concept of association is motion. Motion of some type is necessary if there is to be an associative connection. If we were to exist in a static universe where nothing ever moved, then there would be no connection between anything as no object would ever come in contact with another, and by definition, if there is no connection, there would be no association. Such a situation would be a situation of nothingness or total ignorance. A simple physical example is that if atoms do not move into proximity to each other and bond together, they cannot create molecules. Whether is a photon, a quark, or an organism, if something does not come into contact with something else, then for all practical circumstances they do not exist.

Cognitive processes are similar in that they must utilize association in the development of higher mental functions since higher mental functions are a compendium of information about the external environment. When our environment presents a new stimulus or we initiate a new idea, we usually relate that to information we already know. In other words, they become associated with one another. Actually, the word ***association*** does not completely describe the process by which complex organisms build up cognitive models of their environment since it describes a relationship, but does not indicate how new information can change an existing cognitive representation and how the cognitive representation or model can actually modify or change the interpretation or importance of a new bit of information. A more accurate term is ***interaction*** in that it implies that bits of information interact and can change each other. The term "cognitive interactions" indicates that a stimulus, concept, or idea can become integrated into a preexisting cognitive representation of the environment such that it modifies that representation since it brings new information. Conversely, the preexisting representation can modify the way the new information is interpreted or understood. In that sense, interactions are the most basic process by which we gain knowledge, knowledge that is essential to functioning and even survival. It is the accumulation of knowledge that allows organic forms to react and respond to their exterior and interior environments. Conversely, if there were no interactions between information in the form of environmental stimuli in an organism, there could be no accumulation of knowledge which is a state of intellectual nothingness.

Attempting to define a cognitive model is difficult as it is intangible and a somewhat abstract concept that is constantly changing. Nevertheless, we need to provide a definition. Basically, a cognitive model is an association between an individual and one or more environmental variables in the form of a cognitive energy input such as tactile pressure or sound and light waves. The simplest form of cognitive model is the association between the individual and a single aspect of the environment which provides the individual with a mental picture of that environmental variable as it either remains static or changes. However, in a more complex form, a cognitive model is an association between an individual and a finite number of changing environmental variables which can interact with each other and thus provide the individual with a constantly changing cognitive picture of their universe. Since the environmental variables in a cognitive model interact with each other, then a change in one may bring about a change in one or more of the others. In this situation, the constantly changing environmental variables that are included in the cognitive model present an intelligible understanding of the individuals surrounding environment. As we shall see in later chapters, there are limits to the number of variables and their related interactive associations that can be included in a cognitive model or the model will become chaotic. In less abstract terms, we might say a cognitive model is a mental or sometimes actual picture of the surrounding universe. Like any picture, it can be very simple so that it is an association between the viewer and that object or it can be quite complex as a picture between the viewer and many objects.

At this point, we might want to take a step back to reflect on the vast number of interactions between the many variables in our universe. Most of us never think about such a huge number since our limited minds cannot grasp something that is close to being infinite, and most of the universe is not particularly important to our existence. However, we do live in such a universe where no matter what scale is utilized there are vast numbers of unknown and likely unknowable variables and the interactions between them. In other words, we live in a huge universe of constant change. Comprehending such a vastness could only be done by an omnipotent and all-knowing God. Perhaps, that is why we created the concept of a God since we cannot do it. If we move to a more local scale including only our planet earth, we still could not comprehend the huge number of interactions between an even larger number of variables. There are interactions among the inorganic aspects of the planet such that there is constant change in our climate, our oceans, and even our continents as shown by earthquakes and volcanic activity. If we moved to organic life forms like plants, animals, and we humans, there too we live in a world of constant interactions. Even restricting the scale to the local environment we inhabit, there are still so many variables and interactions that we cannot possibly grasp all of them.

To survive and function even in our local life space, we need to limit that multitude of variables to the minimum number that is important to our existence. Perhaps, that is the central theme of this text. Cognition is the process by which we eliminate the variables and interactions around us to a manageable minimum. That allows us to carry out the principal task of cognition which is to predict the future interactions in our life space, limited or long term. Everything else that is discussed in this book is simply an elaboration of these two facts.

The functional process of cognition is quite intricate and occurs on many levels ranging from a simple representation of an environment such as recognition of a familiar object (a tree, a book, or a loved one), to the complex processes of understanding abstract scientific and mathematical theories (a calculus equation which describes the acceleration of a rocket). In order to understand the behavior of any organism and how a representation of the environment is developed, we must understand the environment of that organism and that is a complicated process. A complete definition of an organism's environment would include the entire present and potential world outside that organism; however, in most cases, we are only aware of a very limited exterior environment, limited to those things of importance around us. In simple terms, an organism's environment is anything that can impact or has the potential to impact that organism. Whether generated by changes in the exterior world or by changes in the behavior of an organism, there is always an environment that needs to be modeled.

Perhaps, an important principle of life is that organic forms have the ability to respond to changes in the external environment by developing representational models.

Inorganic forms (rocks, water, continents) can undergo changes, but they are changed by their environment and do not develop models to represent that exterior environment. A sedimentary rock may be changed by geological forces over time, and even continents can shift due to the circulation of magma in the earth's mantle, but they do not form a model that guides them to respond to or initiate such changes.

Of course, most of our outside environment is not important, so it is not noticed. For example, as you are reading these words, you are likely not aware of the tactile sensation resulting from what you are sitting upon or the quiet random noises in the room. Thus, we have the potential to be aware of and interact with many stimuli from our outside environment, but we cannot attend to all of these as we would be overwhelmed, a very unpleasant state. In reality, we severely limit the awareness of the outside environment and the models we create of that environment. Actually, our models are composed of and created by those aspects of the environment that are of importance to us in terms of our efficient life functioning, our need for resources, our survival, and often our random curiosity. Identifying the important aspects of an organism's environment can be difficult as it is idiosyncratic to each individual organism. However, a clue to understanding what is important is to see what aspects of the environment an organism chooses to interact with. For example, each person in our world is likely to focus on and interpret different aspects of the outside environment to interact with and thus will form different models of that universe. In that sense, every organism and certainly we humans will develop models that differ from each other although there may be a great deal of similarity depending on the structure of the environment, the structure of the organism, and its prior history. Political opinions are a good illustration of this as people develop different political opinions from one another because we have different models of our political world based on what we focus upon and these models can drastically change due to changes in the reality of the environment (although some individuals will doggedly maintain the same model despite such changes).

As an example, the world political environment was very complicated in 1938 with the rise of Hitler and Mussolini and their aggressive territorial grabs. After Britain's Prime Minister Neville Chamberlain met with Hitler during their famous Munich meeting, he returned to announce that he had achieved "peace with honor" and most of England having endured the horrors of WWI were effusive in their praise. The general model developed by most British citizens of Chamberlain and Hitler was positive, but after Hitler continued his aggression by invading Poland that British political model (attitude) changed and Nazism was seen for the evil it was. As a result, Chamberlain was forced from office in favor of Winston Churchill. There are many such examples of the model created with respect to one type of environment, then changing as the environment and its implications changed. The common phrase "I changed my mind" describes this situation, and such a behavior change can be studied by investigating an individual's behavior, but a fuller understanding needs to analyze how environmental changes brought about new and different cognitive models, and this process will be covered in a future chapter.

Chapter 4
How Cognitive Models Form

Abstract Cognitive models form naturally by organizing the associations between environmental variables. Such associations are like complexity attractors in that relevant associations are maintained, whereas nonfunctional associations are discarded. In that sense, we are always organizing associations even though we are seldom aware of this very common form of thinking. Cognitive models are constantly changing over time as the exterior environment changes. In spite of the fact that our cognitive models need to be flexible enough to cope with these changes, they must also have an inherent stability that tolerates the changing environment they represent. If we lose this cognitive stability, we are likely to become confused and experience chaotic thinking. That can occur when environmental changes are too rapid, or there are too many variables, or there are too many dysfunctional and erroneous associations among the variables. Cognitive models of higher life forms must maintain a delicate balance between integrating changes and maintaining a logical understanding of that changing environment. Environmental changes occur at different rates of time, and cognitive models need to be robust enough to cope with different rates of change without becoming chaotic. We can find examples of this thinking process in navigational models, political models, and even our educational activities.

Keywords Cognitive models · Attractors · Cognitive time · Navigation · Cognitive stability

The first thing we must understand is how such cognitive models are formed. Cognitive models are basically a collection of many individual auditory, visual, and other environmental stimuli that are related to each other and which allow us to understand and react to our environment. Such cognitive models must have a purpose in that the individual organism senses some sort of advantage. Cognitive models have basic survival advantages because having an accurate model of the environment allows an organism to adjust its behavior in response to food sources, threats, among other factors, but in addition to survival advantages most species have developed patterns of cognitive models specific to their biology, culture, and

R. Leve, *The Complexity of Human Thought*,
https://doi.org/10.1007/978-3-031-09104-9_4

their common environment. Such cognitive models reflect local environments and provide that individual with local advantages. Likely, proto-cognitive models form around some local advantage in terms of both survival and behavioral efficiency, and over time, other associated stimuli were included in the cognitive model. In that sense, we can say that the emerging cognitive model has a purpose and a function.

Perhaps, a concept from complexity science, attractors, can illustrate how cognitive models form around such advantages. The simplest of these is a point attractor, and a good example of a point attractor is gravity. Gravity is a force that causes all things on the surface of our planet to be drawn toward a point in the center of the earth. In that sense, it attempts to draw all things together and as an analogy cognitive models also draw aspects of the environment that are related to each other into a cognitive model. Thus, a cognitive model is an attractor that attempts to bring together related stimuli and variables in the local environment to form an integrated conceptual understanding of that universe. Of course, this is a metaphor, however, a cognitive model forms around a cognitive concept or idea, and it then attempts to accrete related aspects of the environment to it, and the more variables it can include in the cognitive model, the stronger and more robust the model becomes. Thus, a cognitive model becomes a belief about the exterior environment which has a purpose and a tendency to maintain and strengthen itself by seeking out aspects of the environment that harmonize with the initial concept or idea.

To understand cognitive models and how they are created, we need to analyze the diversity and complexities of an organism's outside environment and how that environment interacts with the life of any organism. Needless to say, even simplest environments are quite complex and the interactions between an organism and its environment can be quite unpredictable. The main reason that environments are unpredictable is that they are constantly changing. Sometimes, the changes are small, and sometimes, they are large, but it is a rare environment that remains constant for any length of time. The common folk saying **"the only constant is change"** does seem to describe our universe. Obviously, organisms need to respond to these changes, and this means that our models and resulting behavior are in constant motion. Whether it is the simple act of a driver reacting to other autos, a sailor modifying the set of sails, or a listener changing their thoughts in response to another's ideas, the exterior environment is changing and forcing changes in our models. The fact that cognitive models are dynamic and ever-changing is not surprising, however, this process is so natural that we are seldom aware of the environmental models as they exist and dynamically change. We can best be aware of such models by using visual imagery as that tends to freeze a model in time. If I close my eyes and instruct myself to imagine a scene such as the lake outside my back door, I can easily "see" in my mind trees on the far shore, the neighbors dock, the color of the water, gentle waves coming into the cove, and a host of other objects. That is a visual model that I can easily recognize as a representation of my lake. Cognitive models are not only visual in nature because if I like I can imagine sounds such as the voice of a friend or the beginning notes of Beethoven's Fifth Symphony. I can probably do this with any of my senses with greater or lesser success though as a human I might have trouble reclaiming a model of an odor; still I am sure my dog would have little trouble as he is gifted with a greater olfactory ability than me. Of course, we can combine sensations from different sense organs in our model, but the main point is that model creation is such an inherent and dynamic process that we are hardly aware of what we are doing. Complexity science describes the formation and constant changing of cognitive models as a complex adaptive system in that cognitive models are constantly adapting to the changes in our environment. This is a complex process by which we are integrating environmental changes to preexisting models so that we adapt to some criteria whether it is individual survival, emotional satisfaction, or just enjoying the stimulation of thought.

Since environments, especially human environments, can be very diverse, the cognitive models that represent the outside universe can come in many forms. Even my cat seems to have a model of me as a provider of kitty rubs as every time he sees me he meows asking me to give him the kitty rubs. In some cases, they are a form of mental picture, but they can be some form of unconscious behavior that responds to environmental demands. Humans use sight as the main coordinating sense organ, but we can also use hearing, touch, and even smell as a form of a model. For example, responding to the soft touch of a loved one is a form of a model representing the environment of that person. Similar examples can be demonstrated with auditory models because when we hear a familiar voice we form a model of the person who is speaking.

Of course, life forms not only exist in an exterior environment, but also are part of their environment in a number of ways, and in that sense, they can respond to their own part of the environment. For example, stimuli that are generated by an organism's own body are responded to and can have a serious influence on that organism's behavior. A simple example is when an organism feels pain it is likely to change its behavior often in a drastic form. The organism will generate a model of the cause of the pain and try out different behaviors in attempt to escape or minimize the pain. Even a common physiological response such as sweating will become part of that person's environment and is likely to produce a behavior in the form of wiping one's brow or cutting back on the intensity of a physical activity. Life forms are constantly in motion and that can and often does affect changes in their environment. Just the act of responding to some part of the environment will change it. The batting behavior of a baseball player at bat will change based on the pitcher's previous pitch and depending on whether it was a ball, strike, foul, fastball, change-up, or some other offering in the pitcher's repertoire. Similarly, the pitcher's behavior changes depending on the batter's previous swings. This duel between batter and pitcher is nothing more than each modifying their cognitive model based on the behavior of the other. Since we are often moving about our life space responding to our environment, we often bring about changes which require minor or major changes in the model that we generate about that environment. This adds to the diversity of that environment and indicates the high degree of flexibility required in constructing an accurate model of the environment.

Though the process of creating cognitive models is usually unconscious, it still requires an expenditure of energy so what is the advantage of having cognitive models and why do we create them. Obviously, the most basic reason is that they allow us to cope with the multitude of stimuli impinging on us from our complex exterior environment, and in that way, cognitive models allow us to simplify that environment. For example, I have a cognitive model of my university office which encompasses chairs, my desk, books, drawers of pencils and pens, tan-colored walls, pictures hung on my walls, and some assorted cycling paraphernalia. My cognitive model allows me to navigate about my office easily finding pens, my laptop, needed books, or any other object without having to deal with the many individual objects and stimuli that compose my cognitive office model. Imagine trying to keep track of the multitude of items in my office environment that would be a difficult task and an inefficient way to pursue my life. However, the cognitive model of my office provides me with a hierarchical concept that is much more efficient. In this example, we are discussing the simple environment of objects in an office; however, more complex environments are dynamic in that the different parts of the environment interact with one another and are constantly changing, and changing the importance of one part may change the relative importance and values of other parts. Trying to keep track of such a situation would often be impossible if we did not have cognitive models. For example, we may have had many different social encounters with a particular friend and may have had many thoughts and feelings concerning that friend, yet the cognitive model of that friend provides us with a relatively robust concept of that person. The cognitive model of that friend provides us with a useful and easy-to-understand concept.

Cognitive models also provide us with another advantage in that they give us some degree of predictability in understanding a dynamic interactive environment. We have already discussed how diverse environments become complex and relatively unpredictable. Our cognitive models provide us with a sense of predictability because cognitive models tend to be stable. We may not know what our particular friend is going to say or do at any given moment, but if we have an accurate cognitive model of that friend, we will seldom be surprised by any particular thought or behavior. Our social and verbal interactions usually will continue seamlessly and without surprise because most of the individual activities of that friend are predictable. Thus, when we construct cognitive models, they have a built-in predictability that helps us deal with and understand the inherent unpredictability in complex situations. Since unpredictability is very difficult for us humans, and likely for any other higher life forms, cognitive models allow us to cope with the inherent unpredictability in the different environments we inhabit.

There is a strong positive relationship between the concept of time and changes in any environment in that the longer the time period the more opportunity exists for an environmental change to occur and the more likely such a change will happen. This presents a cognitive problem to all life organisms whether simple or complex because they need a stable model of their exterior environment. Changes in their model of the environment will require changes in their behavior and that usually requires the expenditure of effort and energy. In many cases, there are absolute limits to what behavioral changes can be made in their existing repertoire due to physical and intellectual structures. As a somewhat silly example, if I fall into a swimming pool, I cannot develop and do not have gills to enable me to breathe, so hopefully I have learned to swim. In terms of structural intellectual limitations, I like to think my dog Finn is very smart for a dog, but I doubt that he is ever going to solve quadratic equations. Like Finn, we both have genetic and structural limitations we cannot overcome.

This presents a problem for every life form because their model needs to be robust enough to tolerate environmental changes while still maintaining sufficient stability for efficient life functioning. The rate of change that occurs in an environment is crucial because if environmental changes are too rapid the organism's model will be dysfunctional and overwhelmed. This is a very uncomfortable situation. In some situations, changes can be so rapid that they lead to cognitive and behavioral chaos which is a painful and precarious situation that most organisms try to avoid. We will need to discuss this important topic further in a later chapter.

A conundrum affecting all life forms is that they are most comfortable with a stable model of their environment; however, the environment does not cooperate because it is changing due to the diversity and complexity of our universe, and this increases with the passage of time. To cope with such environmental changes, any representative model must be flexible and able to tolerate changes. Of course, life forms prefer stability and our memory and experience of prior events lead us to assume that what worked as a previous model for an environment will work again. Thus, we are more comfortable holding on to a prior model of our universe than having to modify or develop a new one. That is easier, more efficient, and requires less mental energy. However, environments do change, and life forms must continually change their environmental models even if they are most comfortable with stable unchanging models. Another way of describing this situation is to say that life forms prefer predictability to unpredictability, but in reality, our cognitive lives exist balanced between predictable stability and unpredictable instability and maintaining that balance is the task of life forms. If the universe were not at all predictable, we could not be able to construct representational models, and if it were perfectly predictable, we could have one unchanging model which might be a rather boring situation.

We are always attempting to achieve stable models, but we never quite get there. However, although we need to change our environmental models, we often can achieve a homeostatic state within certain limits, and often, this is a necessary condition for survival. In that sense, we can only achieve a kind of bounded stability. The limits within which a model can be flexible enough to be stable yet still be pragmatically useful vary with each individual and the models they generate. Physiologically, our bodies have built-in models of how to respond to environmental changes. A good example is the human heart rate which will fluctuate according to different environmental conditions. Obviously, the more physical stress we face in our environment, the higher our heart rate. The lower limit is when we are asleep, and our upper limit will increase corresponding to the intensity of our exercise. This phenomenon is also age-related in that one's max heart rate decreases as we age, thus setting upper and lower limits to our responding heart rate model. In that sense, our bodies have a built-in physiological heart rate model that is robust in the face of environmental demands, but if our hearts were not able to vary, we likely would not survive. Cognitive models are similar in that they tend toward stability, but it is a bounded stability that allows for variation and is always changing.

The process of cognitive model formation is so inherent in normal functioning that life forms are very rarely aware of the process. Rather the focus is on adapting to the environment rather than stopping the process to reflect on what is occurring. In fact, interrupting the cognitive model formation process would be dysfunctional and not helpful for environmental adaptation and in some instances possibly risky for survival. We are much better off to remain unconscious of what we are doing. There are many biological processes and changes that occur in which our bodies carry out complex adaptations, yet we are unaware of them. For example, our heart rate, blood pressure, and respiration are constantly changing in adapting to the demands of the environment. Cognitive model formation is a similar process of environmental adaptation which occurs as part of the neurological system, but allows for cognitive adaptation.

In addition to inherent physiological models, there are also behavioral models that can vary so that they accommodate changes in the environment without having to construct a new model. A simple example is the way we navigate our local world. Most of us have a good grasp of how to get from our home to a work or shopping location in our town or local area. We have formed a mental model, and we usually try to follow the same efficient path in terms of minimizing our time. However, if there is some interruption such as a construction detour or a traffic problem, we can make an adjustment to the path we take without requiring a change in the cognitive model we have of our area. Interestingly, different people will develop different types of navigation models. I tend to orient myself in terms of cardinal directions and distance, so I have a mental map that I use to get around. My wife gets about by remembering certain places and finds her way by going from place to place without any idea of the direction and a minimal knowledge distance from one to another. As a western educated individual, I use the cardinal directions of north, south, east, and west, which are based on the earth's poles and distance along the equator. However, the ancient Polynesian navigators had an even different system. They created directions based on the direction of important islands from their home island, and so they had many cardinal directions each related to a different island. Their model worked well in their environment which involved very few islands compared to the vast distances of the Pacific Ocean, and their success is demonstrated by the fact that they settled all the livable areas of the Pacific Ocean. Now technology has provided us with a GPS satellite solution to navigation which requires much less effort or skill compared to that of our older methods and is such a robust model that it hardly has any limitations when used correctly. As a result, we hardly need to develop a cognitive model of our location. All we need is a simple model of a computer screen which is easier than forming other geographic cognitive models. Of course, if we enter an address wrong or if the navigational algorithm is incorrect, we better have a cognitive model or we might never find our way home.

The example of cognitive navigational models works well because planetary geography seldom changes over time; however, time is an important factor affecting our development of cognitive models. When in a constantly changing environment, our cognitive models need to be constantly modified, and often, we must completely develop a new and different model in order to coordinate our behavior to our outer environment and escape cognitive confusion. Many individuals have had the somewhat unpleasant experience of returning to an earlier address 10 or 20 years later, perhaps a childhood home, and found themselves confused by the changes that have occurred. What were once old familiar places often seem to have moved or are gone completely? Familiar distances between locations may now seem different, either larger or smaller than what was remembered. In that situation, they of course need to scrap their old cognitive model and develop a new one in order to escape their mental confusion.

Perhaps, it is obvious that the rate of change in any environment will have a profound effect on the development and stability of cognitive models and the general rule is that the faster the rate of environmental change the sooner models will become irrelevant, unstable, and nonfunctional. In our example of navigational models, the models are stable since the out geographic environment only changes very slowly. As was stated earlier, lower life forms live in relative unchanging environments, so they can function quite well with simple stable models and did not need to develop sophisticated sensory systems that are sensitive to environmental changes (This may be somewhat of a generalization depending on the individual lower life forms, but as a general rule I think it holds). However, depending on particular circumstances, humans usually live in constantly changing environments, and even though we prefer stable models of our environment, we must often change our models due to changing circumstances. Usually, we try to avoid profound model changes and often we have robust models that can tolerate changes in our environment without affecting our stable models. Unfortunately, there are limits to that adjustment, and many social, political, and economic changes are rapid and require constantly changing environmental models.

The social behavior of other individuals often brings about rapid changes in our environment, and the cognitive model we have of a particular individual may undergo a similarly rapid change. We may have created a positive attitudinal model to a new acquaintance which generated friendly behavior toward that individual, but if he or she then remarks that they are members of the American Nazi Party, or the Ku Klux Klan, our positive model may take a drastic shift as will our behavior toward that individual. There is a multitude of examples demonstrating how a sudden shift in the environment will upset a stable cognitive model which provokes an uncomfortable and often confusing emotional reaction. In the economic sphere, someone who has invested in certain stock and commodities will find that they are confused and upset when the price collapses suddenly. The faster the collapse, the greater the difficulty in maintaining a stable model of their economic situation and the more they may cast about in an attempt to find other more explanatory models.

Their existing stable model is no longer adequate. Creating a new model is not an easy task as most of us are loath to discard a long held and sometimes cherished model. An individual in that situation needs to find new forms of economic logic and new examples that justify the new model which is often an arduous intellectual task. In many dramatic situations, an individual will fall into a chaotic state which can cause a severe deterioration in thinking, behavior, and one's emotional state. We will discuss chaos and cognitive chaotic states and their importance in functioning in a future chapter.

Chapter 5
Human Development and Cognitive Models

Abstract This chapter traces the development of cognitive models from the limited cognitive models of infancy to the mature sophisticated models of adults. This process begins in utero and is a slow but constant effort to understand the myriad of environmental associations across the many stages of human development. By seeking out relationships among variables, human development is a process of seeking stability in a changing world. Starting with the emergence of different infant reflexes and continuing through concrete reasoning to high levels of intellectual abstraction, we humans continue to seek stability by recognizing the relevant and logical associations that surround us. A newborn infant is confronted with a vast number of sights, sounds, smells, tastes, and touches, but that infant does not recognize the associations between these stimuli. Recognizing that there are meaningful relationships between is a slow process, but one that continues through childhood and later life in the form of education. Aside from rote memorization, most forms of education involve understanding the simple and complex relationships in our exterior environment. If we cannot recognize these relationships, we cannot form useful and relevant cognitive models.

Keywords Human development · Cognitive associations · Causality · Imaginary environments · Piaget · Concrete operations · Infant reflexes

Obviously, cognitive models must develop by the gradual accretion of information concerning aspect variables in organism's environment. However, this is not a simple additive process. In the case of humans, it likely begins at some point later in inter-uterine development when neuronal structures begin to emerge and become organized. That means that at some point the fetus begins to form a simplistic model of the inter-uterine environment. This is a rather simple model because the environment available to the fetus is also simple. Although none of us have any recollection of that early time in our development, there was little or no visual stimulation, perhaps a good bit of auditory stimuli in the form of a mother's heartbeats, breathing noises, and other intestinal sounds. In addition, there was likely tactile stimulation as a mother went about her ordinary activities and the infant moved about in the

R. Leve, *The Complexity of Human Thought*,
https://doi.org/10.1007/978-3-031-09104-9_5

womb. Although this is a simple environment, it likely had enough variables to enable the creation of a cognitive model reflecting the simple environment of the womb.

Imagine the explosive visual stimulation created by the infant's emergence at birth. Now, infants have the difficult task of separating the multitudinous new visual stimuli one from another and trying to organize that into a cohesive cognitive model. From this point on, the infants faced a Herculean task of organizing this new, multi-sensory, and complex environment into a relevant cognitive model. Perhaps, the reason that we do not have memories of the early months of our infancy is that there are no cohesive associations that allowed for the creation of logical models. As adults, we access most of our memories because they are related to other memories, thoughts, and ideas. In infancy, we likely do not have this ability to relate one aspect of the environment to another.

The development of cohesive cognitive models takes a long time in humans, and I doubt anyone can identify a definitive point in life where we can say a child has created a sophisticated cognitive model. This developmental process occurs slowly because it requires the recognition of logical associations between aspects of the environment. Perhaps, the first step in this process is the identification of different objects, people, pets, and other important variables that make up a child's environment. However, this is only the first step in the crucial skill of developing cognitive models. The more important skill is the identification of relevant and logical associations between environmental variables. Actually, the recognition and identification of associations between "things" and information are the way we acquire complex information. Trying to understand and predict the consequences of our environment by only identifying and learning separate individual objects is not efficient. The most efficient way we learn about the environment is by understanding the relationships between things. That is, the purpose of our cognitive models and our intellectual life is guided by these associations.

This process of cognitive development involves many mistakes and successes in establishing the accuracy of this crucial process. The consequences of these mistakes and successes are what bring about the increased accuracy, and sophistication in identifying cognitive associations is a crucial life skill and is the main indicator of intelligence. The ability to recognize associations is a process that gradually improves through childhood development, and the acquisition of logical skill is a consequence of this process. Perhaps, a simplistic definition defines logic as the correct association between environmental variables.

The sophisticated creation of cognitive models in humans and other higher functioning organisms is a long process, so perhaps one way to understand the beginning of this process is by imagining a black environment void of any pattern. An organism cannot develop a cognitive model in such an environment because there are no environmental elements to identify or associate in this situation. We cannot be sure when simple cognitive models based on identifications and associations emerge, but it is likely at some early stage in fetal development. As earlier noted, at birth an infant now enters a complicated visual, auditory, and tactile environment with many stimuli that are related to one another. However, the first cognitive models that develop are simple, transient, and rigid since they are composed of early infantile reflexes. I am not sure if we can call these cognitive models because they are pre-programmed reactions to simple environmental stimuli. However, they are specific reactions to environmental stimuli and the beginnings of infantile behavior. A good example of this is the rooting reflex. When an infant's cheek is touched, they will turn in the direction of that cheek and begin to initiate sucking movements. Another is the grasp reflex. If an infant's palm is stroked, they will close their fingers and grasp the object. In these early months, infants respond to stimuli from the outside environment, but they do not yet understand that these encounters are related to the people (maternal and paternal figures) and objects in their environment and that these are relatively permanent. At this point, infants have little sense of past or future time and live in a state of an extended present (Piaget, 1969). They will sense each encounter as a separate event unrelated to other similar past events. In other words, the mother feeding the infant at one point in time is unrelated to that same mother feeding the infant at a different time. In technical terms, they have not developed **object permanence** (Piaget, 1954). The development of object permanence is crucial to the creation of cognitive models because it provides stability and predictability. Throughout the long process of infant and childhood development, human and other higher life forms will naturally seek out the stability and predictability of their environment.

Sometimes in these early months, infants begin to recognize and remember important objects such as a maternal or paternal figure, and this is the beginning of true cognitive models based on object permanence and a rudimentary sense of time. For example, they begin to associate permanent maternal and paternal figures and other familiar people and objects with the comfort of feeding and warm cuddling, and the development of a rudimentary sense of time is shown by their reaction to such people arriving or departing their life space. We have already discussed the advantages of cognitive models in terms of personal and species survival; however, I doubt that infants are aware of such advantages. Infants begin to create these simple cognitive models in order to provide cognitive stability which is much preferable to existing in a form of unstable chaos. This is not only a natural evolutionary ability, but the opposite is believing one's environment is unstable and chaotic, an uncomfortable state of affairs. Knowing that a maternal figure is the same maternal figure no matter when or in what form she appears provides predictability concerning that maternal figure and the maternal pleasures she provides. The alternative is to believe that each time stimuli related to a maternal figure appear it is a new and unrelated individual and that is a form of cognitive chaos. We can summarize this by saying,

The purpose of developing cognitive models is to provide cognitive stability and predictability.

This seems to be a naturally emergent function characteristic of all intelligent life forms. Thus, intelligent life forms over time increasingly and naturally develop many cognitive skills that provide stability and predictability. For example, most human infants by eight months of age will engage in searching for an absent object although only for a brief period of time. By 12 to 18 months, they will engage in a prolonged and more sophisticated search for a lost object which shows that they have developed internal representation of that object separate from the object itself. By two years of age, object permanence is firmly established in children as shown by the fact that they can trace the path of an object that they can no longer see (Piaget, 1954). For example, if they drop a ball and it rolls under a piece of furniture, most children at this age can not only predict the location of the object, but they are likely to find the shortest route to recover it. By age two, most children have developed a robust construction of the space around them and the people and objects that are important to them.

Another crucial skill indicating the developmental construction of cognitive models is the concept of causality. In order to understand the exterior environment, intelligent organisms must understand that when changes occur they can be understood by cause-and-effect relationships. Most children develop an understanding of cause-and-effect relationships between 12 and 18 months. At this age, most children will not only wait for parents to help them with some minor difficulty like opening a door or getting a toy, but they will actively solicit the help indicating that they realize parental help is the cause of achieving their goals and attaining satisfaction in their quest. By this age, they have learned to use rudimentary communication to elicit cause-and-effect relationships. For example, crying is no longer a single diffuse sound indicating some form of the stress and unhappiness, but cries are now differentiated into signals of fright, anger, "I'm want you to change my diaper," and other requests.

The development and sophistication of cognitive models continue throughout childhood, and the quest for stability and predictability undergoes additional changes. Children up to about age 7 or 8 develop rigid cognitive models that do not represent the changes that occur in their environment. Jean Piaget, the famous Swiss Developmental Psychologist, refers to the fact that children up to this time have concrete operations thinking which refers to the fact that children will over focus on one aspect of an event and is unable to shift attention to other aspects of the environment. This provides a simple form of stability and predictability, but at this age they are insensitive or unable to understand changes and complicated associations in their environment.

One example of the concrete models of such children is shown by the following classic Piagetian example. When given two equally sized round balls of clay, they are then asked if the two are the same. They will say they are the same. Then, while they are watching, one of the balls is reshaped into a sausage. Although no clay has been added or taken away, they are then asked if they are still the same size or if one has more clay than the other. Now, the child will say one (sometimes the ball and sometimes the sausage) has more. Another example uses two different shaped jars, and the child is asked to fill each one with the same amount of beads. After filling the jars with the beads, the child is asked which has more beads. Instead of recognizing they are the same, the child will choose one or the other jar and says the one chosen has more beads. The child's error occurs because they simplify the environment of both the clay and container and bead problem by centering their understanding only on the shape of the clay and the container, thus eliminating the more complex variable of total size. Piaget calls these children preoperational because they are unable to perform the mental operation of focusing on the total volume of these problems and instead focus on the simpler variable of shape. By restricting their cognitive model to a simpler environment, they make their environment more predictable because a simpler environment is more predictable despite it being wrong.

After age seven or eight, children begin to solve these problems although the actual age varies with the individual child. At this point, children can easily solve these problems because they no longer center on one simple dimension of the problem. Now, they can attend to both variables, total size and shape, and understand that shape is not important. These more sophisticated children are dealing with and understanding a more complex environment. They can still maintain a sense of stability and predictability in their cognitive models despite the fact that they can allow their understanding of the environment to become more complicated. As was stated earlier, children (and adults) will naturally seek out cognitive models that reflect environmental stability and are predictable even if they have to distort that model toward simplicity.

Around the age of 11 through 15, though this varies with each individual child, there is another change in their ability to develop sophisticated cognitive models. Now, they can manipulate ideas into their imagination because their cognitive models are no longer tied to the individual stimuli of their environment. They can also form hypotheses about events that do not exist and calculate the results in terms of logic. In other words, they are not necessarily bound by an environment that is real, but they can also create an environment that does not exist and perhaps is not even possible and then can predict future outcomes as a result of mental manipulations. At this point, in their development, we are dealing with sophisticated individuals who are able to create cognitive models reflecting complex environments that may or may not exist.

Paradoxically, this presents a basic problem in terms of complexity science. The increasing developmental sophistication occurs because individuals seek out stabile cognitive models that are representative of their exterior environment. Such models are useful because they are predictive of future events which are not only beneficial for efficient functioning and survival, but are likely a personally satisfying state of affairs. However, complexity science tells us that is not the way our diverse and complex universe works. Our universe is diverse and complex with many interactive associations which make for instability and unpredictability, and so our cognitive models which may seek out predictability are similarly limited in achieving perfect stability. Obviously, our cognitive models must have some degree of predictability, or we would be living in a world of chaotic and dysfunctional unpredictability. In reality, our cognitive models exist in a middle area of semi-stability and a kind of bounded predictability. We humans and other higher cognitive organisms would prefer to live in a cognitively stable world, being able to predict our future, but the ideas developed by complexity science tell us that is not possible.

Chapter 6
The Structure of Complex Cognitive Models

Abstract This chapter analyzes the structure of complex cognitive models and demonstrates the flexibility of human thinking through the use of predictive cognitive models. Learning among even lower life forms can be a series of trial-and-error contacts with the exterior environment, and we learn by the consequences of both pleasurable successes and unenjoyable experiences. This type of learning is in the form of **stimulus–response–consequence**. Other cognitive models allow for learning without actual exposure or contact with the exterior environment because we can often predict the future consequences of our behavior. That follows a **stimulus–prediction–response–consequence** form of learning which requires an understanding of time. However, often the consequences of our behaviors are difficult to predict because they can affect unanticipated and unexpected regions of our environment, and we suffer unintended consequences. Errors in this type of predictive cognitive model are demonstrated by propagation of uncertainty equations which attempt to calculate the amount of error. These forms of behavioral learning illustrate how we come to associate our actions (behaviors) and changes in our external environment (consequences) which result in the formation of cognitive models.

Keywords Consequences · Stimulus–prediction–response–consequence · Modeling · Environmental interactions · Law of unintended consequences · Homo habilis · Propagation of uncertainty

Obviously, the creation of cognitive models is a crucial skill if we are to learn about and react to our environment. It is also crucial as it allows us to try out behaviors and ideas without any direct contact with the actual environment. The crucial point is that internal models are flexible in that they can be modified according to the motivation of the organism. There are many situations in which an individual might want to predict the consequences of an environmental structure, but not want to risk the possible negative consequences of enduring such an actual change. Higher-order organisms are able to do that by modifying the models they have created. The common word for that is imagination. Higher-order organisms, especially we humans, are able to modify the models of the environment and then predict the consequences.

R. Leve, *The Complexity of Human Thought*,
https://doi.org/10.1007/978-3-031-09104-9_6

This is common and very useful human behavior and underlies our use of tools. For example, a woodcarver working on a carving needs to select different chisels according to the hardness of the wood, the depth of the cut, and the particular location on the carving. Skilled carvers do not randomly grab assorted chisels and try them out. They have an internal model of their work and select the proper chisel according to the predicted demands of where they are in their work. Thus, they have a flexible model that is constantly changing. I suppose that when they began their work they simply had a block of wood to look at, but in the skilled carver's mind was a cognitive model of the finished carving, predicted to have the form and beauty of a work of art. Similarly, the logger who cut down the tree to provide the carver's block of wood had an internal model of the local forest, but before he cuts the tree he may modify the woodland environmental model, so he can predict where the fallen tree will land. The alternative would be to have a fixed model without modifying his cutting and letting the tree to fall randomly, perhaps at some danger to himself or his crew.

Models are created through interactions with the environment, a process we call learning. The simplest learning model is operant conditioning signified by the relationship between a stimulus, a response (behavior), and a consequence. Basically, an organism senses something in the environment (a **stimulus**) and then emits a **response** to the stimulus (a behavior) and that response has a positive or negative **consequence** for the organism. This is usually coded as **S-R-C** in learning theory. Depending on the consequence, the organism will then change its future response to that stimulus (note that the consequence cannot change the behavior as that has already occurred and is in the past). However, any organism even with an elementary memory can change any future response. That process is a very simple form of learning in that it does not require any internal model of the environment, but only simple memory.

A more sophisticated and useful version of learning that utilizes environmental models can be coded **S-P-R-C** (**stimulus–prediction–response–consequence**), and this is typical of higher-order organisms such as humans. This form of learning states that an environmental stimulus interacts with a preexisting environmental model and the organism can then predict the consequence of its response without having to generate that response. By simply introducing a change in their model, they can anticipate the consequence of that behavior and either engage in the behavior, withhold the behavior, or modify the behavior. This is a much more efficient process in that the organism does not have to randomly try out behaviors and endure the consequences of a maladaptive response.

Of course, being able to predict the consequences of one's behavior is a skill that depends on the accuracy of our models and one's ability to predict environmental changes, and we often make mistakes in our predictions and suffer unanticipated consequences. However, having the ability to modify a model is a powerful adaptive tool. Now, the organism can anticipate environmental changes within the internal model providing an enhanced ability to respond. Humans and higher animals use this predictive form of learning constantly in their everyday relationship with their environment. When selecting a particular article of clothing, we have a model of the future day's environment and we might select a handsome outfit to impress a new business contact or don an old piece of wrinkled clothing if we are going out to a local coffee bistro with a close friend. This is another example of a cognitive complex adaptive system in that we adapt to the complexity of the new and differing environmental circumstances. We not only adapt, but we also create many diverse behavioral systems in response to differing environment, and these systems interact with one another.

Of course, we also might err in our construction of a future model, and this can result in what is commonly called **the law of unintended consequences.** We construct future models based on our models of our present environment and that may have a congruent relationship with a future environment, or it may not be very similar at all. When we attempt to predict the future, we focus on certain aspects of our present environment, and based on those aspects and the relationship between them, we will expect that our predictive model will conform to the future environment. However, there may be other aspects of the environment that we did not include, and so things may not turn out to our expectations.

A good example of the law of unintended consequences occurred in the Paris subway system in the 1970s. At that time, terrorists were leaving bombs in the station's trash cans, so the authorities ordered them to be removed. That may have helped decrease the frequency of terrorist bombs, but it increased the amount of scattered trash and resulted in an unintended and unexpected increase in the number of rats living in the subway stations happily feeding on the trash. Generating future models is quite difficult and easily flawed. The problem is that the greater the diversity of our environment the more likely we are to not include and hence be unaware of important variables because usually there are many things to be aware of and we may not be aware of a variable or understand its importance. Also, if our future environment is complicated by many variables, we are more likely to include irrelevant variables that will have no effect on the future environment. In the case of the Parisian subway system, the effect of rats when dealing with bombs would have seemed quite irrelevant to the authorities at the time, they generated their solution to terrorist bombs.

In reality, using models is such a common and ingrained activity that it is scarcely noticed. Also, it is a continuous process in that the models flow in a seamless and ever-changing progression. Perhaps, we only become aware of our inherent model construction process when we sense something is missing in our construction of a model or when we do not understand something in our environment and we sense that our model is incomplete or dysfunctional. Then, we are likely to increase our attention to other aspects of our environment in an attempt to correct or change our existing model. I suppose model construction is such an innate process that we never interrupt our attention to our universe or say, "Hum," I think I am building a model.

A better way to understand cognitive models is to look at very simple human behavior, and a good example is the tool-making behavior of one of our prehistoric ancestors, Homo habilis. This archaic ape-man was the first to use stone tools which he created by striking one stone with another to produce a sharp flake. The sharp flake could then be used to cut through animal hide, bone, and internal muscle. Striking one stone with another to produce a sharp stone flake involves planning. To plan ahead, our Homo habilis must have had a present model of two stones and a future imagined model of a sharp flake tool emerging from striking the two together. To assume that there was no future model of the sharp stone flake is to believe that this was a random fortuitous act, but the presence of hundreds of such sharp stone flake at archeological sites associated with Homo habilis makes that a false assumption. Neither Homo habilis nor we modern humans can plan without having a future model because trying to plan with an empty model would simply be random behavior. Just as we are constantly creating sophisticated models of our environment, so did Homo habilis in his simple stone environment.

A more mathematically sophisticated version of this discussion on prediction is referred to as "propagation of uncertainty." In all types of prediction, there is always error or uncertainty. The further into the future we try to predict, the more uncertainty we introduce, but whatever the time scale, there is always uncertainity. If there is no passage of time, then our present model is accurate as are the rules that have emerged from that model. However, as soon as we try to predict the future, we are introducing error because we are either eliminating variables or including new variable, and these will interact with the contemporaneous variables that make up our present model. If they interact in an additive manner, then the effect will be less than if they interact in an additive, multiplicative, or power function. Similarly, if we are adding an environmental variable that is stable and does not change, then the effect will be less of a change to our model. Of course, knowing the interactive effects of a new environmental variable is difficult, and we are likely to underestimate the interactive effects. Using the mathematical techniques called propagation of uncertainty provides formulas that can calculate these effects. These formulas are useful in describing such an interactive model and in illustrating the complexity of interactive model creation. However, the formulas only work in the abstract as we usually do not know the exact values to enter into the equations, and in fact, the more complicated our prediction and the farther into the future our prediction, the more we are likely to distort any values we enter into the equations. The equations are illustrative of the difficulties inherent in prediction, but they are derivative equations that cannot yield accurate results when applied in a cognitive realm.

The propagation of uncertainty equations attempts to calculate the amount of error in a situation, and this may work well in a laboratory situation where we can determine limits to the amount of error inherent in our values, but that is more difficult in cognition where the errors are not the kind whose limits (amount of error) can be calculated with any degree of accuracy. In psychological research, we try to do this by using the normal curve and calculating probabilities, but we never know if the many aspects of an environment are normally distributed or how far it may deviate from the norm or an expected value.

Additive formula:

$$\text{If} \qquad Q = a + b + \cdots + c - (x + y \cdots + z)$$

$$\text{then} \qquad \delta Q = \sqrt{(\delta a)^2 + (\delta b)^2 + \cdots + (\delta c)^2 + (\delta x)^2 + (\delta y)^2 + \cdots + (\delta z)^2}.$$

Multiplicative formula:

If $$Q = \frac{a, b, \ldots c}{x, y, \ldots z}$$

then $$\frac{\delta Q}{|Q|} = \sqrt{\left(\frac{\delta a}{a}\right)^2 + \left(\frac{\delta b}{b}\right)^2 + \cdots + \left(\frac{\delta c}{c}\right)^2 + \left(\frac{\delta x}{x}\right)^2 + \left(\frac{\delta y}{y}\right)^2 + \cdots + \left(\frac{\delta z}{z}\right)^2}.$$

Power formula:
If n is an exact number and $Q = x^n$, then

$$\frac{\delta Q}{|\mathrm{Q}|} = |n| \frac{\delta x}{|x|}.$$

Chapter 7
Complexity Principles and Human Thinking

Abstract The basic principles of complexity science describe the emergence of self-organization, and this principle is explained through demonstrations of cycling and sailboat racing. In these situations, self-organization arises as a way of minimizing the energy demands of the local environment. These activities also demonstrate how rules inherently emerge and control the behavior of the agents in that environment. For those individual agents, the rules tend to both simplify the cognitive models directing their behavior and decrease the number of variables and interactions allowing them to better "understand" that local environment. This chapter also illustrates the structure of compound models which may have many variables but no interactions and complex models which will have many variable interactions. Complexity science shows that many cognitive models attempting to represent the exterior universe may be so complex that they are likely to indicate bounded and imperfect representations.

Keywords Cognitive unpredictability · Initial conditions · Butterfly effect · Model stability · Cognitive rules · Compound cognitive model agents

The principles of complexity science provide some insight into how we can understand the process of cognitive model creation as these principles help us predict when a phenomenon is unpredictable. As is true in so many aspects of our universe, the behavioral interactions between an organism and its environment often are a complex and unpredictable process in that they fall outside the exact predictability of scientific laws and cannot be reduced to a theory or an equation. The development of complexity science and its principles is an attempt to understand this universal complexity and provide some insight into this unpredictability. ***In that sense, it attempts to predict and provide an understanding concerning phenomenon that are unpredictable.*** That may sound contradictory, but complexity science identifies the multitude of situations that are not predictable and therefore by contrast tends to identify those situations that are predictable. In Chap. 2, we identified a number of principles of complexity science such as emergence, complex adaptive systems, flocking, self-organization, system adaptation, and others to explain the complexity

R. Leve, *The Complexity of Human Thought*,
https://doi.org/10.1007/978-3-031-09104-9_7

of our universe. In a general sense, complexity science attempts to explain how dynamic complex systems emerge among the multitude of diverse situations in our world and includes our natural environment and our cognitive environment.

For example, as I am writing this I can look out at the well-defined streaks of foam being blown downwind by a strong Nova Scotian wind on the lake outside my backdoor. They have self-organized into separate lines of white foam and have adapted to the gusts of wind racing down the lake. They have "flocked" together into many different streaks that are not less than 7 or more than 9 meters apart, and every now and then, a much larger wave emerges to run down the lake until it crashes on the shore. I cannot predict where the foam streaks will form, whether they will go straight or curve, which ones will die out, when larger waves emerge, and where. This common situation is an example of the utility of complexity science in that it can provide an understanding of the unpredictability of the dynamics of my lake, how it has self-organized into foam streaks, and how unexpected waves can emerge. Complexity science recognizes that although many aspects of the wind-driven streaks are unpredictable (their location, size, speed, etc.), they do self-organize into the patterns I have observed.

Another example is weather prediction. Complexity science has identified the principle of "initial conditions" as being important. That means that slight changes in the initial conditions of a phenomenon can have huge changes at a later time. We have already discussed the classic metaphor of the "butterfly effect" which states that the beating of a butterfly's wings in the Amazon rainforest can produce cascading weather changes that can generate a devastating hurricane that ravages Gulf Coast cities. A better meteorological example of the concept of initial conditions is everyday weather prediction. Weather prediction can be quite accurate four hours in the future, but not very accurate for a week in the future. There are likely to be few initial conditions (changes in the location, direction, height, and speed of jet stream, collision of new air mass, etc.) that affect the weather over four hours of time, but there will be a host of initial conditions that can determine the weather a week in the future. However, even a four-hour weather window with our sophisticated radar, weather balloons, and instruments can be faulty if the sun heats an area of ground adjacent to your personal picnic location causing a parcel of heated air to rise and eventually develop into an afternoon thunderstorm that rains on your about to be eaten sandwich. However, predicting the occurrence of a thunderstorm will be more accurate in a four-hour window than over the span of a week. Thus, the concepts of initial conditions dictate that knowing all initial conditions of the weekly weather environment can be very difficult and has a great effect on our ability to forecast weather and other phenomena.

Just as complexity science provides an understanding of complex phenomenon in the physical realm, it also can be useful in understanding the behavioral and cognitive realm. Human behavior, both simple and complicated, can demonstrate the concept of a complex adaptive system. A complex adaptive system is one that self-organizes into a pattern, a dynamic pattern, often an unexpected pattern, without any directive from a leader or authority. It will occur naturally as an adaptation to the external environment. If you have ever watched a cycling race like the Tour de

France on TV, you may have been struck by the pattern that the peloton (the main group of riders) formed at different times and in different race locations. Since cycle racers can travel at speeds up to and exceeding 50 kilometers per hour, they create a significant wind that requires a great deal of energy to overcome, and the faster they go, the greater pedaling energy they must expend (wind is the primary influence as the rolling resistance of the wheels on the pavement is minimal). If they ride behind another rider, they will use about 30 percent less effort, and as a result, racing cyclists will form a long string behind the lead rider or riders. They are forming a complex adaptive system of riders such that each cyclist rides close (often inches) to the rear wheel of the preceding rider and inches from racers on their right and left. There is no leader that dictated that the riders assume this pattern, but it will occur naturally in order to adapt to and minimize the wind. This overall pattern of a long string of cyclists will often change if the road direction shifts so that now the wind is coming from the side of the road. Then, the string of riders will slant across the road so that the first rider is on the windward side of the road and the rearmost rider will be at the end of a long string of riders on the downwind side of the road. If there are a large number of riders, they may split into two or more groups repeating the same slanted pattern because the road width is not large enough to stay in the wind shadow of the preceding racer. As seen from above, it can seem like a complex ballet of cyclist weaving back and forth according to the shifts in road direction. The cyclist ballet is simply a result of a leaderless complex adaptive system adapting its behavior to the wind direction (Fig. 7.1).

The real situation is even complicated than that simple description. As there are many teams in the race, they will ride in such a way to protect their best cyclist from a headwind in order to save his strength for more critical parts of the race such as an important mountain climb or the final sprint. As a team comes to the final sprint, they will form a line in front of their fastest cyclist, protecting him from the wind and leading him to the final couple of hundred yards, so he can sprint out from behind their wind shadow and win the final sprint and the race. Thus, there are a number of dynamic adaptive systems going on at all times during a cycle race requiring individual riders and teams to adapt to constantly changing circumstances, and what may seem to the uninitiated as a race where the rider with the strongest legs will win is actually a series of dynamic systems of very complex adaptive behaviors responding to an ever-changing environment.

Another behavioral example of a complex adaptive system is the beginning of a sailboat race or almost any other race that involves very complicated human behaviors. The best position at the start line at the beginning of the race is the windward position closest to the upwind end of the line; however, no boat is permitted to go over the line early before the starter sounds a horn. Of course, all the boats are moving since they cannot just stay still in place. That means that before the start boats seem to be milling about in a random fashion maneuvering to get to the favored position seconds before the sound of the horn signals the start of the race. Of course, no boat is allowed to touch or hit the hull of another boat or they incur a penalty. Again, there is no leader directing the position of any or all of the boats yet as they get closer in time to the start a pattern spontaneously emerges such that the boats form into a

Fig. 7.1 Wind direction creating a self-organized racing peloton. (Photograph by Thomas Gaier)

single line just behind the start line. Usually, as the starting horn sounds, all boats are lined up close to but not touching one another and reaching their maximum speed as they cross the line. Seen from the start that too seems like watching a patterned ballet slowly emerge from a previously chaotic mass of milling sailboats (Fig. 7.2).

There is a multitude of other behavioral examples of such complex adaptive systems emerging in a leaderless situation. The overall pattern may be generally predictable, but attempting to predict the position, orientation, and speed of any individual weather pattern, cyclist, sailboat, or other agents will be very difficult. However, they are likely to organize themselves into an adaptive system in response to the demands of the environment, and this seems to be an integral property of our universe. Obviously, inorganic wave and weather patterns will spontaneously organize without any input from the water or atmosphere as a property of their environment, and they are mainly inflexible so long as there is no change in their outside environment. However, organic organisms with simple or complex cognitive processes are different. Though they have no leader or outside authority directing a complex adaptive system, they can be more flexible and better attuned to changes in their environment. Since we cannot explain their behavior by looking at a directive authority, we need to look at the cognitive behavior of the agents whether they be an ant, a cyclist, or a sailor. In order to form a complex adaptive system, each will need to form a model of their environment, and to be an efficient member of the system, they will need to form identical or at least very similar models. Looking at how an

Fig. 7.2 Picture of the start of a sailboat race. (Photograph by Christo Anestev)

agent forms and then modifies its behavior according to that model illustrates the process of model generation. In the case of a bike racer, the overall environment is very complex as each cyclist must take into account many constantly changing variables such as position of other opposing riders, position of teammates, wind direction, road direction, peloton speed, and a host of other factors. Keeping track of so many model variables is a terribly difficult or impossible task especially as humans are limited in the number of variables they can keep track of at any given time (This crucial fact will be demonstrated and explained in later chapters). In addition, our cognitive tendency is to maintain stability in our models of the environment and that is a difficult task in a bike race, a sailboat race, or other complex adaptive systems. A common way in which we humans (and likely other living organisms) cope with maintaining model stability and a limited ability to cope with too many variables is the development of rules. Many systems have inherent rules which serve to simplify such a situation. As an example, there are inherent rules that an agent, racing cyclist, sailor, or ant must obey and these rules are not usually invoked from an overriding authority, but emerge from adaptation to the situation.

Cognitive Rules

Rules are a form of guides that spontaneously emerge from the interaction between a cognitive organism and an outside environment. Cognitive rules are terribly useful in many ways because they form cognitive paths that direct functional behaviors and they eliminate the plethora of irrelevant variables in an environment, and so they simplify cognitive models. Without the emergence of rules, the cognitive models that guide functional behaviors would become overwhelmed and dysfunctional. We have already seen how situations such as sailboat races and cycling races are examples of self-organizing systems, but these systems self-organize according to rules that guide their behavior. In other words, an accretion of individual cyclists (agents) by itself does not predict the dynamic emergence of the constantly changing pattern of a peloton; however, inherent rules emerge from the aggregation of cyclists. A few of these rules are to stay close to the wheel of the preceding cyclist to minimize the drag of the wind, but not close enough to hit his or her wheel (and crash), and do not make sudden sideways movements (another way to start a crash). A psychologically emergent rule is do not be the lead rider for too long (you will use 30% more energy and get very tired), but do not always remain behind the other riders (known as sucking wheel) or you will be seen as a cheat by the rest of the riders. The unspoken social rules are to take your turn at the front, or you will suffer social isolation or more likely the verbal wrath, sometimes physical wrath of other riders. Organisms and especially cognitive organisms are constantly surrounded by such self-organizing rules, and they are so common that they are seldom recognized.

The air traffic control system that controls world aviation is a good example, in that there are specific rules that separate aircraft. In most countries, aircraft traffic is separated according to altitude rules. Depending on their direction of flight, airplanes are required to fly at 1000-foot intervals from one another. For example, in the US ATC system aircraft flying a westerly heading will fly at even-numbered altitudes, while those flying easterly fly at odd number altitudes. The rules will differ and become more complicated depending on the absolute height and whether the aircraft is flying according to VFR rules (visual flight rules, meaning that planes are flying in clear air so they can see each other) or IFR rules (instrument flight rules, meaning that they could be flying in clouds and cannot see each other). These rules are guides to aircraft and air traffic controllers in that they guide their behaviors and keep aircraft safely separated from one another. The rules also provide pilots with a model of the airspace that they are transiting. Image the chaos that would ensue if aircraft flew randomly about the sky. The specifics of air traffic control rules may have been detailed by human minds, but basically, they are self-organizing in that demands of the environment dictated some kind of separation and having 1000-foot intervals between planes is a safe alternative. The ability of aircraft to maintain a specific altitude varies with the skill of the pilot, the accuracy of the altimeter, changes in barometric pressure, and other factors. Thus, the complicated environment of aircraft, atmosphere, and pilot skill dictates that a five-foot separation would produce catastrophic crashes and having 10,000-foot separation would produce an empty airspace inefficient for the demands of travel needs. There is nothing special about a 1000-foot altitude separation in that it could be another safe number such as 800 feet, 1500 feet, or some other useful number, but the fact remains that it is the combined environment of the atmosphere, aircraft instrument reliability, and pilot skill that required some form of air traffic control rules. In that sense, the environment created a self-organizing system of rules. These rules are guides that underlie our very complicated air traffic control system, and they dictated the cognitive models that are used by pilots and air controllers. In terms of complexity science, our air traffic control system is a complex adaptive system because each pilot is constantly adjusting their altitude to the one assigned by air traffic control and each individual and air traffic control is constantly assigning or changing altitudes for each aircraft in accordance with the position of other aircraft and the position of the airplane they are controlling. For example, when an aircraft is taking off and traffic control is constantly changing the altitude, they must pass through to reach their en-route altitude, and similarly when they are approaching their destination airport, air traffic control will be changing their altitudes, so they can be in a good position to descend for a safe landing. Each of the agents in the system (aircraft, pilot, and controller) forms a very efficient self-organized system that constantly changes to create a very efficient and safe air traffic control system. This system evolved over time according to the changing needs of the aviation environment and that evolution produced inherent rules (guides) that are certainly complex in terms of its many interacting variables, but also is adaptive to the demands of its environment.

Another example of a complex adaptive system determined by environmentally generated rules is the common traffic circle. These are numerous especially in England and France. In France, the rule is to enter on the right and autos already in the traffic circle have the right of way. In England, the procedure is reversed in that autos ride on the opposite side of the road. The particular roadside that autos traverse is irrelevant so long as there are rules guiding the traffic and giving drivers a model of that countries' traffic circles. Imagine the automotive chaos if there were no rules and drivers utilized random opportunities to enter and exit traffic circles at any time and in any direction. Certainly, there are yield signs and roadside diagrams to help the naive drivers, but the auto travel environment has dictated that traffic must move in only one direction if it is to avoid random auto movements and the ensuing chaos of crashes.

Many of the rules that determine cognitive adaptive systems are so common and simple that we never even recognize them as rules. A good example is hiking a wilderness trail. Two popular treks in the South Island of New Zealand are the Routeburn and Greenstone trails. The trails are well marked, but they are surrounded by a dense temperate rainforest and wandering even a hundred meters off the trail without a compass or GPS could easily result in getting disoriented and never finding one's way back to the trail. Thus, the unstated rule is never wander off the trail and that serves as a guide to hiking in New Zealand and happily finding one's way to the next hikers' hut. Of course, the trails in New Zealand are not a straight line going from the start to the end. In reality, they must follow a complicated vertical and horizontal landscape of mountains, rivers, marshes (even pastures full of cranky cows), and a host of other detours, but these complications do not invalidate the rule of "stay on the trail."

The preceding examples demonstrate that "good" rules are quite useful in many situations, but how do rules seem to spontaneously emerge. The answer is that if cognitive models are the ways in which we understand our external environments, rules both emerge from the models and guide the changes in models through the inclusion and exclusion of environmental interactions. In that sense, rules "say" pay attention to this variable or event and ignore others. In that way, they serve to make our cognitive models adaptive and relevant because as rules emerge from demands of the environment they become pathways that guide behavior generated by cognitive models to efficient adaptation. Of course, rules that are generated by the exterior environment are still modified by our existing cognitive processes. The example of altitude separation of aircraft in our traffic control system indicates this fact in that the environment dictated that a logical separation must exist, but the fact that 1000-feet separation was chosen rather than 1200 feet or 850 feet is an indication that our cognitive model prefers even and simple numbers.

Complex and Compound Cognitive Models

Complex environments are quite different from other types of environments, and they need to be understood in terms of their unique properties. Coping with complex environments requires first a recognition that they are complex, and then, an understanding that they must be simplified in order to be understood and not understanding the properties of a complex environment is likely to result in cognitive chaos. A complex environment is something that exists in the exterior world, but for us humans and other high cognitively functioning organisms to understand that complex exterior environment it must become a complex cognitive model. Perhaps, it would be more accurate to describe such models as complex cognitive environments. Basically, complex cognitive environments will have a number of variables, but most importantly they will have many interactions between the variables such that changes in one or any can result in changes in the others and sometimes include catastrophic changes. The degree of complexity of an environment does not depend on the number of variables in the environment but rather on the number of interactions between those variables. This situation will be discussed at length in Chap. 8.

An environment that has a number of variables without any interactions between them is not really a complex environment, but might be best described as a compound environment. Compound cognitive environments might have a number of variables, but compound environments are much simpler, will tend to be static, and will be resistant to change. A metaphor for a compound environment is a picket fence. Each of the pickets is part of the entire fence, but they are independent of one another and do not interact. Algebraically, this is a simple additive situation where the complexity of the environment is equal to the sum of the number of variables; however, if these variables have interconnections, then this is a geometric situation and the complexity of the cognitive environment can far exceed the number of discrete variables. It is the existence of interactions between variables that allows for the more confusing properties of complexity to occur.

In one sense, complexity science depends upon and is a study of interactions. In order to understand some of the concepts of complexity science, one must be aware of and study the interactions between variables in a complex environment. For example, self-organization is only going to occur in an interactive environment where the effect of variables can be changed because interactions are a form of communication between variables. In that way, a change in the external environment can bring about a new self-organized pattern. This can be seen looking at a line of ants building a bridge composed of ant bodies when it contacts a water obstacle. This self-organized bridge building can only occur if the ants have some form of interactive communication among themselves. In other words, any ant approaching the bridge under construction must know the position of other ants in order to accurately and successfully and their body to a position that will result in a useful and completed bridge of ants. If they were not able to interact with each other, they would likely form a random pattern of individual ants wandering about near the start of the obstacle.

A similar situation occurs when agents such as geese fly in a V pattern or baitfish form a tight ball flocking together according to simple rules. If the geese had no interaction or a fixed unchanging interaction with one another, they are likely to form a random and disorganized flight pattern. In actuality, the flocking behavior of migratory geese shows that the interaction between them changes within the overall V-shaped pattern of the flock. The V-shaped pattern of the flock may be stable, but there is movement between individual geese such that each individual goose will be in a different position in the flock over time. To do that, the geese must have some sort of visual communication so that they respond to the differing flight positions of their neighbors. If a flock of geese never changed so that each individual goose stayed in the same place that would be a compound flock of geese, it would be a very inefficient form of migration. The few lead geese would quickly get tired and likely quite irritated with the laggard geese who were cruising along in the beneficial helpful air currents.

Similarly, the concept of emergence also depends on interactions between variables and is unlikely to occur if there is no opportunity for the variables to interact over time. Although I am not a great fan of the meteorological butterfly example, it will serve as a useful metaphor to explain this point. The butterfly effect postulates that wind created by a butterfly flapping its wings in the Amazon can create a hurricane that eventually devastates Caribbean islands and coastal American cities. Obviously, for this to happen, the butterflies flapping must interact with another air current which then must interact with moisture differences, air mass heat differentials, weather fronts, and so on, and on until it finally generates the hurricane. In other words, there must be a series of interactions between different meteorological variables to finally produce the hurricane. If our heroic butterfly flaps its wings and the minuscule wind created does not interact with any other weather variable, then it is just an isolated variable with no interconnections and will never produce the hurricane. The interaction between variables in this situation is likely to be critical in terms of its values. We might speculate that the butterfly needs to flap its wings to create the perfect wind current, neither too fast nor too slow, which must interact with a certain humidity level, again neither too humid nor not humid enough, and so on to generate our hurricane. We can describe this situation in another way by saying that the butterfly effect requires a large number of variables with many interactions over some period of time. In other words, we are dealing with a very complex interactive environment that will be extraordinarily difficult to predict. Predicting the hurricane would mean creating a future cognitive model and accurately predicting such an occurrence from our heroic little butterfly is well-nigh impossible.

Chapter 8
Constructing Cognitive Stability

Abstract Two principles inherent in our universe allow for the development of cognitive networks. As a general rule, the **p** concept maintains stability in human thinking and the **k** concept allows for cognitive change. This chapter focuses on the role of the p factor which allows for the inclusion and exclusion of environmental information in the formation of cognitive models and does not allow a cognitive model to become overwhelmed by too much information. The k factor focuses on the interconnections between informational variables and that will be discussed in the next chapter. Examples of how the p factor allows for the formation of cognitive variables are discussed in terms of common everyday activities such as driving an automobile and dangerous behavior such as safely navigating a kayak through the complex rapids of a white water river. Diagrams of the interactions in cognitive models demonstrate the limits of stability in such models and how they can quickly become chaotic and dysfunctional.

Keywords Neuronal models · Dysfunctional life forms · Bounded stability · p process · Inclusion · Exclusion · Cognitive probability · Cognitive nodes

The development of the rules and limitations inherent in the formation and maintenance of neuronal models is likely related to the principles that underlie the exterior universe (Jantsch, 1980**).**

There are two salient reasons why our cognitive models should be subject to the same rules and limitations of the exterior universe. Firstly, life forms are a part of the entire universe, and since they are constructed out of the chemical material of the universe, any construction of such material must reflect the basic rules and limitations of the universe. Life forms may have evolved additional rules and be subject to additional limitations; however, it is unlikely that they could evade such basic processes. Secondly, if the cognitive activities of life forms are to accurately reflect the exterior universe, they must of necessity reflect the principles and constraints of the phenomena they are attempting to mirror. If cognitive constructions were not guided by such constraints and processes, they would create an inaccurate reflection of the universe, and it is doubtful that such a dysfunctional life form could ever

R. Leve, *The Complexity of Human Thought*,
https://doi.org/10.1007/978-3-031-09104-9_8

evolve (Edelman, 1992). The history of science demonstrates that the universe is not completely random, and its events and phenomena are often repeatable (Odum, 1988). So too, our cognitive models of the exterior universe must be nonrandom, stable, and repeatable.

Model Stability and Functional Interconnections

Although we usually conceive of the universe in terms of concrete objects and we have already noted that in reality, all life form information gathering systems detect energy such as photons, sound waves, tactile pressures, and other forms of sensations, and therefore, our construction of stable cognitive models is the result of the interconnections of a vast number of energy inputs.

As noted in the previous discussion of models, constructing cognitive models with a bounded stability is a difficult task as the model must maintain a basic stability in spite of the fact that the energy inputs from the exterior universe are constantly changing (Morrison, 1991) and Stuart Kauffman (1985), (1986), (1993), and (1995) have presented a theory of self-organization in the universe which argues that interconnections in the universe are organized according to specific Boolean rules which result in a generally repeatable stability which avoids random chaos. This theory postulates that two variables called p and k are the determinants by which any system of interconnections, no matter how large, organizes itself on a dimension ranging from fixed stability to random chaos. In general, p is the process that describes how we maintain stability in our cognitive models and k is the process that allows models to change without degenerating into a chaotic state.

The central problem in developing effective cognitive models is that the model must be an accurate reflection of the changing exterior universe, and so it must receive constant relevant information, but it must not take in too much information or it will go into a chaotic state. The number of energy inputs a life form receives from its environment is enormous, but all such energy inputs cannot be incorporated into a cognitive model, meaning that cognitive processes must be effective at screening out irrelevant information. Of course, we must assume that a cognitive model of the organism's life space is always present, but this does not seem to be a drastic assumption as even simple observation confirms that some cognitive model of the exterior universe, no matter how simple, always seems to be present (James, 1950).

Inclusion, Exclusion, and Cognitive Models

The inclusion and exclusion aspects of cognition are analogous to the factor p in that the connections between important environmental stimuli must be significant enough to initiate an inclusion process. Viewed from a probability perspective, if the energy information in an environment is relevant to a contemporaneous cognitive model, then $p = 1.0$. That indicates perfect inclusion. When $p = 0.0$, there is no inclusion. These are the states by which we include and screen out irrelevant variables, and discrimination at these extremes is easily identified. However, when the correlation between the model and the variable is somewhere between $p = 1.0$ and $p = 0.0$, there is ambiguity and a life form is more likely to become confused and even fall into a chaotic state. In other words, we are confused as to its relevance and importance and whether it should become part of our environmental model. The closer a relationship approaches a probability of 0.5, the more likely that instability and chaos will occur. Such a situation is easy to understand as a correlation approaching $r = 0.5$ leaves an organism in doubt as to whether an environmental stimulus warrants inclusion which introduces ambiguity in the model construction process. Humans and other life forms will likely sense such a state as confusion, and this will produce an interruption in the continuous functioning that is necessary for life forms (Hoyert, 1992).

There is always the possibility that an organism will connect a stimulus to a model because it seems to be relevant to the organism, but is actually irrelevant as a valid reflection of the exterior environment. Such an erroneous inclusion will lead to a model that does not accurately reflect the exterior universe. Though such an error may lead to later problems in efficient functioning and even survival, it will at least temporarily maintain the stability and repeatability needed to avoid organismic chaos and confusion. A problem of human cognition is that often we are able to distort a model to include an irrelevant variable without realizing that we have distorted that model (Goudsmit, 1989). However, in higher forms of cognition such as in creative scientific model building, an individual may be able to integrate seemingly irrelevant aspects of the environment that are actually integral to a model and this may reflect some of the highest kinds of cognitive creativity. An example is the grand unified theory in physics which recognizes that seemingly distinct forces in physics, gravity, the electromagnetic force, weak nuclear force, and strong nuclear force, all reduce to one at high energy levels.

From another point of view, the function of p implies a relationship between mathematics and human functioning (Vandervert, 1995). In mathematical terms, the cognitive process of p is accurately described by set theory and the mathematical signs of = (equality) and ⁻ (inequality). If we view a cognitive model as a set of interrelated elements, we can deal with a vast number of elements from a multitude of other sets so long as they either fit or refuse the inclusion rule. As long as inclusion is close to $r = 1.0$ or $r = 0.0$, our model will remain stable; however, if we attempt to deal with inputs that are closer to $r = 0.5$, then the inclusion rule which serves to maintain stability will lead to a slowing of model change and possible confusion.

A cognitive example of how this inclusion factor operates is illustrated by the following. Imagine paddling a kayak on a white water river. To avoid a dunking, our paddler generates a model of the river in terms of rocks, current speed, and rapids. Restricting our example to only vision as a source of information, we can easily recognize that our paddler is seeing trees, clouds, water, rocks, and a host of other objects in his journey. A large number of these objects can be included in his visual scan without deteriorating into a chaotic state so long as these objects are recognized as irrelevant and not included in his model of the river. However, approaching rocks, increased current, and changing and narrowing of the river banks will be included and may change his model of that section of the river and thus enhance his chances of a dry journey. The p function enables higher life forms to restrict a rich environment of potential environmental stimuli to those relevant to an existing model, thus avoiding a chaotic cognitive state.

A common human error in the inclusion–exclusion process is the judgment involving political figures. Creating such a model involves many different variables and the inclusion–exclusion process can have an overwhelming number of factors, so we often ignore important ones related to the health of our well-being and the well-being of our nation and choose one or two that appeal to us for emotional reasons. Unfortunately, such factors may be irrelevant to an accurate understanding of a particular political figure, but it does create a simple and stable cognitive model. Oftentimes, we are quite reluctant to give up that model and we may reject new and important factors that could produce a more accurate model of our cherished political figures. This is especially true when our inaccurate model becomes emotionally pleasing, and then, we refuse to recognize new variables as worthy of inclusion. Often, in political judgments, we resort to a kind of binary thinking and separate any new information into positive and negative valences based on whether they fit our existing model or seem to conflict with it. Of course, we then reject those variables that seem to conflict with the model and remain with a stable, but inaccurate model. The present political system in the USA, dominated by two political parties, likely causes individuals to create their models (and their subsequent voting behavior) based on news and opinions that are congruent with their political affiliation. In this way, they likely reject information that would increase the accuracy of their political model, but that process does insure the satisfying state of model stability.

There are so many historical examples of this process. A salient one is the rise of Adolf Hitler. After World War I, Germany was politically and economically an unstable country and the great majority of German citizens focused on the simple militaristic variables espoused by Hitler for their political model. Complex variables such as the hyperinflation after World War I, Germany's shameful defeat, and the loss of colonies and territories such as Alsace Lorraine were disguised into simpler issues such as Jews, communists, and the victorious powers of England and France being responsible for all Germanys woes. Most maintained this simplistic model throughout the obvious destruction and disintegration of their country and even throughout the latter part of World War II.

Networks and Cognitive Models

Our discussion of cognitive models has thus far focused on how new environmental stimuli in the form of information become integrated into existing cognitive models. As we have seen the p factor of inclusion or exclusion is a relatively simple factor in the construction of cognitive models and the inclusion or exclusion of a new bit of environmental information will occur very quickly and most of the time is quite predictable because the new environmental information will be related to an existing cognitive model. However, since cognitive models are amalgamations of environmental information, they must have had a starting point and the study of complex networks provides a useful analogy in understanding this process. In our earlier brief discussion of complex networks in Chap. 1, we learned that in any environment there are nodes and hubs, and the construction of new cognitive models may reflect how hubs are formed. If we can visualize our informational environment as an initial collection of unrelated bits of information, these are similar to nodes. However, for whatever reason or perhaps for no discernible reason, one node may develop associations with a number of other nodes (which are unrelated to each other) and that node may become a cognitive hub or in our case a cognitive model as in Fig. 8.1. The increased importance of a particular node may be due to content repetition, clan membership, social pressures, or a random and seemingly unimportant piece of emergent information. It may even come from resource and economic insecurity and will be likely to form a cognitive model of selfishness and greediness which we will discuss in a later chapter.

As this node becomes in some way important and predominant, it can begin to establish associations with other nodes through the p process of inclusion. Of course, it will not develop an association with other nodes through the exclusion process since they will be seen as irrelevant. In this way, a reasonably simple cognitive model in the form of a belief, understanding, or even a prejudice will be established. This form of cognitive model will be simpler than those we will discuss in the next section because they will only have interactions between the hub and certain nodes, but the nodes will not have interactions among themselves (that is, a more complex situation). We live with many of these simple cognitive models. For example, racist cognitive models usually take this form in that a central belief, a hub, only includes information that is related to the central racist belief. A racist cognitive model prejudicial to African-Americans is likely to include only negative informational nodes such as they are lazy, they are less intelligent, and they are

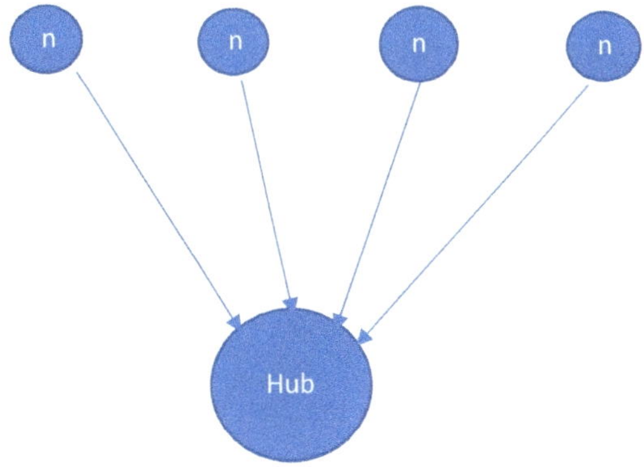

Fig. 8.1 Accretion of information nodes leading to the formation of a cognitive hub

more violent, whereas it would exclude a valid informational node such as they are Nobel Prize recipients, are caring individuals, and are tender parents.

Attitudes and adherence to dictators and autocrats can easily become cognitive hubs because they simplify many complex political issues by only including information that agrees with a dictator and ignoring contradictory information. This is an important observation because certain political issues can seem to have great salience and most people may have limited access to complete information. This simple dictator hub can be maintained over long periods of time when the leader has control of information access since a dictator can eliminate access to certain informational nodes. In addition, the simple inclusion–exclusion process to a central hub, being a simple cognitive model, requires less cognitive energy and is less susceptible to falling into chaos. Because of its simplicity, it is more predictable since it has fewer interactions between bits of information. For example, predicting the continuation of a dictatorship over time is likely to be more accurate than predicting the winner in a democratically organized election.

Although we may see networks as a useful analogy to the formation of cognitive models, we must realize that this is a static model in that it tries to freeze bits of information in time, whereas cognitive models involve a much more dynamic process. Not only are we constantly forming and changing cognitive models, but a multitude of cognitive models are always in existence and likely have been in existence in some simple form since birth. Of course, the number and sophistication of such models increase as we became more aware of the complicated and complex environment around us.

Time, Stability, and Model Change

Time is an important variable that needs to be considered in any discussion of cognitive models. An important aspect of any variable is not absolute time, but **cognitive time**. The relativity of cognitive time depends upon the speed at which an organism can process new stimuli. In our discussion of p or the screening function, cognitive time is usually very rapid for higher life forms as evidenced by the fact that humans are able to screen large numbers of variables quickly. Cognitive time refers to the time it takes to identify the relevance of a new variable in the environment and the time it takes to then integrate that variable into the preexisting matrix comprising that model. Generally, cognitive time is very rapid when excluding irrelevant variables as that is an easier process because it only involves simple recognition, and once the variable is discarded, it will not need to be integrated into the model matrix. Inclusion is a process that takes more cognitive time as it involves decisions and often difficult decisions, and after it is seen as relevant to the model matrix, it must be integrated with the other variables comprising the matrix.

If we return to our white water paddler, we have seen that variables such as clouds and shoreline trees are rapidly seen as irrelevant to the safe progress of our paddler though they are seen in his visual field. However, the sight of a series of rocks in his path requires the paddler to first decide on a path that allows safe navigation of the river without hitting any of these obstacles. Then, he must integrate that into other variables in his model such as his position in the river, the changing speed of the current approaching the rocks, the angle of the boat, and the present speed of the boat. This will take some cognitive time in his decision process although an experienced paddler will complete this problem much faster than a novice.

We have discussed how models are constantly changing as they react to the constant presentation of new variables. These new variables must be integrated into preexisting models so that the model changes to stay relevant to the exterior environment and maintains its stability. We have already seen that if a model attempts to integrate too many new variables at the same time, it will become unstable and fall into a chaotic state; however, another factor that can affect the stability of a model relates to the properties of the variables. Whether new models are being created or existing models are being modified, the stability of a variable has a profound effect on the structure of that model.

As a general rule, stable variables are predictable and such variables will create stable models that are not likely to become chaotic. Obviously, variables that are unpredictable will create unstable cognitive models, which is because stable variables will form stable interactions with a preexisting model, whereas unpredictable variables will form unstable interactions. To integrate a new variable into an existing model, that variable must interact with the other variables composing the model in a stable and predictable way. If the new variable is constantly changing its values or direction, it will affect other variables and the existing interactions between them which means that the model will be constantly changing, thus becoming unstable and unpredictable. In our white water kayaking example, if the current is constantly changing in unpredictable ways due to side eddies or severe sudden increases in water speed, then the interaction with oncoming rocks, the stability of the boat, and the curvature of the river will all be changing and unpredictable. Consequently, the model of our kayaker's "river sense" will become affected and perhaps will become chaotic and dysfunctional resulting in a dunking or worse.

Once an aspect of the environment is identified as important enough to be included in an interaction with an existing model, there are three general categories of predictability that will determine how they will be included in the model and how the model will change. We can categorize the new variable as a constant which does not change or as an additive variable that has small and relatively predictable changes or as a variable that changes in a geometric fashion and undergoes large and unpredictable changes. A new variable that is constant will interact with, but not change other variables in the model. In that sense, it just adds another factor to the model. Thus, it may increase the accuracy and utility of the model (if it is relevant and correct), but in most cases the model is little changed. For example, when driving down a highway, a driver may notice another auto stopped and waiting at a cross street with a stop sign. That auto may be included in the driver's model of the road, but it does not require him to change his speed or direction or any other variable that comprises his model of the street because it is a constant and predictable situation. He simply takes note of the waiting auto, but continues on his way (Fig. 8.2).

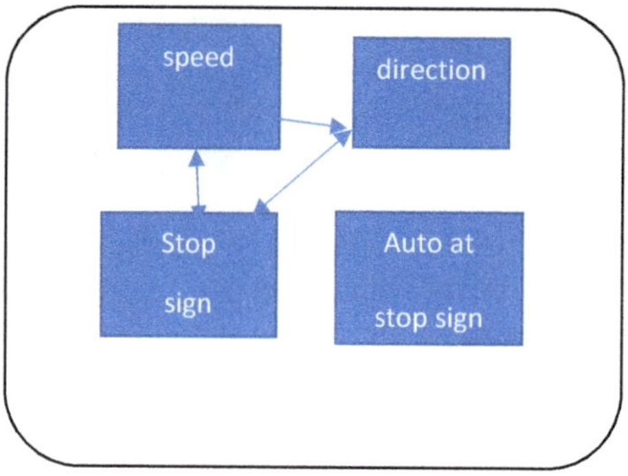

Fig. 8.2 Cognitive model of new variable that does not interact with other variables

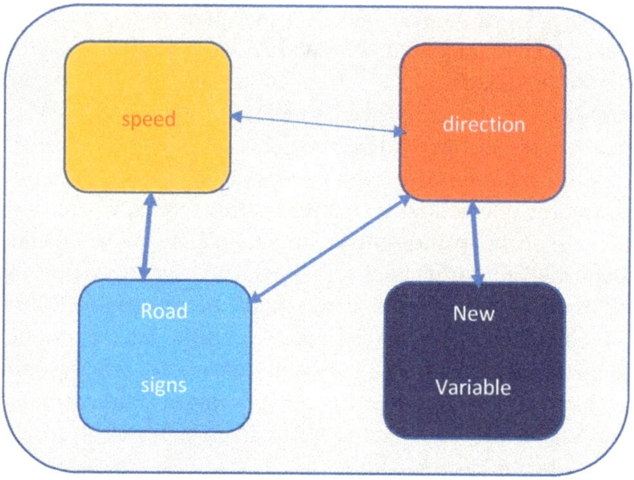

Fig. 8.3 Cognitive model of a new variable interacting with one other variable

Now imagine our driver going down the road and seeing a yield sign ahead. This new variable will be included in his model of the road and will cause him to change his behavior. The yield sign will interact with his sense of speed such that he slows down, checks any merging traffic, and may slow enough to allow the other traffic to pass or he may see there is no merging traffic and continue on his way. In that way, the new variable of the yield sign interacts with the variable of auto speed. It does not interact with the direction of the car unless he wishes to turn at the point in the merge (but that is a different variable) or his cognitive map of the road. The yield sign simply is additive in that it becomes another part of the overall road model road and this situation though requiring a change of behavior is relatively predictable. Its effect is to change one existing variable, but does not result in a profound change to the driver's model of the road (Fig. 8.3).

The third instance of integrating a geometrically changing variable is quite different and more complex.

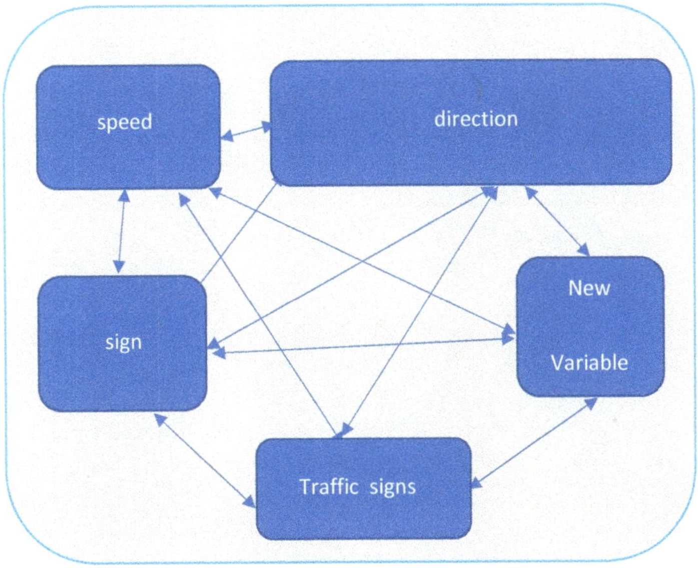

Fig. 8.4 Cognitive model when new variable interacts with all other ariables

A useful example would be an automobile driving toward a destination on a two-lane highway. The variables involved in this situation are the speed of the vehicle, traffic sign indicating approaching curves, changes in speed limits, and other traffic information. If our driver tries to introduce a new variable such as talking on a cell phone, this is likely to interact with and change all the other variables. Now, the driver's speed is likely affected by the distraction of talking on the cell phone, so our driver may slow his speed, pay less attention to traffic signs, and avoid changing traffic lanes. In other words, a change in one of the variables may result in a change in all the others, so the introduction of the new variable such as talking on cell phone will have a compounding effect on the driver and make the cognitive model more complex. If we continue to add additional variables such as a passenger asking a question, additional directional destination signs, realizing that the auto is low on fuel, or snow beginning to accumulate on the road surface, our driver is now in a difficult situation in which there are too many variables to safely cope with and our driver may become overloaded and make mistakes increasing the risk of an accident (Fig. 8.4).

Remember, when a cognitive interaction occurs, it will change the preexisting model, but there is also the possibility that the model may also change the value and meaning of the variable.

Chapter 9
Interactions and Cognitive Models

Abstract When a new variable is included in a cognitive model, it may interact with one or more variables or it may remain separate and have no interactive influence on other variables. In this chapter, we need to discuss how these interactions between variables occur and how they may influence a cognitive model, thus changing our perception and understanding of our exterior environment. Incorporating additional variables that interact with one another will make our cognitive model more complex, and this can lead to a better understanding of our environment; however, we shall see that there are limits to the number of interacting variables that can be included in a cognitive model, and incorporating too many will cause emotional overload and cognitive chaos. In other words, we always run the risk of our environmental model becoming dysfunctional.

Keywords Interaction limits · k process · Cognitive replication · Time and cognitive models · Complex reasoning · Higher-order concepts · Factorial analysis of variance · Complexity of bridges

The second factor to consider in a study of cognitive models is the process through which models change according to the number of interconnections between variables in a cognitive representation of an exterior environment. Stuart Kauffman finds an important relationship between the number of interconnections in a physical system and the stability of that system (Kauffman, 1993, 1995). In his writings, he postulates that k represents the number of interconnections in a Boolean network. As a general rule, when there are a small number of interconnections between each element of the network, then stable and repeatable patterns emerge, in other words a stable environmental model; however, as the number of stimuli and their interconnections increase, the model that emerges becomes more chaotic.

When there is only one new stimulus to be integrated into an existing model, the number of interconnections is small. Those particular environmental stimuli may interact with the existing model and modify it, and/or the model may interact with the new stimuli and modify that. This is a two-way interaction, which can be coded as $k = 1$ as the new stimuli form an interconnection with the existing cognitive

R. Leve, *The Complexity of Human Thought*,
https://doi.org/10.1007/978-3-031-09104-9_9

model. This yields a relatively stable pattern of model change, but when we attempt to integrate many new stimuli into a model at one time the number of interconnections quickly increases and the resulting pattern becomes chaotic (Kauffman, 1993; Langton, 1990; Holden, 1986). If we attempt to integrate two environmental stimuli into our model, then each stimulus can modify the models; they can modify each other, and the model can modify each of the two stimuli because in an interactive situation every part can have an effect on every other part. Of course, some stimuli may be a constant and cannot be changed; they can only change the existing environmental model, so the interaction only moves in one direction. If the interactions are bidirectional, then the matrix can become quite complex and is likely to become cognitively chaotic. In simple terms, we humans (and other life forms) cannot take in too many things at one time or we become confused and likely dysfunctional. This is illustrated in Fig. 9.1 which shows how quickly the number of possible interactions increases with each new stimulus that is added. By attempting to include 4 new stimuli into an existing model, we generate a possibility of 20 interactions and that is a situation that at best would strain anyone, but is more likely to make that individual fall into a confused state of unpleasant chaos.

The central requirement of any cognitive model is that it must be able to change while still maintaining its stability or *the ability to replicate itself on demand or revert back to its original state* (Little, 1974). Maintaining replication is a central requirement because we understand new experiences by comparing them to previous experiences. This is another way of saying that we integrate new experiences or changes in our outside environment by incorporating such changes into already existing models. If we think of a cognitive model as a matrix of individual elements with interconnections between them, then incorporating a new variable dictates that we establish a new pattern of interconnections. Kaufmann's observations provide evidence for the fact that there are severe limits to the number of new variables that can be incorporated into our existing models at any one time because each new element requires an organism to readjust the pattern of interconnections. Common

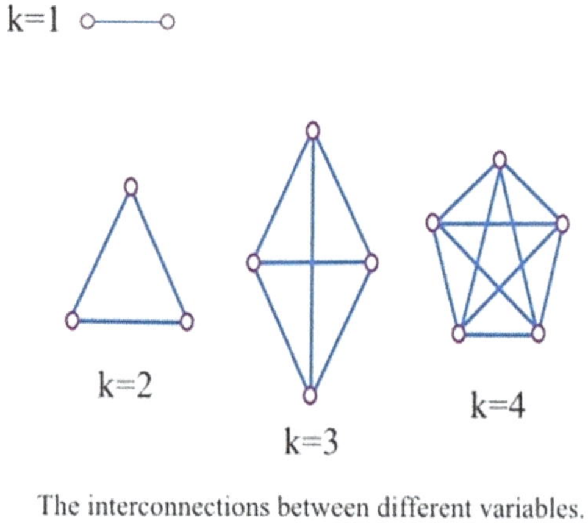

Fig. 9.1 Diagram showing geometrically increasing variable interactions

observation confirms that humans can accept only a limited number of new stimuli or new bits of information before they become overwhelmed (Schmid, 1991).

If we return to our example of the paddler making his way down the river, we quickly realize that as he scans the river ahead he is limited by how much information he can utilize. He cannot incorporate every rock, standing wave, current change, and eddy that is within his visual scan. Rather he limits himself to those of immediate proximity to his proposed path and is likely to provide immediate and crucial information. As he proceeds, he will sequentially incorporate others, but to attempt incorporating all the hazards is likely to result in a chaotic dysfunctional model of the river and perhaps a cold swim. Initially, this new k pattern is likely to be more complex containing a larger number of interconnections than the original model. The benefits of increasing the k interconnections are obvious for a number of reasons. First, the more informational elements we can integrate into existing models, the more accurately our models will reflect the outside environment. Second, the more rapidly the outer environment changes, the faster models will need to change to remain useful. Third, the more we can detect relationships between variables, the more accurate the new model will be. However, the increased number of interconnections is likely to be a temporary phase and will have a strong tendency to revert toward simplicity or to reduce itself to a minimum number of interconnections. Likely, it will revert back to a pattern of $k = 1$ or $k = 2$.

The process by which an increased k is reduced to $k = 1$ or $k = 2$ occurs by developing higher-order concepts that reduce the interconnections between variables. The higher-order concepts include the original variables; however, they no longer need to be individually considered since any influence they might have on other variables of the matrix is already included. For example, the concept of speed can include any number of objects in motion without needing to establish an interconnection between each and every moving object and whatever base it is measured against. An even higher-order concept can be developed if we relate speed to mass. Rather than having to deal with whatever interconnections exist between speed and mass, we can reduce these to a higher concept called the total energy of an object.

As a practical example of this process, imagine that our paddler sees an approaching rock downstream. He must take into account at least five variables to avoid the rock: the speed of the current, direction of the current, speed of the kayak, distance to the rock, and available time before hitting the rock. Each of these is observable variables, and a novice paddler will shift his concentration successively from one to another in an effort to avoid the rock. Calculating the interconnections between these variables is a time-consuming process, and if too many rocks and changes in the current appear rapidly, an accurate and repeatable solution may not occur and our novice may become an unhappy swimmer. The experienced paddler has learned that there is a reciprocal relationship between these variables such that speed can be converted into increased time by back paddling. Time before hitting the rock is related to distance, and distance (and force of an ultimate collision) is related to the speed and direction of the current. He does not focus on any one variable, but rather on the relationship between them. In terms of k, the interconnections between the variables have been collapsed into $k = 1$ or $k = 2$. This new relationship which is not directly observable is usually called "river sense" by the paddler, but is known as "total energy" to the more scientifically minded, that is, the total energy of the kayak in relation to any fixed object. Whatever it is called, the interconnections between the original variables have been reduced, and as a result, the experienced paddler traverses the river in a less chaotic and panicked state. In this case, the cognitive interval may be quite long or short depending upon the native talent and practice available to our paddler.

As already mentioned, the process of cognition consists of relating one event, object, or concept to another. Usually, we relate a new and unfamiliar observation or object to a familiar one. Perhaps, the essence of the process referred to as "understanding" is detecting the relationships or connections between the unfamiliar object or concept and a familiar model (Barton, 1994). In our attempts to establish a congruence between our cognitive models and the real universe, we can almost never reach an equilibrium state because there are always new changes that must be incorporated into our cognitive models. Thus, we are constantly involved in the process of adjusting cognitive models. If we could freeze a cognitive model in time, we are likely to find that it is stable in that the model tends to approach the $k = 1$ or $k = 2$ number of interconnections between elements of that model.

Model Change and Time Factors

An important if obvious observation with respect to k is that the process works backwards in time. When we attempt to incorporate a new variable into a model, we are introducing new interconnections into a preexisting model. If we take our time frozen model as reflecting a $k = 2$ matrix, then k is likely to increase, and the more new variables we attempt to incorporate, the more interconnections we will introduce. If we attempt to introduce a number of changes that increase the number of interconnections beyond $k = 5$, we will produce chaos and the model will become dysfunctional and suffer a catastrophic collapse. Since we are always facing changes in our universe, one may wonder how we ever avoid a $k > 5$ situation. Kaufmann suggests three general situations: $k = 1$ and $k = 2$ indicates stability, $k = 3$, $k = 4$, or even $k = 5$ indicates creativity, and $k > 5$ produces chaos. To avoid $k > 5$, we must restrict any cognitive event so that it produces less than $k > 5$ interconnections. Time is the important factor here, and the process occurs as follows. When a change is introduced and the number of interconnections increases beyond $k = 2$, the cognitive model detects commonalities between elements in the matrix (the development of higher-order concepts) which then simplifies the model, thus reducing the number of interconnections to $k = 2$ or k reduces to a stabile minimum number of interconnections. During this reduction, no new changes can be introduced into that model until k again reduces to a stabile minimum (Cordier et al., 1994). At that point, the process of model change can begin again and new changes can be integrated into the model. Perhaps we might describe a *cognitive interval* as the time needed to reduce new information to a $k = 1$ or $k = 2$ or minimal interactive pattern. A cognitive interval is rather elastic in that it may be quite short or rather lengthy depending upon many factors such as the number of interconnections needed to be reduced, the rate of change in the environment, the complexity of the problem, preexisting talent of the individual, and extent of available experience.

Complex Levels of Cognitive Reasoning

So far we have only considered simple cognitive reasoning which does not accurately describe higher levels of cognitive abstraction as might be utilized in scientific enterprises. One characteristic of such abstract cognitive efforts is the ability to seek out and discover higher-level concepts, thus quickly and efficiently reducing a high number of interconnections to $k = 1$ or $k = 2$. The process of theory construction in science may be an example of this process of reducing k to some stabile minimum, and we will look at an example of this process in Chap. 11 when we analyze how the Wright brothers understood and developed the many interacting principles of flight. The classic eq. $E = MC^2$ is a good example in that by reducing the vast number of interconnections in the universe to the higher-order concepts of energy and mass, and speed, the equation achieves a $k = 2$ state. Obviously, discovering higher-order concepts, although a difficult process, is necessary for the integration of information and the progress of any scientific endeavor. Figure 9.2 illustrates this relationship.

The crucial question centers on the process of how the number of k interconnections is decreased to a stabile $k = 1$ or $k = 2$. The simplest way of reducing interconnections to $k = 1$ or $k = 2$ is the straightforward process of sequential comparison. For example, if confronted with a $k > 2$ task, an individual would be able to sequentially compare the interconnections between each environmental variable to every other in turn and detect those interconnections that are identical. If this is done sequentially, then the information reduction is in fact a series of single comparisons, and even when done quickly, it is basically a k reductive process. This is likely the method that is used in most lower-order cognitive processes. Figure 9.3 illustrates a diagrammatic view of this type of cognitive data reduction.

Fig. 9.2 Diagrammatic example of interactions among Einstein's equation

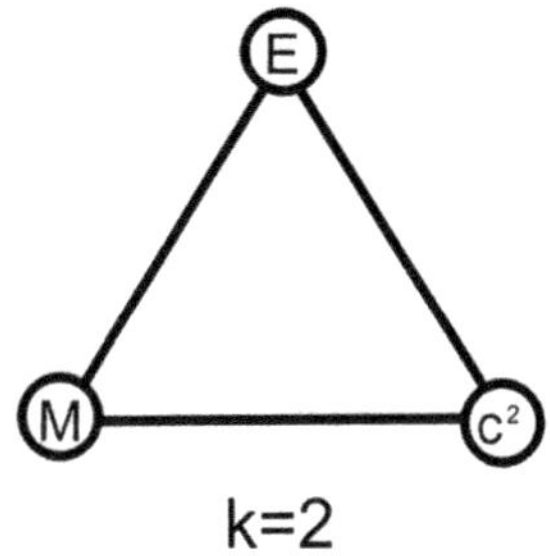

The k = 2 connections underlying Einstein's classic equation.

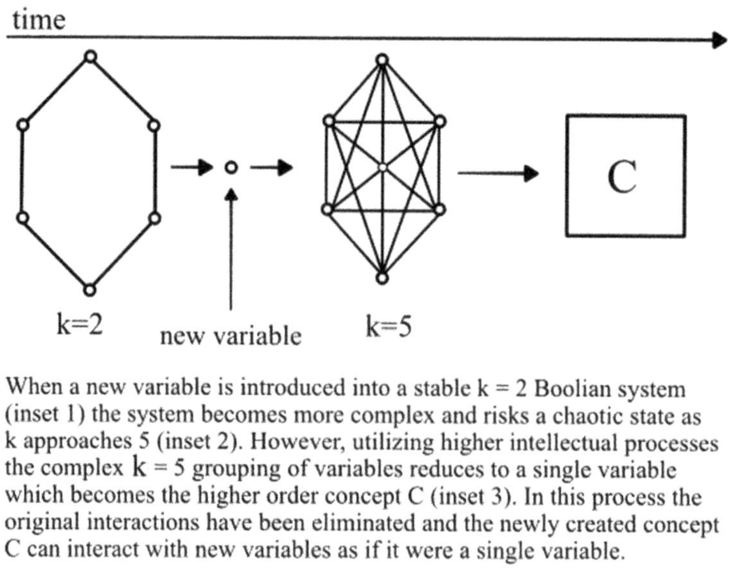

Fig. 9.3 Diagram showing how complex interactions are simplified

However, higher-level cognition as is needed in processing higher-order scientific information necessitates a more rapid and complex form of data reduction. In this process, the reduction involves a very high level of abstraction because the reduction of interconnections centers on the interactions between interconnections, rather than on individual variables. To clarify this somewhat obtuse concept, imagine five bits of information, identified as A, B, C, D, and E. Each bit of information is in some way related to the others in that if the value of one changes, then its relation to the others will change. Thus, if A changes its value in relation to B and C, then D will change in relation to A because they are interconnected such that a change in one will affect the relationship between any other. In other words, the value of D is a function of the relationship between A, B, and C.

This is similar to the classic nonadditive interaction effect in mathematics. The unique and difficult aspect of this type of cognition is that the relationship between individual variables and elements is not the focus of attention, but rather the reduction occurs among the relationships themselves. Thus, one is reducing complex relationships rather than simple informational interconnections. More to the point, the process is a reduction among the abstract relationships between concepts, and this produces the higher-order concepts that then provide a k minimum reduction. Figure 9.4 illustrates a diagrammatic view of this type of cognitive data reduction.

Mathematics again provides an analogous method to this cognitive process in the form of the statistical procedure known as factorial analysis of variance. This procedure identifies levels of significance between variables which is another way of saying it tells whether they are related or unrelated (at some chosen level of significance). At its simplest, it performs a comparison, testing the relationship between

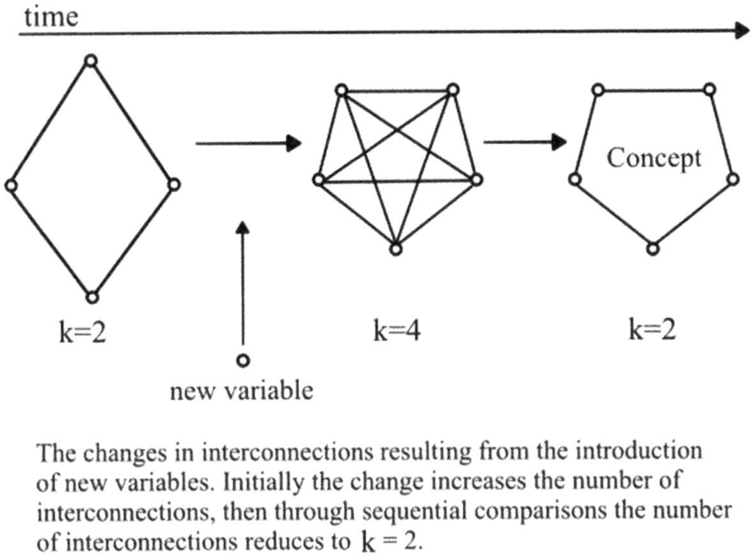

Fig. 9.4 A higher-order concept simplifies a complex set of interactions

two variables and a series of such analyses is similar to sequential comparisons in lower-order cognitive activity. However, a factorial analysis of variance not only detects these simple relationships between variables, but also detects interactions. That is, it determines whether there are relationships among the interconnections between variables. An interaction between two variables (a two-way interaction) is usually easy to understand and interpret. It means that the relationship between an independent variable and the dependent variable may be affected by another independent variable. For example, the efficacy of a drug (independent variable) may be affected by one's gender, male or female (independent variable). In other words, we may find that an antidepressant medication may work much better to alleviate depression in men than it does in women. However, if we try to test the efficacy of the antidepressant drug and include gender, ethnicity, and age, f(our independent variables) that will generate so many interactions that in most cases is too complex to be interpreted or understood. Perhaps this is similar to a $k > 4$ or $k > 5$ complexity, and both situations if not reduced will result in informational chaos.

In summary, the development of higher concepts seems to be a process that has definite limitations and these are well described by the inclusion–exclusion function of p and the creation of higher-order interconnections described by k. As we develop concepts that incorporate new information about the universe we inhabit, we must be sure that the models we create incorporate new variables at a cognitive rate that allows for creative model change without producing cognitive chaos.

Of course, the main purpose of a cognitive model is not to simply generate a fixed and stable cognitive model but rather to generate models that predict future environments. Such cognitive models are most efficient when they tell us what changes are going to occur in the environment that we must adjust to. Our models are always changing since the environment is always changing. For example, I have a static model of my desk as I am sitting there, but as part of my model I know there is pen in front of me. Having knowledge of the location and existence of the pen is useful, but the real purpose or advantage of my cognitive model is in the future when I decide to write myself a note, then I know the pen is on my desk and available to me to write the note.

The Development and Purpose of a Cognitive Model

Trying to define or identify a cognitive model is quite difficult because it can refer to an almost infinite number of aspects of an individual's environment, and it is a mental concept and not a tangible thing that is point-at-able. It is a cognitive process that attempts to put understanding and stability into a constantly changing environment, allowing a life form to create a limited sense of stability and a bounded predictability. This is a difficult task! Life forms live in a universe that is constantly changing which by its very definition is unstable and unpredictable. Complexity science is an attempt to understand the limits of this unpredictability to understand what phenomena are unpredictable and what are the principles that describe predictable phenomenon.

In respect to cognition, complexity science indicates that there is a progression in the process of cognitive reduction which tends to generate simple and useful cognitive models. The progression follows a particular cognitive sequence. The starting point is the preexisting cognitive model or preexisting thoughts. Since we live in a rich environment of constantly changing variables, there is likely to be some emergent factor arising out of the multivariable environment that interacts with the preexisting cognitive models; thus, any emergent stimuli can produce a change in the cognitive model as the first step in this process. Perhaps the best way to understand the effect of an emergent variable is to think about the interactions between factors in a cognitive model. Sometimes, the introduction of a new stimulus will not have an important effect on those interactions, whereas at other times it may result in a complete reorganization of the cognitive model. In terms of complexity science, new and unexpected cognitive relationships may emerge which results in new, novel, and unexpected occurrences. We can think about this as the emergence of a new and unique understanding concerning a political issue, historical or contemporary event, scientific phenomenon, or almost any event.

We might better understand the concept of emergence by looking at emergence in the physical world. For example, when atoms of oxygen and hydrogen which are both gases come together, there is an abrupt phase transition and they produce a chemical liquid, water. Similarly, a number of inorganic atoms including carbon, hydrogen, oxygen, and many others result in the emergence of organic life forms and the multitude of new and unpredicted complex biological and mental activities associated with such life forms. Just as we would not expect such unusual novel changes to occur at a physical level, a similar emergent process occurs on a cognitive level.

Any emergent stimuli that are relevant to the preexisting cognitive model will modify the interactions between cognitive variables, thus initiating a process of change or adaptation that is not predicted by a simple accumulation of cognitive stimuli. The process of changing existing interactions to the introduction of a new emergent stimulus is a form of cognitive adaptation. In that sense, human thinking is a complex adaptive system because we are always making adaptations to our thinking. Neurologically, our cerebral cortex and lower structures of the brain are constantly modifying the host of neurochemicals enabling negative electrical potentials to travel across synaptic connections. However, seen from a cognitive perspective, we are dealing with a myriad of different thoughts that interact with each other, which are constantly being modified. Thus, looked upon either from a neurological or cognitive-behavioral perspective cognitive activity is a complex adaptive system, adapting to the exterior environment with a constant inclusion of new events and changing interactions between variables to generate a new cognitive model.

As a result of this adaptation, we tend toward self-organization which is the next step in this cognitive process. In other words, there is a natural process through which we tend to find the most simple and efficient cognitive models that often arise spontaneously because they are an obvious and simplistic adjustment to our environment. The last step in this process of cognitive reorganization is similar to the concept of flocking in complexity science. In flocking, a pattern is established that is simply followed by each agent according to the rules that have emerged. There is little need for cognitive activity because the behavior of the agent simply follows elementary and well-established rules. A cognitive model now has been established which is a form of a solution to the vicissitudes and demands of our ever-changing cognitive environment. Of course, once we have reached this solution, we are back at the original starting point because it is likely that a new cognitive emergent phenomenon will appear that will require this sequential process to begin again. In that sense, this is a constantly repeating cognitive activity such that any preexisting solution is simply a starting point whereby environmental changes, as a possible form of emergence begins this sequential process again so that we generate a new cognitive model or solution that continues this sequential cognitive activity. In a way, this is quite similar to how philosophers of science describe the purpose of scientific activity. Science tries to answer questions not to generate a permanent solution to a problem but rather to continuously generate more questions. We also need to keep in mind that this is a process of cognitive reduction by which we are constantly reducing the interactional complexities of our environment into a simpler form which then guides our behavior so that we can better adjust to that environment (Fig. 9.5).

Perhaps the preceding discussion seems somewhat abstract and obtuse and might be better explained through the use of examples, and almost any episode describing scientific or engineering discoveries will suffice. An interesting example is the development of boats and bridges. We might imagine a migratory band of Homo erectus encountering a river at the boundary of that territory. The land on the other side of the river becomes a stimulus for crossing the river because they might see

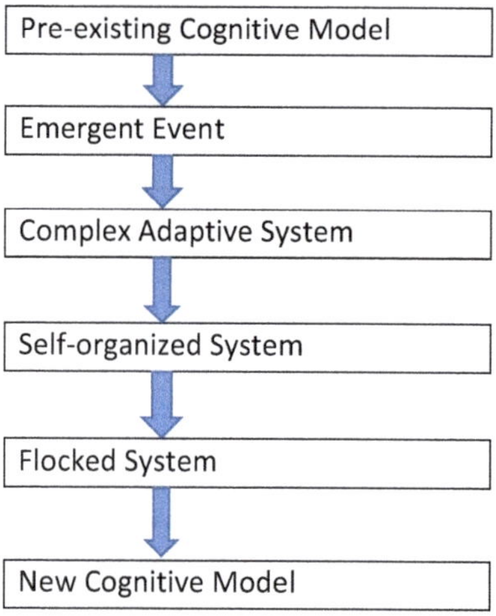

Fig. 9.5 Sequence in the continuous evolution of a cognitive models

edible plants or animals across the river or might simply be curious as to what is there. This stimulus might initiate an emergent process related to river crossings. Assuming our fictitious little band has never crossed a river, they might initiate a number of behaviors. They might start by trying to wade until they found the water was too deep. Perhaps one member stepping off into a hole would naturally kick her feet and flail her arms thus both staying afloat and moving toward the far shore. Thus, learning to swim solved two important principles inherent in any river crossing problem, staying above the water and propelling oneself in the desired direction, for example, the far shore. This adjustment might be sufficient for our swimmer, but it would not suffice for the band member who wanted to take a child or their possessions with them. Now, she needed to solve a third river crossing principal, carrying capacity. At this point, an observant member might have noticed a log floating on the river and decided to hold onto the log to get across the river. Now, one's possessions, and at some risk, one's child, could be put on the log and with some frantic kicking all could attain the far shore. There might be many adaptations to this "use a log to cross the river" such as selecting the correct size log to keep one's self, child, and possessions safely afloat. With some experience, perhaps the band might use fire and stone hand tools to hollow the log. They might even shape the ends, so it now had a bow and stern and it moved more efficiently requiring less kicking. We can see that this is only the beginning of a series of adaptive steps from our simple river crossing tree trunk to the sophistication of modern boats and ships using complex materials, sophisticated hull designs, and sails and engines as propulsion (see illustrations and pictures of these in Chap. 10). We might not think of a log as a terribly sophisticated watercraft, but it is the product of a complex adaptive system that encompasses all the principles needed to cross a body of water. The different types of boats that have emerged from this need to cross rivers and oceans illustrate the continuing complexities and adaptations required by the many different requirements involved in water crossing. Obviously, a simple log is insufficient to cross the

Pacific Ocean, but the human cognitive process has provided many creative maritime adaptations needed for many diverse watery circumstances. Interestingly, many cultures have developed many different types of boats such that they are useful in almost any marine environment from the Inuit kayak in Arctic waters to massive nuclear aircraft carriers that can carry military dominance into any ocean. Every one of these crafts is a simpler or more version of a complex adaptive system in the way it functions Our complex cognitive adaptive systems have even led to the development of the submarine, perhaps the essence of a complex adaptive system since to maintain perfect stability at different depths it is constantly ingesting and expelling water into its buoyancy tanks, changing the angles of its diving fins, varying its speed, and changing a host of other electromechanical devices. It even adapts its power systems, electrical, diesel, or nuclear in accordance with the submarine depth. In modern nuclear submarines, navies have been able to go to incredible depths using atomic reactors which are in themselves a complex adaptive system.

So far, we have seen how an environmental circumstance initiates a cognitive emergent process that is modified by continuous complex adaptations such that it forms a host of useful and efficient vessels. The next step in this process often generates a process of self-organization in that once an adaptive solution is found it usually produces a repetitive pattern. In our simple example of a dugout log, once our Homo erectus band has discovered this method of crossing the river they are likely to continue to go back and forth forming a repetitive pattern. Seen from above, it is likely to form a somewhat curved line (taking into account the current) stretching from one bank to the other and constantly repeating itself depending on the number of river crossings our band engages in. Thus, when crossing the river, our dugout tree is always in motion; however, the line going from bank to bank always remains the same with only slight changes due to vagaries in the river current. Usually, a self-organizational process is generated as a simplistic and efficient solution to a problem. In our example, the repetitive pattern has evolved out of many adaptive river crossing attempts. The pattern of a relatively perpendicular route to the far shore is the most energy-efficient method that has emerged out of the many possible complex adaptations that could have been selected.

The concept of self-organization is easier to see when it has many agents such as a bicycle racing peloton group of riders) which self-organizes such that each individual cyclist moves about the group, but the group pattern remains stable. I am often surprised at the self-organization that occurs in my college classrooms when once students have chosen a seat on the first day of class they continue to take that same seat throughout the remainder of the semester. I do not assign seats, but this stable pattern almost always occurs. I am not sure of each student's reason to take the same seat, but perhaps it provides each student a degree of behavioral stability and lessens any anxiety concerns that might result from trespassing on another student seat. I have even asked them why they self-organize in the same classroom pattern, but they cannot come up with an explanation either. Usually, they say it just feels right.

There is another river crossing example of the progression from emergence to complex adaptation and then to self-organization, and that is the bridge, which in its many different forms solves the problem of crossing a river. Using a bridge in a contemporary form to cross a body of water may require a very sophisticated amount of cognitive adaptation, but in its simplest form it requires more accidental discovery than thinking. The simplest form of a bridge is to simply walk along the riverbank until one might fortuitously find a tree that has fallen across a stream. Discovering such a tree does not require a great deal of adaptation, other than walking, but it does solve the emergent problem of getting to the other side. Perhaps a further step in solving this emergent problem would be to find a tree that leans across the river and then cut it down with a stone axe. This may not seem like a great intellectual leap, but it does follow a complex cognitive path. Once a need emerges to cross a river, due to simple curiosity or a better food source, swimming or wading will be seen as inefficient (and wetter) compared to simply walking across a log. Thus, a rather simple adaptive system of transportation has emerged, and now, the behavior patterns of the band have now been changed by adaptation to the increased efficiency of a simple log bridge. I might imagine that once one has had the luxury of crossing a stream by walking on a log rather than swimming in cold or even crocodile-infested water that individual will certainly use an adaptive cognitive model of log crossing as a better adaptation to get across a stream.

If this simple example seems rather insignificant compared to the classic examples of a complex adaptive system such as a city, an economic market, the human brain, or an electric power grid, it does illustrate the intellectual development of an adaptive system. The early Chinese culture provides a good example of the development of many different types of bridges as a complex adaptive system. There are many variables that must be understood in building a bridge among them the width of the river, the current, available material, composition of the river bed, and many others. Building a bridge involves adaptation to all of these many variables yet by -first millennium China had developed the concept of a beam bridge, a cantilever bridge, arched bridges, pontoon bridges, and suspension bridges using iron, wood, stone, rope, and bamboo (Needham et al., 1971). They had also developed the concept of a cofferdam and dredge to set bridge foundations and even included draw bridges to allow the passage of ships. Early Chinese bridge building is an excellent illustration of a complex adaptive system in the building of a bridge because it is obvious that they not only adapted to the hydraulic geography but likely used a good bit of trial and error in this process. Their success in solving this multivariant complex problem is shown by the fact that in 1059 they had constructed a beam bridge 3600 feet long across the Lo-Yang River (Fig. 9.6).

The process of constructing such a bridge and the many others of various bridge types across China is an excellent illustration of a cognitive complex adaptive system resulting in a finished product that changed the transportation behaviors of people living on different sides of the river. We can assume that the bridge created a greatly modified complex adaptive system in the way in which social and economic interactions were changed with citizens going back and forth according to their needs.

There are many examples in more modern times of how a bridge created a new complex adaptive system. The Brooklyn Bridge constructed by John Roebling and his son Washington Roebling in 1883 spanned the East River in New York City

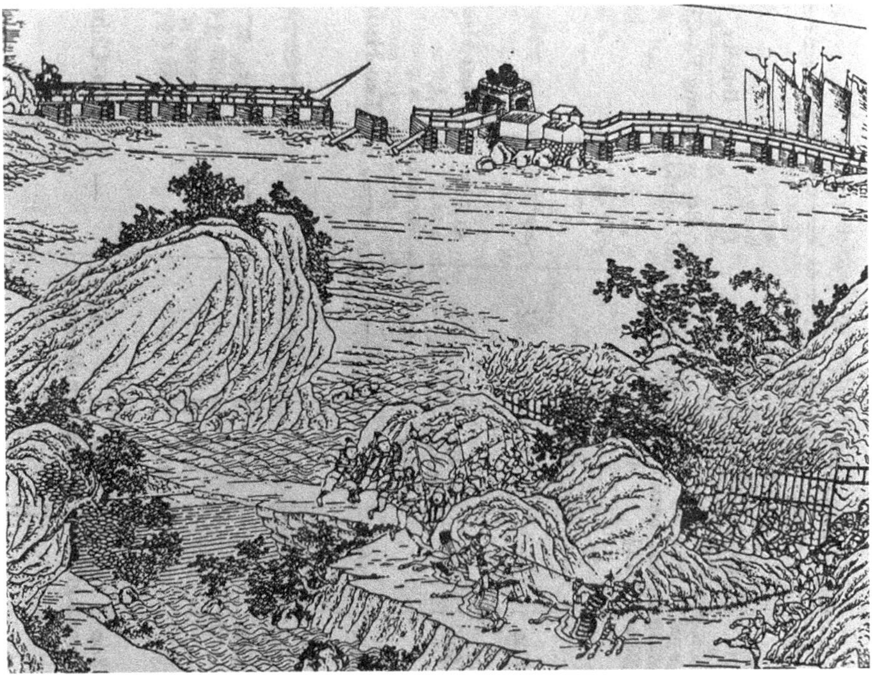

Fig. 9.6 Picture of the Lo-Yang Bean Bridge

linking Brooklyn and Manhattan. Before the Brooklyn Bridge was constructed, crossing between Brooklyn and Manhattan crossing was by ferry and the population of Brooklyn in 1850 was approximately 590,000 individuals. By 1900, the estimated population was 3,800,000 individuals. Obviously, the bridge created a population migration as people adapted to the ease of moving people and now vehicles from one side of the river to another. As of 2000, the population of Brooklyn is approximately 18 million people and approximately 150,000 people go back and forth across the Brooklyn Bridge every day. Thus, people initially changed their social and economic pre-bridge ferry-based systems into systems based on the newfound ease of the East River crossing. Now without any overall authoritarian direction, goods services and people go back and forth and Brooklyn has become integrated into the greater New York City complex adaptive system. We might speculate as to whether the bridge across the Lo-Yang River created a new complex adaptive system that changed and hopefully improved the lives of the local citizenry. We might also speculate on whether the creation of a complex adaptive social system in either Brooklyn or the Lo-Yang River area could have been predicted. I imagine that although the changes might have been guessed at by a keen observer, the actual details and structure of each complex adaptive system would have been very difficult to predict.

Chapter 10
Overload, Confusion, and Chaos

Abstract Overload, confusion, and chaos are mainly the result of including too many variables and their interactions in the creation of a cognitive model. Life forms tend to seek out simplicity in terms of cognition since complexity in thinking requires a greater expenditure of energy and results in cognitive fatigue. Cognitive chaos in a cognitive model can occur when stimuli from an exterior environment become too complex or there is not sufficient time to develop a logical cognitive model. Generally, humans have been programmed through evolution to avoid these unpleasant cognitive states. When they occur, they produce emotional reactions such as anger, fear, and sometimes even panic states that will interfere with logical thinking. Examples are discussed illustrating chaotic thinking, and methods to avoid this dysfunctional cognitive state are presented.

Keywords Cognitive confusion · Chaos · Avoiding overload · Simplicity and stability · Cognitive salience · Panic states

We have already discussed the observation that cognitive models are continually changing because we live in a changing environment and that means that we are constantly adding new variables to the matrix that composes our cognitive models. To cope with these changes, life forms incorporate relevant variables according to the previously discussed p factor of inclusion (discussed in Chap. 8) and these new variables are integrated into preexisting and new models through the k factor (discussed in Chap. 9). However, coping with new variables presents a problem because there are important limits on how many variables can be included in any model and the rate at which new variables can be included. Basically, cognitive overload can occur when the environment presents more variables than an organism can integrate into an existing cognitive model or when a number of new variables are presented in a very short period of time, perhaps even instantaneously. In such a situation, the cognitive models that represent the exterior environment become overwhelmed and dysfunctional. That is, the model falls apart and the organism is left in a state of confusion which is another way of saying it does not understand its environment and that produces an unpleasant emotional state. These unpleasant

R. Leve, *The Complexity of Human Thought*,
https://doi.org/10.1007/978-3-031-09104-9_10

cognitive-emotional states are difficult to describe, but likely we all have experienced them. In some cases, we might say, "I can't think," and at other times we may freeze and not be able to do anything. In my long-ago military training, my instructors always said when facing an emergency "Do something, anything, but do something." That was the military's way of saying never freeze.

Organisms create environmental models, so they can represent and respond to their environment, but when these models fall apart they may find themselves in a dangerous situation. However, even if the situation is not life-threatening, it will sense environmental confusion, an unpleasant state. This is true of all cognitive organisms although the sophistication of their cognitive models may vary depending on the extent of their neurological structure, their ability to remember prior experiences, and their inherent ability to learn new situations. In other words, higher organisms may be better able to cope with such a situation because they have a better ability to handle more environmental variables and at a faster rate.

As an example, imagine an eight-year-old child playing second base in a little league game. A simple situation occurs when no one is on base and a ground ball is hit the child. The child's model of his environment focuses on the speed and location of the ball, the position of the runner, getting the ball to first base, and thus getting the runner out. In this situation, the child's model of the game has few variables, and so the model is representative of the situation and guides the child's correct response of throwing the ball to the first baseman. However, if there are opposing players on the first and third bases, the model of the game becomes more complex and decisions must be made quickly. In addition to the previously mentioned variables, the child must decide how fast the groundball is moving toward him, the location and speed of the runners, the position of his teammates, the score of the game, and likely other confusing variables such as teammates shouting instructions. In that situation, our poor unexperienced eight-year-old child is easily confused by this new and overwhelming model and his behavior is likely to become chaotic. He may not know where to throw the ball, or he may throw it to the wrong teammate, or he may even freeze and hold on to the ball doing nothing.

Perhaps it is surprising that humans who live in such a changing and complex environment do not continuously fall into an overload situation. Somehow, we seem to exist in a complex adaptive system in terms of cognition in that we are constantly adapting to new situations and our cognitive models undergo continual change, yet we adapt and manage to avoid overload and confusion. Surprisingly, we manage to navigate our complex changing environments when the expectation is that we should constantly fall into overload situations.

In this chapter, we will discuss the many ways we humans have learned to avoid that situation; however, the answer may be that our evolutionary and developmental history has programmed us with methods by which we easily and automatically use some form of cognitive simplification. Both our evolution and our personal development have produced these skills because the effects of cognitive chaos are too traumatic and not having these skills would have produced dysfunctions in humans who are unlikely to cope with changing environments or have survived. Generally, variable overload and confusion are rare events in human functioning for which we should be thankful because as already noted it is not just a cognitive experience; it also produces very unpleasant if not painful emotional reactions. Although our evolutionary history may have provided us with the ability to avoid overload confusion, our cognitive development is another important factor. Infants come into the world with simple reflexes which are like simple models that help them cope with their environment. For example, when their cheek is touched, a week-old infant will turn in that direction and initiate sucking movements. This is an adaptive behavior in that turning in the touched direction might help the infant locate the breast and sucking movements initiate feeding. Called the rooting or orienting reflex, it is a simple model of responding to a simple environmental stimulus. This model becomes more complex as stimuli from their vision, hearing, smell, and especially touching senses improve, and they begin to form the concept of a maternal figure with all stimuli associated with their mother.

However, if they are exposed to other people, especially many other people, they may become confused, upset, and cry. Obviously, they become overwhelmed by the new sights, sounds, and smells which are at odds with the model of their mother. This does not happen to all infants, but such behaviors are not uncommon for five to nine-month-old infants and are called the stage of stranger anxiety. As they grow older, all children overcome this as they have formed models associated with other adults in their life, and so they no longer become confused and upset. Their increasing and gradual sophistication decreases their confusion and allows for an increase in the number of people models they possess.

Methods to Avoid Cognitive Overload

When we are in situations that bombard us with too many environmental variables, we will avoid cognitive overload by restricting the number of environmental variables we take in. This is the process referred to as the *p* factor discussed in Chap. 5. In our everyday functioning, we are always doing this with little difficulty, but in overload situations we are likely to significantly increase such restrictions. For example, in a social conversation where many peoples start talking at the same time, we cannot attend to what everyone is saying, so we will focus on one person because trying to understand what everyone is saying would lead to verbal chaos. This would be especially important in an emergency with many people shouting conflicting advice, and hopefully, we would attend to the person providing relevant helpful advice.

In most situations, we form complex models which are composed of many interacting environmental variables which we described in Chap. 9 as the *k* factor. However, there are limits to how many variables we can attempt to utilize to create a functional model. When faced with too many variables humans typically stop trying to include certain variables and often will restrict their environmental model to focusing on one or two. This is especially true in emergency situations. Faced with an emergency, airplane pilots are always told to just concentrate on flying the airplane and ignore other less essential variables. A friend flying a glider faced such a situation when suddenly his canopy came open while being towed to release altitude. There were a host of variables to cope with such as, his sunglasses askew, the open and vibrating canopy, a 70-knot wind in his face, needing to stay in position behind the tow plane, maintaining safe airspeed, and many others. Correctly, he ignored these variables and concentrated on just staying in proper position behind the tow plane. When he reached a safe altitude, he released the towrope and restricted his attention to flying the glider at the correct airspeed back to the runway.

Dr. William Neese and I (2011) have conducted a series of experiments investigating how subjects deal with cognitive overload. We presented undergraduate students with problems having a great many interacting and changing variables to see how they dealt with such situations. In one scenario, we asked them to decide which of three autos would arrive first leaving from the same spot and arriving at the same destination. Each car took a different route with different distances, went at different speeds, encountered varying speed limits according to the number of curves, and had different probabilities of hitting slowed construction and different probabilities of encountering police stops. This is such a complex set of changing and interacting factors that it is likely impossible to solve without the aid of a computer program. Surprisingly, none of our subjects gave up saying it was unsolvable. Rather, each student would come up with a decision as to which car arrived first. We then asked them to tell us how they came to their answer and the process that they used in all our subjects indicated that they focused on only one variable and ignored the others. Some focused on the speed of the particular car, others on the distance involved, and others the number of potential stoppages. Not only did they ignore all the other variables, but they were quite confident in their answer. When asked how confident they were in their answer, almost all said they were 90–95% certain they were correct. Despite the obvious complication inherent in the problem, they were not upset about being asked to solve it and did not find it to be a very frustrating experience

We carried out a similar study using clinical psychology graduate students, asking them to form a clinical diagnosis using the Diagnostic and Statistical Manual V and a treatment recommendation based on a complex of information from a series of different psychological tests, patient interview material, and social demographic information for mentally ill patients. This kind of clinical data contains many different pieces of information, and they interact such that one piece of information can change the significance and meaning of other information. For example, an individual with agoraphobia is likely to also experience depression and panic attacks. Another individual with a bipolar disorder, I may in addition, experience dysthymia and paranoid symptoms. In other words, this is a classic problem of attempting to solve an unsolvable complex data matrix where any one data point can significantly change the ultimate diagnosis and treatment recommendation.

Despite the obvious difficulty, all of the subjects formed a diagnosis and treatment recommendation though their recommendations were different from one another. This is not surprising since many studies show that even experienced psychologists and psychiatrists often disagree and have poor inter-judge agreement in diagnosing patients. The main reason they have such poor agreement is that they tend to focus on a very few, in some cases one, diagnostic variable, and by using so few variables they tended to select different variables which produced different diagnoses.

This situation is not only characteristic of clinical psychology graduate students, but has been a chronic problem in psychiatry. Many studies have found that psychiatrists do not agree on a diagnosis or a choice of treatment. Studies indicate that their degree of agreement ranges from 04% to 26% and averages about 16% across many studies which are very poor (Levav et al., 1984), (Ash, 1949), (Aboraya, 2007), (Allsopp et al., 2019). These findings were and still are upsetting to the field of psychiatry and were thought to be due to inadequacies of judgment in the field of psychiatry or inadequacies in the DSM-V. However, additional research studies investigated the degree of agreement among cardiologists and internal medicine physicians. When given detailed case material about a patient and ask to recommend the medical diagnosis, their inter-judge agreement was similarly poor and they agreed with each other only about 16% of the time (that is, food for thought next time you visit your physician). The same problem was given to bankers who were asked on the basis of financial information to decide whether someone should be approved for a loan. Once again, the bankers disagreed with one another, and their percent agreement averaged about 16%.

The problem does not seem to lie in any inherent problem with the techniques or inadequacies of psychiatrists, cardiologists, internal medicine physicians, or bankers, but rather any individual faced with making decisions involving a cognitive matrix of many interacting variables is not likely to agree with any other individual. In other words, a basic axiom of living in a complex universe is that individuals are going to disagree. Unfortunately, that is a sobering, but valid truth of complexity. Since we humans live in a complex environment, we are going to disagree, and the more complex that environment, the more likely we are to disagree.

Integrating many interacting variables into a stable model is quite difficult, and as we learned in Chap. 9, there is a limit to how many variables can be included. This is especially true if it needs to be done in a short time span. The obvious solution is to decrease the number of variables which simplifies the situation and that seems to be what our graduate students did when they were presented with a large number of variables that interact such that a change in one will change others. Trying to form a stable model of this particular clinical environment when there are too many things to include would have resulted in cognitive overload so they automatically chose to simplify the situation.

"Organized around a series of laboratories, this course surveys projects, methods, and controversies in digital humanities scholarship. Students will develop skills in digital methods potentially including textual analysis, network analysis, data scraping, visualization, mapping, and sound studies, while exploring the digital humanities as a way of knowing; the uses and abuses of data-based humanities; the politics of race, gender, and labor in collaborative scholarship; and the problems and possibilities of thinking the humanities at scale. Students will reflect on their experience with the digital and assess the ways digital methods (re)mediate analog forms of scholarship. Students will practice reviewing digital humanities projects and create low-stakes DH artifacts of their own. A final project investigates a substantive humanities research question using digital methods".

This can occur in verbal situations where there are so many abstract words; it may be impossible to understand what the writer is describing. I came across the following example in a description of a college course.

This is an example of a large number of abstract words that most people would have a difficult time integrating together in an effort to understand and develop a cognitive model of the content of the course. In other words, an attempt to form a model of what the course is about is likely to fail because each word is so diffuse that trying to put them together to develop an overall meaning results in confusion. Most people would likely only focus on one or two keywords that they feel have some overall meaning as a way of simplifying the description. They may even feel confident that they understand the description of the course, but they are likely to form a verbal model that is an incomplete or even erroneous model of the course. Although most people would need to simplify the description to cope with this situation of verbal overload, a university professor or other individual well versed in this particular academic area is likely to understand the terms and has little difficulty forming a cogent model of the class and its contents. I learned this when I gave the description to my daughter assuming she would agree that this was an example of cognitive overload. However, as an anthropology professor, she had no difficulty putting all aspects of the description together and explaining it to me in a form I could understand. She provided a good example of how humans can overcome verbal or any other type of overload by using prior training and memory.

The process by which humans handle overload and confusion is such a common occurrence that is usually an unconscious process. We humans live in such complex environments that we are constantly eliminating variables. We either ignore them completely because they do not seem relevant or we delete them from inclusion in a model because we sense that including them will cause confusion. This was shown by the results of our studies on overload. When we asked why they had chosen the variables, they used the students replied that that one was the important one. When questioned further about why they did not try to use other variables, they were usually dismissive saying those were not very important. Once they focused on what they decided was the most important information, they paid no attention to any other factor. After, they were reminded about the other data variables that they still did not include them. Most replied that trying to include more information would have been confusing so they just ignored that.

In another part of the study, we asked them to first make a snap judgment on their answer to the problem within 15 seconds, and then, we asked them to take as much time as they wished to modify or change their answer. Even though they now had as much time as they wanted to consider other variables, none of the students changed their answer indicating that once they had selected the information they needed, they did not include or reconsider variables they had deleted or ignored, which indicated that they were unaware that they were automatically simplifying a complex problem. As previously noted, another surprising finding is that they had confidence in their answers. Despite only using part of the information provided, almost every subject reported that they were 90% certain that their answer was correct.

Although ignoring and deleting variables are the most common way we cope with potential overload and confusion, in some instances we are able to cope with a multitude of variables by using our cognitive processes of intellect and memory to form complex and relevant models that correctly reflect our environment. If we anticipate an overload situation, we can simplify it ahead of time through practice and memory. In some ways, this is similar to an "if–then" statement in computer code (if this happens, then automatically follow a selected sequence of responses). When confronting situations with many variables, we can develop and practice alternatives for each situation. In other words, we have developed models of behavior and thought that are triggered by particular stimuli. This process is a form of cognitive simplification in that with time to analyze a situation we can delete irrelevant variables and then integrate a limited number of variables into a cogent model. Through this process, we can likely limit our cognitive model to only relevant and important variables in a rigid sequence. In doing so we have changed a complex situation to a compound situation because we have not only decreased the number of variables, but more importantly we have eliminated the host of interactions between those variables. In that we have a simpler cognitive model readily through simple memory.

Coping with emergency situations is a good example of this process. When faced with a life-threatening emergency, many people become confused and do nothing; in essence, they freeze and cannot form a relevant and useful model of the situation. Often, people will pass a serious automobile accident and do not stop to help because they are overwhelmed by the situation and do not know what to do. Contrast that with an experienced EMT who will stop and help because they are trained to deal with that situation. They have many models, they have learned and practiced over time, and they follow a sequence of actions to help the injured. They stay calm which another way of saying they are not confused or overloaded. Then, they follow a sequence of attempting to stop any bleeding, next begin CPR if needed, next immobilize injured individuals, and finally administer other needed medical procedures. Most untrained people in a medical emergency will do something by focusing on what they think is the most important thing to do, but they are not likely to think out all available possibilities. The usual and obvious positive action is to use a phone or cell phone to call for help and that is a simple, if not complete solution. Of course, doing something even if it is a simplified solution model is usually positive. As I mentioned earlier, the military recognizes this fact and when soldiers are facing combat they are trained to "do something, anything, but do not do nothing." In essence, they are told that a simple action or a wrong action is better than no action.

Aircraft pilots, and especially military pilots, function in complex interactive situations which have the potential for instantaneous emergencies. To cope with such situations, they are trained to memorize a sequence of responses to deal with the many types of emergencies that can arise. In essence, they are taught to develop a series of models related to each emergency situation whether it is deteriorating weather, a mechanical emergency, or the explosive violence of the enemy. A different way of stating this situation is that the environment has changed in an untoward way, and each different environment requires a different model. Training airplane pilots is a long-term learning process because there are so many different types of emergencies.

Pilots cannot be expected to try to suddenly create a useful and relevant model to deal with an emergency when under stress. They need to identify the relevant variables and integrate these into a sequence of actions to handle the situation. An example of a simple emergency model in a common single-engine, four-seat, private aircraft is as follows:

Emergency Engine Failure in Flight—(Cessna 172 airplane)
Sequence

1. Airspeed	65 knots
2. Carburetor heat	On
3. Fuel selector	Both
4. Mixture	Rich
5. Ignition	Both or Start
6. Primer	In and locked
7. Radio	Mayday
8. Transponder	7700
9. Landing area	Select

This is a very simple list for a single-engine airplane, and it is only a model for one type of emergency, however trying to generate this sequence quickly into a useful model for a novice pilot will prove very difficult. An experienced and competent pilot must have emergency models for engine failures on takeoff, at altitude, and on approach. Also, checklists are needed for communication failures, turbulent weather, and many, many, others. Military pilots who are dealing with many more complex systems related to weapons, radar, stealth, and much more will need to memorize a host of models to safely fly modern military aircraft. Memorizing emergency models is only one way of dealing with emergencies, but pilots must also practice the action behavioral aspects of traumatic changing environments by continually practicing in flight simulators. Military and commercial airline pilots are required to cope with a host of emergencies presented by simulators. Practicing the behavioral aspects of emergency models is crucial as it teaches pilots to recognize the type of emergency (the type of changed environment) and then select the correct model to best cope with that situation.

Aside from learning specifically trained models to cope with changing environments, generalized experience is another important factor. We humans obviously have a fund of environmental models that we have accumulated through age and experience. Many of these are simple and instinctual requiring little or no previous learning. For example, soldiers in combat do not need to learn to hit the ground at the sound of an artillery shell hitting nearby. Most individuals whether they are soldiers or naive civilians will react.

Cognitive Overload and Emotions

Describing emotions is a difficult process as words usually do not accurately convey the intensity of an emotion. Words such as anger and sadness can identify the emotion, but they cannot capture the intensity of a rage reaction or the profound and lingering unhappiness that causes a person to burst into uncontrollable tears. Not surprisingly, cognitive overload is an unpleasant situation that tends to produce unpleasant emotions such as stress, anger, emotional lability, and emotional confusion. This is a strained and dysfunctional situation that we always try to avoid. These unpleasant emotions are both a reaction to the cognitive overload, and a signal to the individual that cognitive level overloads has occurred. Emotions tend to be a simpler mental activity than cognition in that it has all or nothing quality. Though we may have varying intensity of an emotion, that feeling is one dimensional in that we just feel an emotion such as anger or sadness or stress, and it does not have the multidimensionality and complexity of cognition. Emotions tend to blind us to the many aspects of our environment, and we are likely to over focus on the internal state of how we feel. That is quite different from cognition, a process that tends to focus on our environment and integrate environmental variables into cogent cognitive models. For the most part, the all or nothing aspect of emotions does not facilitate the positive process of cognition and is detrimental to the creation of accurate environmental models.

Experiencing an emotion also tends to produce a behavioral response, and that too is a more elemental activity than cognition. Thinking tends to be an activity that does not involve a great deal of physical activity. Emotions are different in that they tend to generate physical and often times intense physical behaviors. The feeling of anger often results in verbal complaining, social sulking, shouting, and even throwing things. Stress usually produces a sense of frustration and eventually exhaustion. These behavioral concomitants to emotions are common behaviors, but they are not conducive to a positive and logical cognitive process. Temper tantrums in young children illustrate the deleterious effects of emotions and their accompanying behaviors on a child's intellectual processes. In the midst of a temper tantrum, the child may be yelling, flailing about, and sobbing uncontrollably. In that state, they are only attuned to their inner feelings and the environment around them is ignored.

Usually, when children are in that state they are unaware of adults trying to control or console them and are hardly aware of where they are or what else is going on about them. The cognitive process of learning is completely shut down. This is not a time when they can form cognitive models of their environment.

However, there are certain situations in which mild emotional responses can be facilitated in that they can activate thinking by initiating new and increased attention to the exterior environment. Mild frustration can motivate an individual to increase the cognitive searching process which can result in discovering new aspects of the environment to include in existing models. This can result in a creative cognitive process. However, intense unpleasant emotions are likely to have the opposite effect in that useful thinking and cognition will be ignored because the individual is likely to focus on the emotional feelings and reactions. When an individual experiences cognitive overload and the ensuing emotional reactions, thinking is going to deteriorate and there is likely to be an increased chance of including erroneous or irrelevant variables in the cognitive activities. This will lead to a poor or wrong cognitive solution, and it will also create erroneous or irrelevant models of the environmental situation. Obviously, when a cognitive activity has entered into an emotional state, it will be difficult to engage in creating relevant environmental models. Hopefully, an individual realizing that they have entered an unpleasant state of emotional overload will try to get out situation, but that is not very easy. One can try some sort of distracting activity like a time-out procedure, counting to 10, physical exercise, or just putting aside the cognitive activity and doing something that is completely different and requires sustained attention. However, that is easier said than done when one is involved in an important or engrossing problem. In cases of severe cognitive overload, the emotional reaction will be so acute that instead of having a stable model that allows predictability and understanding of the environment we are faced with confusion as to what are the important variables in our model. At that point, the logical flow of interconnections between models breaks down and we can become confused as to which environmental variables are important and which are irrelevant resulting in the creation of erroneous and confused cognitive models.

The Effect of Salience

There are certain events, situations, and people, which are so noticeable and prominent that they seem to take over our normal and logical cognitive activities. I refer to these things as salient phenomena because they have a powerful effect similar to emergence. They are so cognitively and emotionally powerful that they eliminate the normal stimuli of existing cognitive models and destroy the interactions between them. As a result, they simplify the complexity of cognitive models because they cause an individual to only focus on the one salient variable and ignore the other relevant variables. Salient phenomena often produce a very serious and sometimes catastrophic change in a person's thinking and behavior. The difference between salient phenomenon and emergence is that although both can produce huge changes, emergent phenomena are usually insignificant variables not recognized as particularly environmentally significant in terms of the ultimate results they generate. Salient phenomena are usually obvious and are quite environmentally significant. They will seem urgent and essential to a particular aspect of an individual's life and will seem to require immediate and consistent attention. They are likely to seem all encompassing and will sweep away our usually reasoned thinking processes. Salient phenomena are important because they can produce irrationally emotional behavior and one salient event can fix a social or political belief such that it will not be changed despite more logical environmental information. Sometimes, a single powerful salient event can even generate self-destructive emotional behaviors.

Salient events are especially prevalent in religious, social, and political environments because these phenomena are associated with strongly held beliefs that are difficult to change. For example, the custom of honor killing in certain religions is initiated by a salient event such as a family's daughter choosing to fall in love with or marry a man from another religion or unacceptable social group. This violation of the family's religious honor becomes a simple and overriding cognitive variable that is so powerful that it will erase or render unimportant all previous variables related to the daughter's previous place in the family. In this situation, the cognitive model of the daughter's position as an integral member of the family with interactive relationships and responsibilities to other family members, including an established status in the family, and loving attachments, become simplified to a single violation of religious honor. As a result, the cognitive model is now a simple one of violence which can result in the death of the daughter often by beheading.

Similar salient phenomenon can be found in social and political situations. One of the most important political controversies in the United States centers on abortion, and the many subissues such as fetal viability, fetal neurological and physiological stage of development, a woman's choice, definition of the beginning of life, and the morality of terminating a pregnancy. These and other cognitive variables associated with the termination of a pregnancy are many and complex in that they interconnect such that changes in the perceived validity of one will affect the perceived validity of others. A thoughtful person would attempt to develop a cognitive model that encompasses the total complexity of this issue and how it might affect other aspects of a person's social and personal environment; however, individuals on both sides of this issue often use salient phenomenon that allows them to come to a simplistic cognitive model defining this issue. For example, those against abortion may focus on pictures of a well-formed healthy fetus or reports of an aborted fetus being born alive and having an existing heartbeat. Those in favor of abortion may focus on stories or news video examples or the plight of an impoverished mother trying to raise an unwanted child under terrible economic circumstances. Both of these examples are an attempt to use dramatic and emotionally salient events to simplify what should be a complex intellectual moral and biological decision.

Unfortunately, there is a price to pay for the cognitive simplicity generated by salient phenomena and that price means that we lose the data and complexity needed to reach accurate decisions and a better understanding of one's real environment.

Since salience leads us into ignoring or rejecting many variables, especially those that conflict with preexisting social and political beliefs, we are seduced into a cognitive situation described in Chap. 4. We discussed the p factor that determines the inclusion or exclusion of environmental data in terms of its correlation with existing cognitive models. If p equals 1.0, then that information is included, and if p equals 0.0, the information is ignored. Obviously, if new data are ignored in a p equal 0.0 situation, then that data are not included in a preexisting cognitive model which allows for simplicity in that the cognitive model does not change and any interactions remain constant. If we apply this to social and political beliefs, then an individual is able to stubbornly hold on to their beliefs rather than letting new data change such beliefs. Thus, people tend to seek out salient events that agree with their beliefs and ignore events, no matter how powerful, that conflict with their beliefs. In the real world of political beliefs, I am often amazed at some individuals' ability to distort the relevance of an important and correct salient event by coming up with reasons to reject it. This is especially true when data or information seems to be contradictory. In that situation, which is similar to a relationship of p equals 0.5, an individual may be unsure about including that information in an existing cognitive model. In other words, people are confused by conflicting information and will try to change the information so that it completely agrees with a preexisting belief or is rejected and ignored.

The salient issue of the relation of American historical figures to slavery presents such conflicting data. This political issue becomes salient to many people as they cheer or fear the removal of historical statues in public places or even in the US Capital Building. Some groups actually called for the removal of the Washington Monument and the Jefferson Memorial because both presidents owned and sold slaves. Such a demand has major salient importance since it upsets the historical acceptance of long-standing and cherished monuments, and many people will have a strong emotional reaction. This is a conflicting cognitive situation. Should these men be honored for their great contributions to our nation or vilified for their participation in a horrible social injustice? Including this kind of conflicting salient information is very difficult for most people to integrate into a cohesive and stable cognitive model.

The great Union General and President Ulysses S. Grant is another excellent example of such conflicting information. Grant not only made perhaps the most important contributions to ending the confederacy and slavery, but also supported constitutional amendments to abolish slavery and give former slaves the right to vote. However, there is evidence that before the civil was he used slaves belonging to his wife's family and actually owned slaves himself. To complicate the issue further, there are data showing that Grant emancipated a slave named William Jones prior to the Civil War. In order to develop a cohesive cognitive model of Ulysses S Grant, we can decide to accept that he owned slaves in order to develop a negative cognitive model of Grant, except that he was a great general and president that contributed to the end of slavery. In order to have a positive cognitive model of Grant, we might ignore the issue completely, or generate a more accurate, but complex cognitive model incorporating both aspects of this great American historical figure.

However, maintaining a simple if inaccurate positive or negative cognitive model of Ulysses Grant requires less cognitive energy, maintains existing cognitive model interactions, and allows one to maintain a preexisting belief. Unfortunately, that belief is flawed in that it rejects or ignores important information. It ignores information, including salient information, and provides for simple and usually inaccurate explanations and decisions. It ignores the fact that our environment is full of complex and contradictory bits of information that are related through complex interactions and the same was true in the 1800s of Grant's time. Ignoring complex contradictions allows individuals to maintain simple cognitive models that easily support racist beliefs and can lead to genocidal decisions. Sometimes, maintaining a simplistic belief about historical figures is a naive historical and educational error that is not particularly dangerous. However, when this simple noncomplex thinking is applied to people and groups, it results in a simple cognitive model that is unlikely to change and can justify the worst of human behaviors.

Of course, the most accurate cognitive model of U. S. Grant is that he was an amazingly talented military mind and a socially thoughtful individual who also had temporary and typically human flaws. One of Grant's personal flaws was the fact that at times he abused alcohol. This not only was true during his military career in the Civil War, but also became so severe his early military days that he had to leave the Army. He was vilified by his enemies because of his inability to control his alcoholism and Abraham Lincoln suffered many complaints about Grant's drinking. Reportedly, Lincoln's humorous response to these complaints was to say that if he could find out what brand of whiskey Grant drank, he would send the barrel of it to all his other commanders. This remark shows that Lincoln in his wisdom understood the cognitive complexity of Ulysses Grant as an individual understanding that Grant was both a great military tactician and someone with a serious drinking problem, thus avoiding a simple salient cognitive understanding of his best general.

Such a complex cognitive model requires a great deal of effort to maintain as it is likely to change according to the influx of new information. Of course, that is also an advantage of this complex cognitive model in that it accepts and likely may motivate us to seek out new information which gives us a more accurate understanding of Ulysses S. Grant. Thus, such a cognitive model is not static in the form of a fixed belief, but allows for the inclusion of new information and a continuously modified cognitive model. In this case, the emotional salience of, "Grant was a slave owner," can be mitigated and put in proper perspective.

Chapter 11
Correlation, Canalization, and Cognitive Models

Abstract Using the examples of simple and canonical correlation, this chapter demonstrates how cognitive variables accrete to form a stable cognitive model that provides a control on overloaded and chaotic thinking. However, cognitive models are constantly changing since the exterior environment is changing, and so as a cognitive model is modified, it maintains a basic stability by controlling the degree of relationship between new variables and the cognitive model. Once a functional model is created, both individuals and cultures often become fixed and are reluctant to allow further cognitive changes. This process called canalization shows how human thinking restricts creativity and the introduction of new ideas. Middle Eastern, Chinese, Western European, and Polynesian cultures created significantly different methods of constructing boats even though all solved the same problem of safely crossing oceans, Each method became crystalized in that culture and never incorporated successful foreign ideas. Examples of that cultural disparity are discussed.

Keywords Linear correlation · Canonical Correlation · Beta weights · Cognitive dissonance · Dhow · Outrigger

In Chap. 9, we looked at how higher-order concepts are formed by integrating different variables together, thus combining those variables into a single concept. In this chapter, we need to look at how we select environmental variables to form a complete cognitive model of our environment. The basic process is one of selecting relevant aspects of the environment that appear to be associated with previous models while being open to the introduction of new and seemingly unassociated environmental variables. To understand this process of cognition, we need to break it down into its component parts; however, human thinking is a continuous process, and as we engage in that process, we are usually unconscious of the constant selection and integration of environmental variables. Of course, selecting relevant environmental variables also involves the rejection of many other environmental variables; otherwise, we would face perceptual overload and chaos. For the most part, we tend to select new variables that are related to previous environmental

R. Leve, *The Complexity of Human Thought*,
https://doi.org/10.1007/978-3-031-09104-9_11

models we have constructed. In that sense, it is like going from A to B to C to D to E and so on. That means that when we integrate variable A into our existing model, it then modifies the model. Now, we integrate variable B into the modified model which produces a somewhat different perceptual model to which we then integrate variable C and so on. However, if we try to jump from variable A to variable E without the intervening variables, of variables B, C, and E, there may not be enough of a relationship with which to integrate the new variable into the preexisting model. In that sense, cognition is a process by which we are constantly integrating something new and perhaps unfamiliar with something that is already known and familiar, our previously constructed cognitive model. The greater the relationship between the new variable and the existing model, the easier it will be to integrate that new variable into our model. There are times when we might attempt to include a non-related variable into a preexisting model, but that will likely produce a chaotic and confusing state. There are some situations in which there are no obvious relationships between new environmental variables and existing models; however, there may be hidden relevancies that allow unfamiliar and seemingly unrelated variables to be integrated into previous environmental models. Such situations are indicative of highly creative and clever thinking. For example, the cognitive model of birds such as the white-breasted nuthatch, ruby-throated hummingbird, and goldfinch that I see at my bird feeders seem completely unrelated to a Brontosaurus or Tyrannosaurus rex. Yet, it turns out that such seemingly disparate species are intimately related through the process of evolution and unearthing that relationship required a great deal of clever research. Of course, once those associations are established, we have little problem in putting the Tyrannosaurus rex and a tufted titmouse in the same cognitive model.

Actually, our analysis of this process is somewhat flawed in that it requires us to break it into components for simplicity; however, human cognition, whether based on an external or internal variables, is most similar to a fast-moving stream or an interesting video documentary that continues without any breaks. As I am writing this chapter, I am engaged in that continuous process because one concept or sentence produces a new, but related thought that leads into another sentence. Hopefully, my sentences are correlated to each other in a progressive verbal stream and I am able to have those relationships make sense to a reader. The common term "stream of consciousness" is another way to capture the continuity of the process.

We have spoken earlier about the process of how different aspects of environmental information become associated with one another and then integrated into a cognitive concept.

A useful and simple mathematical metaphor for how cognitive models are formed is the statistical process of correlation which shows the relationship between two variables. The formula for simple linear correlation is

$$(r) = \left[n\Sigma xy - (\Sigma x)(\Sigma y) / \text{Sqrt} \left(\left[n\Sigma x2 - (\Sigma x)2 \right] \left[n\Sigma y2 - (\Sigma y)2 \right] \right) \right]$$

In terms of demonstrating the degree of association between the environment and the model representing that environment, we can have x representing the environment and y representing the cognitive model. (r) indicates that relationship and when $r = 0.0$ that indicates that there is no relationship and as r approaches $r = 1.0$ that indicates a perfect congruence between the environment and the cognitive model. A typical example of a strong if not perfect relationship is the correlation between IQ and academic grade point average. If we know someone's intelligence, we can predict their grade point average within some limits. Similarly, if we know someone's grade point average, we are able to make a good, if not perfect prediction concerning their IQ. Notice that this relationship goes both ways.

In terms of cognitive models reflecting the exterior environment, there needs to be a relationship between the two; otherwise, the cognitive model would not reflect the environment that the organism inhabits and will generate dysfunctional models and dysfunctional behaviors. However, a simple linear correlation does not do an adequate job reflecting the association between an exterior environment in a cognitive model because it only looks at one element of the environment and one perception of a cognitive model, whereas the process is much more complex. Obviously, the exterior environment has many elements or parts and the cognitive model also is composed of more than one representation.

A more robust description of the process is a complex mathematical process called canonical correlation. Canonical correlation illustrates the relationship between a number of environmental and perceptual variables, and the significance or power of each variable in the formation of cognitive models. The formula for canonical correlation is as follows:

Canonical Correlation

$$\beta Ve + \beta Ve + \beta Ve + \beta Ve + \beta Ve = \beta Vp + \beta Vp + \beta Vp + \beta Vp + \beta Vp$$

Ve indicates environmental variables.

Vp indicates perceptual or mental variables.

β is a beta weight that is multiplied by the relevant variable (beta weights describe the power or importance of the variable).

On the left side of the equation are different stimuli or aspects of the environment, Ve, that we live in and an on the right side of the equation are the simple perceptions (Vp) that we humans use to create our cognitive concepts. Each variable has an associated beta weight which indicates the importance of the variable to the overall solution of a canonical correlation equation. In this case, the values of the variables are not exact values that yield an exact solution to the equation, but rather it indicates the process by which we form an integrated cognitive concept or model. In a purely mathematical solution, we would have definitive values for each of the variables. However, obtaining exact values for environmental or/and cognitive variables is likely impossible because both the environment and human perceptions are constantly changing and will vary from one individual to another.

This is also true of trying to generate accurate values for the beta weights. They indicate the importance of the inclusion aspect of each variable and that too is likely to constantly change given that we live in an imprecise and constantly changing complex environment. Thus, the utility of the equation is not in its ability to precisely calculate cognitive model formation, but to illustrate the complex process by which we form cognitive models of our environment.

Although we cannot calculate exact values for the variables and beta weights in canonical correlation equations, we can roughly approximate bounded values because our cognitive models comprise a series of complex adaptive systems reflecting important aspects of our exterior environment. In the process of adaptation to our environment, we are constantly changing the environmental variables we are attending to and their beta weights, which constantly changes the perceptions that we use to create cognitive models. Nevertheless, we maintain a generally homogeneous state of stability with respect to our environment.

As an example, we may have a cognitive model of professional colleagues based on a personal history composed of comments, achievements, emotional reactions, opinions, perceived biases, and a host of other past social interactions. Since the behavior and cognitions of our colleagues are never rigid and unchanging, these will be modified over time due to changed circumstances in those individuals, in ourselves, or in some aspect of our work environment. In our daily contacts, our colleagues may interpret a particular situation in a different way from us, or they may feel more strongly about certain issues, and that will induce changes, smaller or larger, in our cognitive model of these individuals; however, we will make social adaptations to these changes and our cognitive models of our colleagues will remain basically intact. Like any complex adaptive system, we adapt to such common changes, so our cognitive model remains a stable system in terms of maintaining a homogeneous collegial relationship.

Our complex cognitive adaptive systems can usually cope with most normal social and organizational changes, but we may not be able to adapt to massive and unusual social thoughts and behaviors which may destroy our cognitive model of a colleague. If the colleague suddenly announces they just joined a local chapter of the Ku Klux Klan and starts to pass out violent and racially offensive literature to coworkers, adaptation to such a massive change will be difficult to maintain and our complex adaptive system concerning that individual is likely to become chaotic and confused because our cognitive model cannot adapt to such an unexpected and profound change.

Canonical correlation demonstrates another important aspect of the complexity of the human cognitive process. There are limits to how many environmental variables we can include in the equation and a similar limit to how many perception variables that can be included. If we try to include too many environmental variables, we risk entering an overload situation that can result in cognitive chaos. In terms of perceptual variables, we face a similar limit because if we refer back to how higher-order concepts are formed, there is also a limit because of the geometric increase in the number of interactions. Referring back to Chap. 9, we see that the usual situation in the formation and maintenance of higher-order concepts is two. As we increase new perceptions resulting from the inclusion of environmental variables, we find an HOC of three has 6 interactions, a higher-order concept of four has12 interactions, and a higher-order concept of five has 20 interactions. Attempting to integrate so many interactions into the formation of a new cognitive concept would put a great strain on our intellectual abilities and is likely to fall to a chaotic situation.

Another factor that we need to be aware of is that when cognitive concepts are generated they are quite difficult to change. Once people have formed an opinion, a concept, or a belief, they are reluctant to change that opinion, concept, or belief. Perhaps it is too much of an effort for people to dismantle a cognitive concept consisting of many interrelated associations and then go to the trouble of understanding new associations to form a new cognitive concept. The first step in this process is to delete some of the associations between various cognitive elements which then means identifying new associations between the remaining cognitive elements. The next step is to include new cognitive elements and establish those associations. While this may seem easy to facilitate, in reality this usually is a difficult cognitive transition and one which most people would rather forgo. Likely, retaining the original and established concept requires much less cognitive effort. Once we have crystallized the associations between different environmental and cognitive elements, we can reduce this to a $k = 1$ or $k = 2$ cognitive situation and that is much easier than dealing with establishing all the new associations in a $k = 3$ or $k = 4$ situation. Also, most people prefer the cognitive stability of just retaining a concept that is known and familiar. Most of the time we humans prefer a situation of homeostasis to one of change, and this is likely true of all sophisticated life forms. A simpler way of saying this is we would rather not change our minds.

Canalization

An old psychological term called canalization describes this mental process because it is like traveling down a canal where you can only go in the direction of the canal and have no flexibility to explore other places. Not only do we rigidly hold to a cognitive concept once it is established, but also we will tend to ignore or reject conflicting situations from the environment. This is the common psychological phenomenon of cognitive dissonance. There are a myriad of studies that demonstrate that people will go to great intellectual lengths to exclude new information or deny obvious evidence that would seriously compromise a cherished belief. We have already discussed that it is easier to not include new environmental elements than it is to add new ones into a pre-established concept and form the many interconnected associations that are required to change the cognitive concept. The process of cognitive dissonance allows us to engage in this simpler form of cognitive exclusion. We humans are quite facile at rejecting ideas, opinions, and beliefs that we do not like or seem foreign, and we have an amazing capacity to disregard logical associations and obvious realities. Another way of saying this is that we will go to great lengths to argue against something even if we realize it is correct. In many situations, we commonly cease our intellectual processes in favor of emotional reactions, and as mentioned in Chap. 10, emotional reactions have a simplistic all or nothing quality that tends to either accept or reject new environmental information. In simple emotional reasoning, we no longer are attempting to understand the complexity of associations between cognitive elements, but simply reject any sort of intellectual inclusion.

A history of sailboat design and construction across different cultures can illustrate the emotional reluctance to change cognitive concepts and the process of canalization. There are many ways to construct boats that are simply solving the problem of conveniently crossing a body of water. However, different cultures developed different methods to solve this basic problem and once adopted these methods were not changed. This can be illustrated by looking at the ways in which European, Polynesian, Arabic-Indian, and Chinese designed, built, propelled, and navigated their boats. Basically, boats, with the exception of a floating log, are simply built to be containers that float and can carry people and cargo in a useful and efficient fashion. Likely, the first boats across all cultures were hollowed-out logs called dugouts and I have seen these simple boats still used in places like Nepal and Myanmar to cross rivers. We can speculate about how different groups developed different methods to build even these simple boats. Some groups used fire to hollow out the log and some cultures used a stone adz. Likely, a combination of these was also used and cultures developed different tools and methods for measuring the dimensions as they worked (Fig. 11.1).

Fig. 11.1 Photograph of dugout made from one log

As more sophisticated and useful boats began to be designed to cross oceans rather than rivers, the boat builders of various cultures developed quite different types of seagoing craft that reflected the available materials, tools, and environmental requirements demanded by their particular geography. Whatever their original differences, once the underlying techniques and cognitive differences emerged, they did not change despite the fact that all were excellent vessels capable of crossing vast stretches of the Atlantic, Indian, and even the immensity of the Pacific oceans (Fig. 11.2).

Figure 11.3 shows typical Arabic dhows that were used for centuries to cross the Indian Ocean. The hull was constructed of planks and frames that were tied together using knotted coconut cord. This produced a single-hulled boat that achieved its

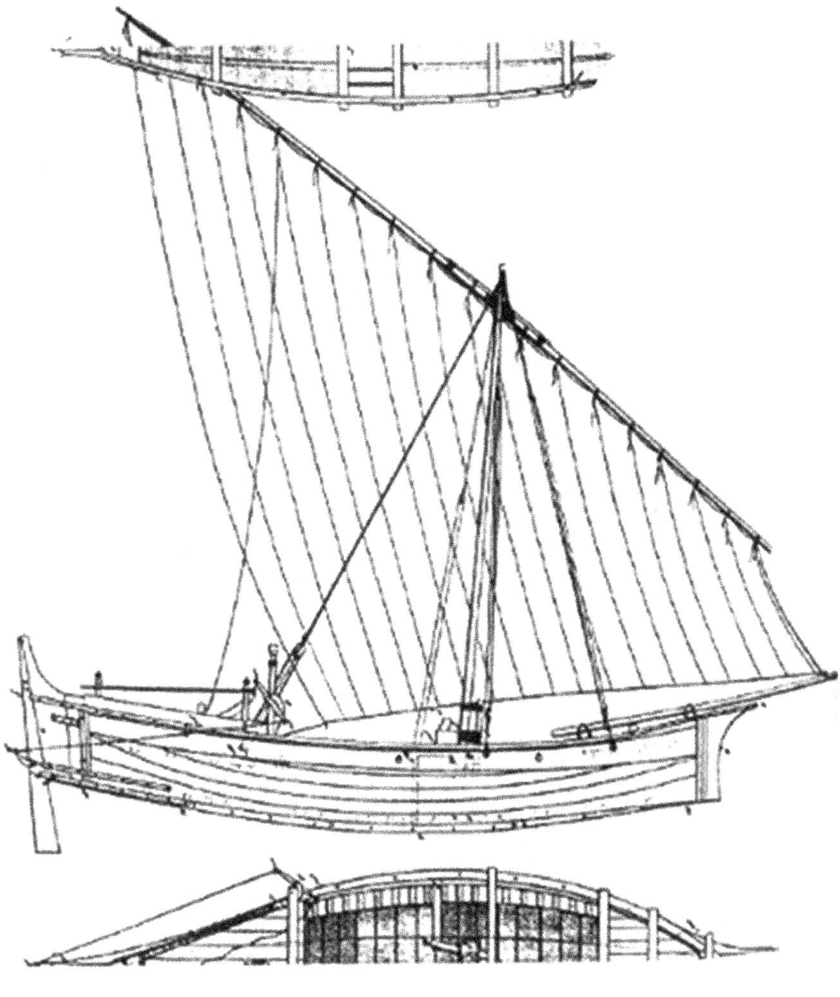

Fig. 11.2 Arab-Indian-type dhow showing lateen sail and hull construction using coconut cord

Fig. 11.3 Arabic dhows capable of crossing the Indian Ocean. The planks and frames are held together with fiber cords

stability (remember sailboats heel with wind and can capsize in a strong storm wind) by placing their ballast weight in the bottom of the hull, thereby achieving a right-side-up stability. Most western sailors would think that a boat tied together with cord could hardly be seaworthy, but these craft were quite seaworthy and able to cross from the Arabian Peninsula to India. Their sails were a modified triangular lateen sail that used a different type of mast, boom, and sail arrangement than in any other culture.

Figures 11.4 and 11.5 shows two different examples of Polynesian and Melanesian sailboats. These are basically boats with two hulls attached together or a boat with one hull and a stabilizing outrigger. The hulls may be dugout logs on smaller boats or planked hulls on larger catamarans (catamaran is a Tamil word meaning "logs tied together"). They are inherently stable and heel much less than sailing boats from other cultures. In addition, they are much faster and require less propulsion power. Certainly, the catamaran and outrigger is a drastically different designs than European, Chinese, or Arabic-Indian boats. The sails were also different in that they had the main part of the sail area near the top of the mast rather than near the bottom as found in boats of the other cultures. This was achievable because the catamaran did not heel very much and so could utilize the increased wind flowing higher off the water.

Fig. 11.4 A small boat typical of the Polynesian–Melanesian culture using an outrigger attached to the main hull. The outrigger provided excellent stability such that these boats hardly heeled in most winds and made for an excellent working platform. (Photograph by Zombaba)

Fig. 11.5 A large seaworthy catamaran of the Polynesian–Melanesian culture. These craft were able to sail the huge reaches of the Pacific Ocean in safety and over time reached all the Pacific islands and likely the West Coast of South America. (Photograph by S. Watson)

Adob

Figures 11.6 and 11.7 illustrate the construction methods and the ships used by western cultures. They built single-hulled boats with many planks covering the frames that produced the shape of the hull. The planks and frames were attached in a rigid fashion using treenails. With this method, a round hole is drilled through the

Fig. 11.6 Diagram showing the typical hull construction of European and American vessels. After a boat frame is built, the wooden ribs and planks are attached to the frame with treenail made of wood dowels or in later time bronze screws

Fig. 11.7 Diagram of a typical sailing ship of western cultures. Stability was maintained by filling the bottom of the hull with stones, lead weights, or heavy cargo. Full decking sealed the sailboat and insured adequate buoyancy. (Photograph by Kirstin Reimer)

plank into the frame and a hardwood pin is pounded into the hole. After the hardwood pin swells by being immersed in water, it joins the plank and frame securely together. After different metals came into use, the treenails were replaced by iron nails or bronze screws, but the basic method of constructing a watertight hull was the same. Smaller European boats used triangular sails like the Arabic-Indian sailboats, but differently. They only used a mast and boom to control the sails and did not have the boom on top of the sail. Larger boats as shown in Fig. 11.6 such as a barque or brig split the sail area into many smaller square sails which was a significant departure from all other cultures.

An expanded view of a seagoing Chinese sailing vessel shows the compartmentalized hull and easily reefed sails.

Figure 11.9 shows a Chinese junk (a rather poor western name for a very fine and efficient sailing vessel). The interior of a junk was composed of a limited number of bulkheads that split the vessel into separate internal compartments rather than the numerous structural frames of European and Arabic-Indian ship. As a result, the junk was less likely to sink if it began to leak as any flooding could be limited to one compartment, a very beneficial safety feature that was eventually introduced into modern liners and warships. This type of construction mimics a stalk of bamboo which also is segmented into sealed compartments. Another significant difference was the shape of the hull which had a flat bottom that increased the initial stability in rough water. A disadvantage is that a flat bottomed boat slips to leeward easily and so will not be very able at sailing into the wind. Chinese boat builders were aware of this and built centerboards or leeboards into the sides of the hull to counteract this problem. Other cultures did not make use of leeboards and centerboards which were only used on Dutch barges at a later time in history. The sails on Chinese junks also were quite different from that used by any other culture in that they had many full-length battens across the sail as shown in Figs. 11.8 and 11.9. This made reefing very easy in storm conditions, but these sails were not very efficient at tacking upwind. These battened sails were quite different from the sails of all other cultures.

Predictably, when the sailors and builders of one culture did come in contact with another, they usually were dismissive of that sailing craft assuming their sailing vessels were far superior. Usually, they thought that such boats indicated the simple uninformed thinking of the other simpler culture. For example, when the English explorer Captain James Cook reached the Polynesian islands and saw double-hulled catamarans and boats with outriggers, he thought them primitive and assumed they could not survive an ocean journey. This, in spite of the fact that they were faster and easily more maneuverable than his 143 foot three masted barque. He also missed the fact that this clever culture settled all the scattered islands and conquered the vast distance of the entire Pacific Ocean in their catamarans.

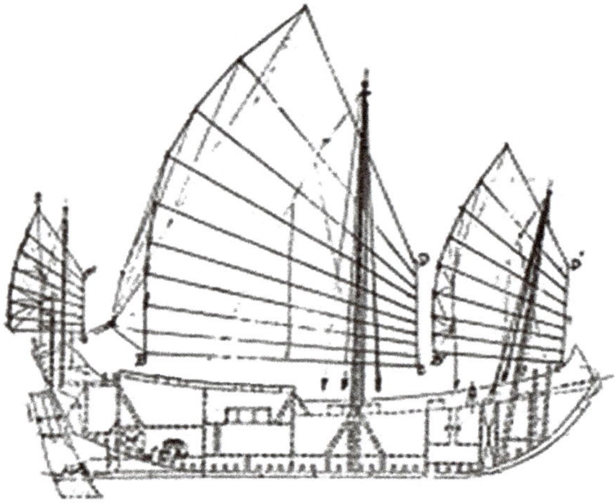

Fig. 11.8 A schematic diagram of a typical Chinese sailing vessel showing the collapsible sails and a hull separated into individual compartments

Fig. 11.9 Photograph of an ocean-going Chinese junk

Chapter 12
Creativity and Complex Scientific Models

Abstract Using the historical development of human flight by the Wright brothers, Otto Lilienthal, and Octave Chanute, as an example, this chapter demonstrates the cognitive reductive principles used in the creative solution of abstract complex problems. Much of the work of scientific discoveries is made through simplifying inherently complex problems, and this chapter presents a number of techniques through which such scientific problems are solved. Techniques such as identifying identities, sequencing, eliminating interconnections, and understanding the salience of variables are described and explained through examples. This chapter has been recognized as having significant pragmatic importance for the solution of complex scientific problems. In addition, these problem-solving techniques are applicable in understanding social, political, and cultural issues.

Keywords Principles of flight · Cognitive reductive methods · College selection principles · Postdictive analysis · Wright brothers · Otto Lilienthal

Solving scientific problems is a difficult endeavor as it usually involves many interacting abstract variables. Although most problems in science involve a large number of variables, the main problem is one of reducing those variables to a successful solution. As we saw in Chap. 3, if we have a matrix of many variables and those variables interact, it may cause a complete and sometimes sudden reconfiguration of the matrix which can be cognitively confusing and will not yield a viable solution. On the surface, complex scientific problems seem to involve the inclusion of many variables; however, the main difficulty is in the process of reducing the number of variables such that it develops a stable, logical, and understandable cognitive matrix. If trying to solve a problem by getting rid of information seems counterintuitive, it is! However, the essence of the problem is that we must include many relevant variables and then reduce them, and the reduction or elimination of variables is the most difficult cognitive part.

In order to understand this difficult cognitive process, the work of the Wright brothers in developing the principles of flight in 1903 provides an excellent example because they provided detailed documentation of their thinking from 1895 when

R. Leve, *The Complexity of Human Thought*,
https://doi.org/10.1007/978-3-031-09104-9_12

they began to 1903 when they achieved the first successful powered flight (Wright & Wright, 1953). In addition, we are able to study the cognitive process used by other inventors such as Octave Chanute, Otto Lilienthal, and Samuel Langley which resulted in the failure to achieve stabile and useful powered flight (Jakab, 1990; Chanute, 1997). Contrasting the successful work of the Wright brothers with the failures of other scientists demonstrates the different cognitive techniques which led to their success and which provides a template to understand how all complex scientific problems are solved. Perhaps even more enlightening is the fact that Orville and Wilbur Wright illustrate how the most complex scientific problems can be solved by simple thinking that appears to be and perhaps is reflective of genius.

Orville and Wilber Wright began their work with very little prior information to guide them, and much of that existing information was wrong. Of course, the principles of flight have been known for countless eons; however, they were only known to birds and certain insects. These species had utilized all of the principles of powered airplanes, gliders, and helicopters. However, these species had the advantage of scale in that being relatively small they had the ability to overcome the effects of gravity and were able to utilize smaller and less rigid structures. The problem of manned human flight is much more difficult because the scale of carrying a heavy human and the strong structures needed for internal integrity introduces a vastly greater amount of complexity. When Wilbur Wright began his investigations into the problem of manned flight, he studied birds, especially hawks. Even the simplest observer would notice that hawks have flapping wings as a form of propulsion, tail feathers as a form of pitch control, and wingtip feathers as a form of roll control. They even have legs that serve as the landing gear although these are not crucial in terms of flight. Of course, transforming these simple structures of birds into the structures, operations, and principles into a craft capable of lifting a human into the air under control required a form of cognitive expertise and insightful creativity. Because the principles underlying manned flight are so complex, the brothers needed to solve a multivariable interactive cognitive matrix in order to create the first viable aircraft and analyzing their work illustrates the six cognitive principles they used in reaching their solution.

Developing the principles of flight and utilizing these principles to create the first aircraft in 1903 was a task of great difficulty. Although many other experimenters had tried to achieve manned flight and some principles of flight were known, Wilbur and Orville Wright were unique in utilizing specific cognitive processes to solve these problems. Analyzing the methods they used is a useful postdictive analysis of how scientific problems are unraveled in a complex interactive environment (Jakab, 1990; McFarland, 2001a, b). As we saw in Chap. 3, the basic problem in understanding complex systems as identified by Stuart Kaufmann (1993) is that as the number of interactions between variables increases, the complexity of the system increases exponentially and such complex systems become incredibly difficult or impossible to solve. A complex system may include a large number of variables so long as there are few interconnections between the variables. Kauffman (1995) defined the number of interconnections as k and concluded that when k becomes large, $k > 5$, such a system usually becomes insoluble.

In science, complex multiple interactions can be reduced through the creation of higher-order concepts and that process is illustrated in Fig. 12.1.

A higher-order concept includes the effects of subordinate variables, but reduces the group to one variable. Since manned flight involves many interacting variables such a problem ought to be unsolvable, we can identify certain cognitive reductive procedures which allow for the solution of such complex problems. Wilbur and Orville Wright faced such a situation in attempting to create the first aircraft and a diagram of some of the multiple interconnections, ($k > 5$), between flight variables is shown in Fig. 12.2.

Many aviation predecessors such as Pilcher, Lilienthal (2001), Chanute (1997), and Langley (McFarland, 2001a, b) had identified some of the variables involved, but none had been able to solve the interactive relationship between these variables, such as lift, pitch, angle of attack, airspeed, center of pressure, center of gravity, and wing area. Each of these variables may have multiple states, and even if we assign only two states to each variable and include 10 variables, the number of possible interactive states can be 2^{10}. Obviously, such a complex system cannot be solved by attempting to include all variables in a time constricted overall solution. To achieve a cognitive solution a reductive procedure involves a thorough understanding of each variable, its possible states, relevant experimentation, and a good bit of creativity. This chapter is an analysis of how cognitive reductive procedures accomplish the simplification of complex systems and documents the processes that were used by the Wright brothers. This situation is similar to many complex scientific problems which involve many variables with a large number of interactions. The

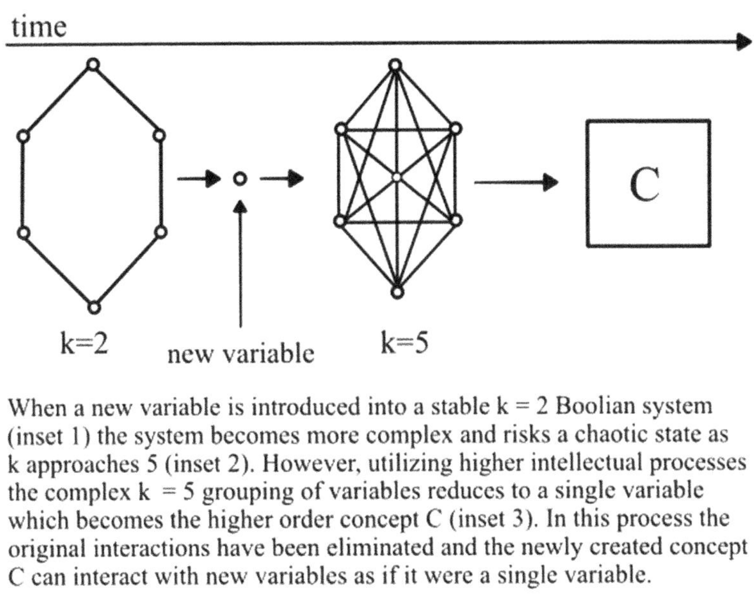

Fig. 12.1 Diagram illustrating the introduction of a new variable into an existing cognitive matrix

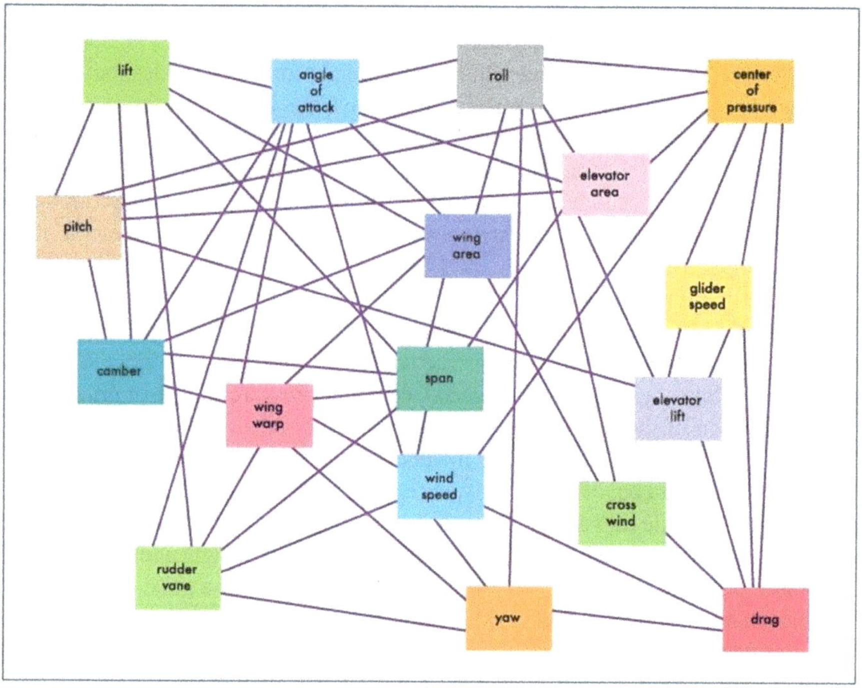

Fig. 12.2 Interactions between numerous flight variables

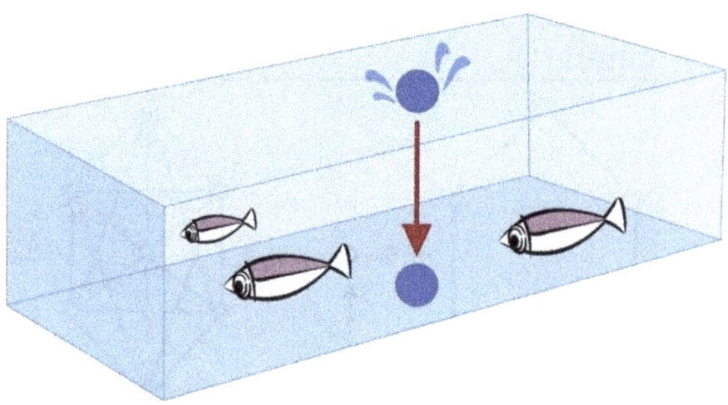

Fig. 12.3 Stability of an object in a fluid. Drawing by Linda Olender

difficulty faced by Wilbur and Orville Wright was that of attempting to keep an object (aircraft) moving in a defined position laterally and horizontally within a fluid as shown in Fig. 12.3.

Of course, the only two stable points for that object are resting at the bottom of the fluid due to influence of gravity or floating at the top of the fluid if the specific gravity of the object is less than the fluid. This situation is further complicated by the fact that the object needs to follow a stable path despite turbulent variations in the fluid as shown in Fig. 12.4.

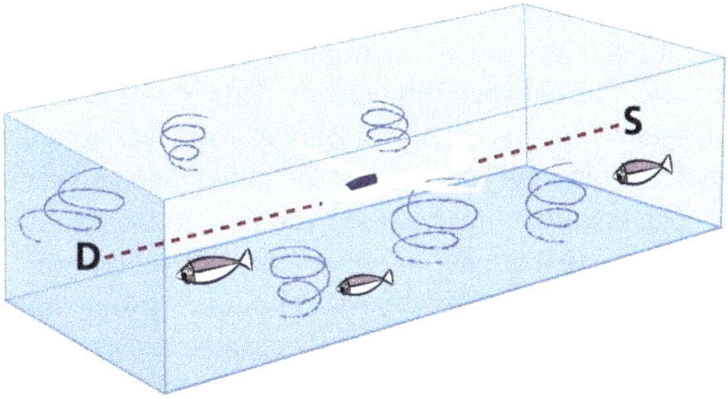

Fig. 12.4 Chaos in atmospheric turbulence. Drawing by Linda Olender

To maintain a stable defined pathway through a fluid such as our atmosphere means that the motion and position of the object are dependent on such variables as lift, drag, yaw, pitch, roll, mass, center of pressure, and center of gravity. The Wright brothers were facing a classic multivariate complexity situation and earlier attempts to solve such complexity resulted in chaotic solutions in which the designs were not able to fly and inevitably resulted in chaos as evidenced by a crash and at times the deaths of the investigators. Wilbur and Orville Wright followed a different approach, and the methods they used were successful and produced the first viable aircraft.

Perhaps the most unusual aspect of the Wright brothers' accomplishment is that unlike Lilienthal, Chanute, or Langley, they had no formal training in engineering or mathematics. In fact, neither had graduated the high school they attended, and although both could have received diplomas, they did not go to the bother of completing the administrative requirements. Also, the study of science was not a common aspect of the Wright family. In fact, aside from some dabbling in printing a local newspaper, they were bicycle racers and bicycle mechanics. Their interest in aviation was serendipitous in that upon reading of Lilienthal's death Wilbur decided to investigate the problem of flight and he later interested Orville in this work. Perhaps this seeming inexperience might have been an advantage in one respect. They were not wedded to one particular approach and were aware that they needed to solve many problems including the airframe, aircraft stability, and power in the form of a reliable engine. By contrast, earlier investigators of flight tended to fixate their approach on a single problem. Otto Lilienthal put most of his attention on the shape of the wing and generating the lift needed to support the weight of a pilot. Octave Chanute emphasized the strength and stability of the airframe structure which is not surprising as he had been a famous bridge designer in his career. Samuel Langley put this attention on constructing an engine that could be light and yet powerful enough to provide enough forward speed for flight. All of these aviation pioneers were subject to canalization in that their thinking focused on only one aspect of the problem, and so their contributions were limited to certain aspects of this cognitive problem to the exclusion of the other. More importantly, they did not realize that there were important interactions between the different variables of flight and solving these variables without understanding how changes in one would affect others could not result in a viable airplane. Adapting a canalization approach to the problem is insufficient in most scientific and other complex problems because it not only limits ones thinking to one dimension of a problem, but it ignores the interactions between dimensions. This is an important error because most complex problems have variables and dimensions that interact with one another, and ignoring such interactions will provide an incomplete and static solution.

The cognitive methods they utilized in their solutions are illustrative of the processes use to a greater or lesser extent by all scientists attempting to solve complex interactive problems. Almost all complex problems need to be solved by reducing their complexity. The remainder of this chapter analyzes the different methods that Wilbur and Orville used to come to their solutions and will illustrate how such methods are utilized to solve most complex scientific problems (Wright, O. 1989; Wright, W. 1909).

Cognitive Reductive Principles

Detecting Underlying Identities

An important cognitive technique in reducing multiple variable matrices and their interaction is the recognition of identities that underlie variables. Often two or more variables may seem discrete when in reality they may be reduced to one variable. In such a situation, the number of variables is reduced, and consequently, the number of interactions is also reduced. Of course, such identities may exist under certain circumstances and not others. For example, lift generated by a wing and the weight of an aircraft are two seemingly different variables; however, in-flight lift must equal weight, and realizing this, Wilbur and Orville knew that if they calculated weight they would have a measure of lift. As a result, they were able to calculate the amount of lift they generated from their first glider wing during experiments at Kitty Hawk in 1900 by flying the glider attached to ropes and fish scales borrowed from the local fisherman. Using this system, they were able to calculate not only the amount of lift of their wing shape, but knowing the wind strength with an anemometer, the amount of lift as measured by the fish scales added to the weight of the wing was equal to the weight the wing could support at that given airspeed. This is shown in Fig. 12.5.

When they had achieved balance and control with their 1902 glider, the addition of an engine and propeller was a logical next step. However, having no experience in constructing a propeller, they turned to the data on ship screws and found that was inapplicable to a propeller in the thinner fluid of the atmosphere. Finally, they realized that a propeller is nothing more than a wing generating variable lift in rotary motion, and so the knowledge they had in developing a lifting wing was used to create an efficient propeller. In fact, their propeller was 66% efficient compared to a modern propeller which averages around 68% efficiency. In this way, they realized that the underlying theory for a wing and a propeller was similar and so they were able to reduce the two variables to one.

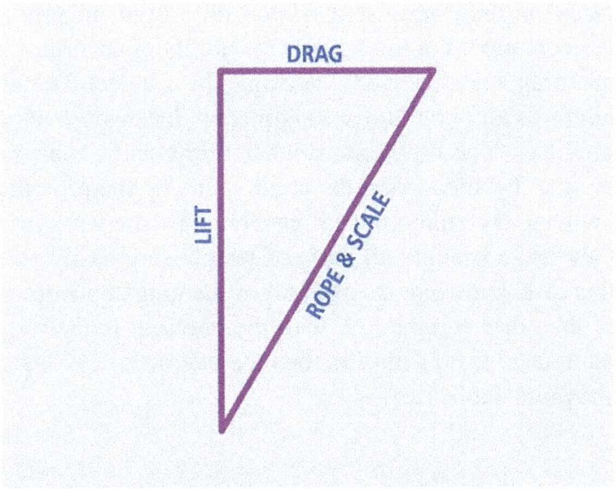

Fig. 12.5 Using rope and a borrowed fish scale to calculate lift and drag of the Wright brothers' Glider. Drawing by Linda Olender

Perhaps the most obvious and simplistic example of an identity is the relationship between wind speed and speed of the aircraft. In other words, the wind coming at an airplane is the same as the wind created by the speed of an airplane. In terms of generating lift, these variables are identical, and so in calculating lift, they are one. Knowing this, Wilbur and Orville constructed a well-controlled wind tunnel as there was no difference between the wind created by their fan or the more cumbersome procedure of moving the wing into the air. In fact, this procedure was tried by other early aviation enthusiasts by mounting the wing shape to be tested on a rotating arm. Of course, this procedure gave inaccurate results compared to the sophisticated wind tunnel used by the Wright brothers. In this instance, what appears to be an identity is not quite an identity because the properties of a rotating wing are somewhat different than the stable wing that the Wright brothers created in their wind tunnel. In fact, they were very careful in their use of the wind tunnel as, for example, they spent over a month manipulating shrouds and honeycombs grids in order to obtain a straight wind and they did not allow anyone other than the observer to come near their apparatus when in use.

Reducing Opposing Variables to an Identity

There are conditions when variables that are opposites in their function are in reality equal or can be canceled out in their basic operation. Under such conditions, the calculation of one variable may yield a direct calculation of the other. A good example of this principle is the calculation of lift and drag which might appear to be opposite in their effects on a flying object since lift is a force that keeps a wing aloft and drag is the force that retards its forward motion. When Wilbur and Orville first began their study of the lift produced by a wing, they used a model bi-wing glider; however, in addition to calculating lift, they also realized that they needed to calculate drag because a wing with a high lift producing profile also produces a greater amount of drag. Since the ability of an aircraft to fly is a function of both lift and drag, they needed to calculate the drag coefficient of their wing. Obviously, an aircraft's ability to move a significant distance forward will be limited by the drag it produces. The brothers calculated drag using their borrowed fish scales and rope system. By measuring the angle made by the rope that was holding the glider and knowing the amount of lift generated by the wing (as measured by the fish scales), they had a triangle all parts of which were easily solved through trigonometry. In this case, knowing one of a pair of seeming opposite variables allows the calculation of the other variable. As with the previous reductive principle if a variable can be eliminated from a matrix, then the interactions will also be reduced. This process is shown in Table 12.1.

Separate Multiple Variable Problems into Relevant Groups

An important principle in reducing any complex system to manageable proportions is to separate the variables into smaller related groups so that there are fewer interconnections between the total numbers of variables. To do this, the smaller grouping must contain relevant variables that can contribute to solving one part of the overall solution. Many early aviation experimenters attempted an overall solution by building an aircraft and then trying to fly that structure. In this way, they summed all the variables together, but were not able to understand the subtle and crucial interconnections between them. The central problem recognized by the Wright brothers was the problem of balance and stability, and this property of flight depends on the interaction of the center of pressure and the center of gravity. The Wright brothers correctly focused on that central variable which then determined the type of airframe structure they would construct. Actually, this is somewhat of a simplification in that to solve stability they did have to take into account variables such as lift, drag, and airspeed; however, balance and stability were central to all others because if this was not solved then the problems of power, lift, and airframe structure could not be effectively tested. Wilbur illustrated this fact in an invited address given to the Western Society of Engineers in 1901.

> The difficulties that obstruct the pathway to success in flying machine construction are of three general classes: 1. Those which relate to the construction of sustaining wings; 2. Those that relate to the generation of power required to drive the machine through the air;

Table 12.1 Same variables determine both lift and drag

Variables determining lift	Variables determining drag
Speed	Speed
Wing shape	Wing shape
Angle of attack	Angle of attack

> 3. Those relating to the balance and steering of the machine after it is in flight. Of these difficulties two are already to a certain extent solved, however the inability to balance and steer still confronts students of the flying problem, although nearly eight years have passed. The balancing of a flying machine is very simple in theory. It consists of causing the center of gravity to coincide with the center of pressure. But in actual practice there seems to be an almost boundless incompatibility of temper which prevents their remaining peaceably together for a single instant, so that the operator, who in this case acts as a peacemaker, often suffers injury to himself while attempting to bring them together. (Wright, O. 1998)

The position of an object in motion in a fluid is affected by movement around three axes, pitch, roll, and yaw, and those are the central variables that the Wright brothers focused on in their experimentation as shown in Fig. 12.6.

They realized that an aircraft is inherently unstable and must have adequate controls to return it to a stable position. To do this, they incorporated a horizontal forward canard to adjust pitch, a system of differentially warping the wings to control roll, and eventually a rudder to adjust yaw. Other investigators such as Langley and Chanute largely ignored the problem and tried to build a structure that was inherently stable. Lilienthal tried to attain balance by shifting the position and thus the center of gravity of the pilot. Langley and Chanute never were able to create aircraft that could sustain significant flight, and Lilienthal unfortunately was killed because shifting the pilot's position was only sufficient to control small winged aircraft and could not cope with wind gusts that exceeded his ability to regain balance.

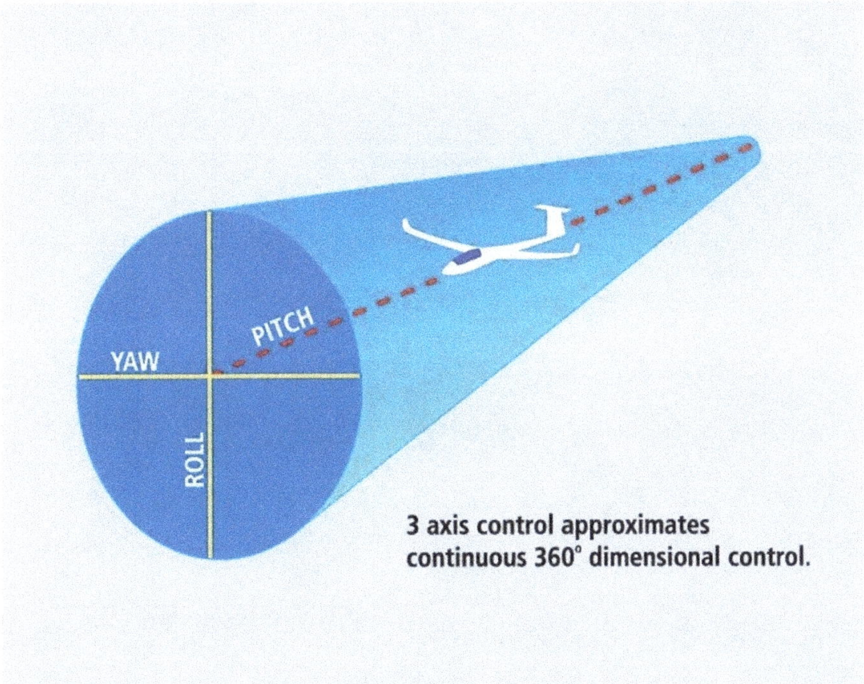

Fig. 12.6 Controlling an unstable aircraft with yaw, pitch, and roll variables. Drawing by Linda Olender

Separating a multivariate problem into relevant groupings is only the first step in this reductive procedure. The more difficult task is finding the group that is basic to all others and this principle requires a thorough understanding of the overall problem and significant creativity on the part of the investigator. Perhaps, in addition to thorough knowledge of the problem and creativity, sometimes scientific serendipity also plays a role. Unfortunately, if the wrong grouping of variables is focused on a complex problem may not be soluble and many early aviation pioneers did that and failed in their endeavor. Samuel Langley focused on the problem of power, Octave Chanute focused on the structure of the airframe, and Otto Lilienthal focused on the problem of lift. All of these variables needed to be investigated and solved, but a solution to these was very difficult if not impossible until the more basic problem of balance was solved. This seems to be a classic example of cognitive canalization. By over-focusing on one variable, Lilienthal, Chanute, and Langley not only ignored other crucial variables, but also were not able to identify the crucial interactions between all these variables, and thus, they were not able to reduce the number of variables and interactions to form a simpler and more stable matrix. Figure 12.7 illustrates diagrammatically how the multiple interactions in the complex problem of soaring can be decreased by using a relevant subgrouping of the variables such that a higher-order concept may be generated.

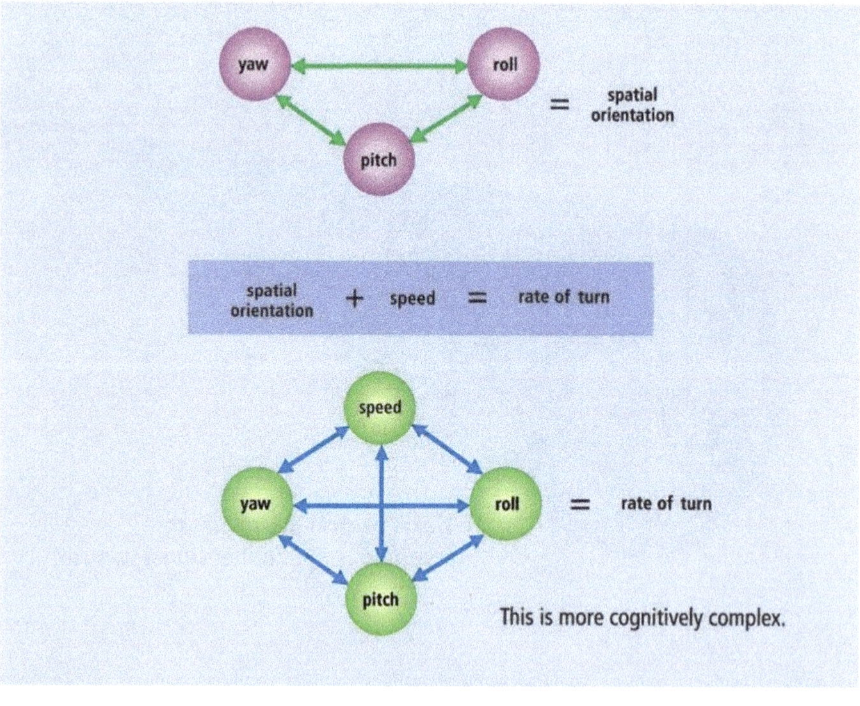

Fig. 12.7 Reciprocal interactions between aircraft speed and control variables

Assessing the Importance of Each Variable

In a multivariate problem, it is likely that different variables have varying degrees of importance in their contribution to an overall effect. This may occur because a particular variable may produce a catastrophic outcome if not properly understood, while another variable may produce an undesired effect on the ultimate outcome, but its influence is of lesser importance. Thus, to achieve a solution to a complex problem involving many interacting variables, an investigator must have some knowledge of the weight that each variable contributes. Unfortunately, when trying to solve a new problem or achieve a breakthrough in a new area of research, an individual is by definition unfamiliar with that variable matrix, and so identifying the importance of each variable in its contribution is difficult. Of course, any experienced scientist will rely on previous work found in the literature, consult with others, study the variables through experimentation or experience, or rely on their "intuition."

In the case of the Wright brothers, they used all these methods. As soon as Wilbur became interested in the problem of manned flight, he wrote to the Smithsonian Institution, a repository of early information on flight, to obtain their literature. Throughout their early work, they met with and consulted with Octave Chanute although they quickly outstripped his expertise. Perhaps, Wilbur's immediate identification of control and balance as the central problem was done through intuition; however, identifying a psychological factor such as intuition as a causal agent is speculative. If intuition was a factor, then it was likely influenced by the fact that two early aviators, Lilienthal and Pilcher, had died investigating the principles of flight. Perhaps Wilbur did not need a great deal of "intuition" to realize that in order to stay alive long enough to solve the problem of manned flight, balance and control were critically important variables.

In science, the most common method to assess the importance of variables is through experimentation, and this was another method used throughout their work. Perhaps the best example was the method they used to calculate the amount of lift produced by a wing. At the present time, the common wing shape is familiar to most people with even a scanty knowledge of aviation; however, in 1901, the data on wing shapes were mainly the work of Otto Lilienthal and his data included an erroneous Smeaton number (a figure expressing the relationship between pressure, wing surface, and velocity in a fluid) and overestimated by one-third the lift generated by a wing. When the Wright brothers built their first wing and experimented with it at Kitty Hawk, they quickly realized it did not generate the lift needed to carry a person's weight and that Lilienthal's data contained errors. In their situation, the total amount of lift depended upon airspeed, wing area, and wing shape and surface. Airspeed could not be varied as it depended on the Outer Bank's wind, and wing area was limited by the strength of construction materials. The most important variable was wing shape, and once that was recognized, they built a wind tunnel, and through experimentation with different shapes, they were able to identify the optimal wing shape for the conditions at Kitty Hawk. Wilbur Wright described the complexity of their task in a 1908 article as follows.

> The pressures on squares are different from those on rectangles, circles, triangles, or ellipses; arched surfaces differ from planes, and vary among themselves according to the depth of the curvature; true arcs differ from parabolas, and the latter differ among themselves; thick surfaces differ from thin, and surfaces thicker in one place from another vary in pressure when positions of maximum thicknesses are different; some surfaces are most efficient at one angle, others at other angles. The shape of the edge also makes a difference, so that thousands of combinations are possible in so simple a thing as a wing. (Wright, W. 1909)

In their wind tunnel, they experimented with many different shapes until they found the shape that produced the greatest ratio of lift to drag. Identifying that wing shape was the most important variable in understanding lift and that discovery reduced this variable group. Identification of the crucial variable or variables is a very important step in reducing the complexity of a multivariate system as it allows an investigator to greatly decrease the number of interactions between variables, thus simplifying an overall solution. This reduction leads to a smaller k complexity and opens the possibility of allowing that variable to be manipulated, while others are held constant.

Hold All but One Variable Constant

Once the most important or significant variables have been identified, the complexity of a multiple variable problem can be reduced by holding all variables constant while manipulating the most important one. This is a useful principle whether attempting to reduce the overall variable matrix or a subgrouping of variables. When only one variable is manipulated with all others held constant, the effect on an overall solution can be detected and calculated. In essence, this is a way of reducing a complex matrix to only one variable or to a $k = 2$ relationship since there can only be one reciprocal interaction between two variables. In this simplified situation, the only interaction that exists is between the identified variable and the overall concept or solution, and such a small matrix can be more easily solved.

Wilbur Wright realized this in developing his understanding of what he called "the angle of incidence" which we now call the angle of attack. The angle of the wind meeting the leading edge of a wing is crucial because if it exceeds a certain value the laminar flow over the wing will rather suddenly become chaotic resulting in a sudden loss of lift (a stall) and if not corrected a crash.

> The angle of incidence may be calculated in any case where speed, lift, and area are commensurable. Of these, area may be obtained by actual measurement. Lift is equal to weight supported, and can also be exactly measured. Speed alone requires to be calculated at the instant the observation is made. Thus, the opportunity for error is reduced to a single item, and this the one which affects the result least seriously in case of a slight error. It is easier to measure speeds than angles, and the results are less costly. … *Rule*. The angle of

> incidence is fixed by area, weight, and speed alone. It varies directly as the weight, and inversely as the area and speed, though not in exact ratio. (Wright, O. 1998)

By watching birds, Wilbur noticed that the "angle of incidence" does not change very much no matter what the angle the wing makes with the horizon. In other words, a crucial variable is the angular relationship between the wind and the wing, and other variables such as wing area, wind speed (when held within a certain value), and wing camber are not as crucial and can be held constant in order to solve the effects of lift. Once that relationship was understood, the Wright brothers could design a viable wing and ultimate a powered aircraft.

Perhaps an inherent definition of genius or creativity in science is the ability to single out the most important or most crucial variable rather than the unimportant ones. Once Wilbur had identified the crucial aspect of angle of incidence and identified the small angular range required to produce lift, he and Orville were then free to use their wind tunnel to manipulate the less crucial variables and improve the lifting ability of their wing shapes. By singling out the "angle of incidence" as the crucial variable and holding the others constant, they were able to decrease the number of *k* interactions defining the complexity of flight which was an important observation since as the number of interactions increased exponentially, so did the difficulty of a solution increase exponentially.

In addition to selecting and manipulating the most important or crucial variable, having an estimate of the weight of other variables is also important. Kauffman's initial work on the complexity of *k* interactions assumed that all variables were equal and did not take into account that variables likely have differential weights. If variables have differing weights, this will affect the pattern of interactions in the variable matrix. In most multivariate problems, variables will have differential contributions to an overall solution, and this should be taken into account. Another way of defining a variable with a low weight is that it likely has fewer interactions with other variables and that decreases the overall complexity of the cognitive matrix, allowing the development of a higher-order construct as shown in Fig. 12.7. In developing their understanding of flight, Wilbur and Orville did ascribe varying weights to their problem and treated them accordingly. For example, they gave the development of an engine a very low initial priority and ultimately had a bike shop employee, Charles Taylor, build it once they calculated the needed power. In this way, they first eliminated all variables associated with engine power which enabled them to focus on the subgroup lift variables, and second, they used their wind tunnel to focus on the crucial angle of incidence holding all others (wing shape, wing area, wind speed) constant. Identifying the weights of relevant variables is a crucial aspect of theory construction in science, and Wilbur and Orville were able to reduce the complexity of flight by weighting variables and manipulating crucial ones while holding others constant.

Correctly Sequencing Subgroups

The solution of every multi-interactive problem requires a sequencing or order in which the different aspects of the overall problem are resolved. As the previously discussed processes are utilized, they must be applied in a sequence and obviously certain sequential paths are more efficient than others. In many situations, maladaptive sequencing may prevent a reductive solution. Often, the sequencing of a solution may be obvious; however, this can also be very difficult to predict and is a common reason for scientific failure. Sometimes, a particular sequencing of problem-solving steps may seem obvious, when in reality there are subtleties and hidden difficulties that mislead an investigator into an erroneous sequencing. When a problem seems impossible to solve or leads to dead ends, the difficulty may be an incorrect sequence of steps. This is understandable because the essence of recognizing the correct sequence requires an investigator to predict the future which is often difficult as there are steps that cannot be foreseen in the initial stages of a scientific problem. Most scientific problems are quite abstract and that makes the process of future predictions even more difficult. Analyzing the correct sequence in problem-solving often requires a certain amount of creativity and the ability to anticipate unknown variables that are not recognized at the beginning of a problem. A creative investigator is able to include a wide range of variables and in that way can foresee unanticipated interactions that will determine the best sequence of attack for a problem.

There are times when the correct sequence of a scientific solution seems so obvious that it is often overlooked, and sometimes, seeing the obvious is a form of creativity. For example, the fact that the Wright brothers realized that the balance of an aircraft is the first and most critical step to be solved seems obvious because almost everything in motion needs to be balanced in respect to its surrounding medium. Humans need to be balanced in respect to the ground as we move about. The fastest sprinter and marathon runner will not do very well if they are unbalanced and continually falling over. Similarly, a boat must be balanced in its seawater medium or it will capsize and never reach its destination. Certainly, balance in respect to the surrounding medium of a viscous fluid such as air is more difficult, yet this obvious principal remains the same. This fact is so commonplace in the world around us that it is a surprise that the Wright brothers were the only ones to discover that fact.

Most early investigators of manned flight focused on the obvious variable of lift to the exclusion of other variables. Although lift seems to be the most crucial and therefore the first variable to be solved, Otto Lilienthal and the Wright brothers were unique in realizing that balance and stability needed to be dealt with first (Wright, O. 1998). Their genius was in realizing that they could not experiment with lift until they had achieved flight stability. Unfortunately, Lilienthal's method of control (body movements) was inadequate for the size of his wing area leading to his untimely death. In a 1908 speech, Wilbur Wright documented this understanding saying,

> In the field of aviation there were two schools. The first represented by such men as Professor Langley and Sir Hiram Maxim gave chief attention to power flight; the second represented by Lilienthal and Chanute, to soaring flight. Our sympathies were with the later

> school partly from impatience at the wasteful extravagance of mounting delicate and costly machinery on wings which no one knew how to manage.... The balancing of a flyer may seem at first thought to be a very simple matter, yet almost every experimenter had found in this the one point he could not satisfactorily master. We therefore resolved to try a fundamentally different principle. We would arrange the machine so that it would not tend to right itself. (McFarland, M.W. 2001a, b)

Whereas other experimenter had mainly dismissed the problem of balance by trying to build inherent stability with dihedral wings or self-correcting fins, the Wright brothers were unique in accepting that an aircraft is inherently unstable and they needed to first focus their efforts on developing the structural controls to control yaw, pitch, and roll. The variables involved in lift and power cannot be tested or calculated in an aircraft that is uncontrollable as a crash is likely to ensue before either of these variables can be understood in an actual flight situation. Table 12.2 illustrates the fact that an incorrectly sequenced solution leads to untestable or unsolvable problems.

They also recognized that building adequate flight controls was only one part of the solution. Early on, they recognized that an interactive three control flight system composed of a canard (elevator), wing warping (ailerons), and a controllable rudder had to be controlled by a human feedback mechanism. As any student pilot learns, using one's brain and four appendages to control an aircraft is a time-consuming and difficult skill even with a modern aircraft. The Wright brothers' 1902 glider and the 1903 flyer were very difficult to control and present-day experiments have shown that even experienced test pilots are usually unable to fly replicas of these early aircraft. Thus, a crucial part of their experimentation was developing piloting skills (without the benefit of an instructor), and this was a very complex set of skills that took a great deal of time to develop. Even at the beginning of their work, they recognized that they would need a great deal of practice if they were to learn to control their aircraft, and they also recognized that this was something that other investigators had neglected. Wilbur documented his understanding of this in writing the following:

Table 12.2 Problem solution pathways for the development of flight

Lift	Power	Stability
Wing area	Prop speed	Pitch
Angle of attack	Prop chord	Roll
Airspeed	Engine horsepower	Yaw
↓	↓	↓
Unstable aircraft	Unstable aircraft	Testable
↓	↓	↓
Not testable	Not testable	Lift and power
		↓
		Flight possible
		1903 Wright Flyer

> By long practice the management of a flying machine should become as instinctive as the balancing movements a man unconsciously employs with every step in walking, but in the early days it is easy to make blunders. Skill comes by the constant repetition of familiar feats rather than by a few over-bold attempts at feats for which the performer is yet poorly prepared.
>
> As yet we consider ourselves little more than novices in management. A thousand glides is the equivalent of about four hours of steady practice, far too little to give anyone a complete mastery of the art of flying. Progress is very slow in the preliminary stages…. (Jakab, P. & Young, R. 2000)

Throughout their time at Kitty Hawk, Wilbur and Orville carried out experiments on variables affecting lift and that was an integral part of their early gliding flights. However, that experimentation was ancillary to their major focus on balance and stability of their gliders. Had they not adopted that sequence in their work, they likely would have met with the same failure as Lilienthal, Pilcher, Langley, and Chanute; all of whom were talented scientists, but who put their initial experimentation on the wrong subset of variables.

Example of Cognitive Reductive Procedures: A Practical Application, College Selection

Using the Wright brothers' development of the principles of flight shows the utility of cognitive reductive procedures in solving scientific problems; however, these methods are useful with any complex problem composed of many interconnected variables. Applying to and selecting a college or university are often difficult for many students because of its complexity, and this issue arose in a discussion with my freshman seminar class at the university, so we decided to analyze the college admission selection process using cognitive reductive techniques.

The first step in this process is to generate a list of the many variables involved, and to our surprise, we found that we were able to identify 46 relevant variables. A list of these variables is shown in Table 12.3.

Even a cursory glance at Table 12.3 illustrates that keeping track of all these variables and the interconnections between them would be an impossible task, but somehow each aspiring college applicant must find a way to simplify this complex interconnecting matrix. The fact that hundreds of thousands of students enter universities every year shows that they do find ways to master this situation for better or for worse. Using the methods and the sequence of cognitive reductive procedures provides a useful method of organizing this complex of information so that it is understandable and allows for a cogent decision.

Table 12.3 A list of variables in selecting a college

Opportunity for athletics
Sport divisions I, II, and III or club sport
Making friends
School spirit
Tuition costs
Scholarships
Available student–family finances
Area cost of living
Campus living conditions
Campus safety
School spirit–athletic teams
Size of school
Permission for auto on campus
Number of students
Average class size
Geographic location
Rural versus urban
Public or private
Availability of many majors
Quality of faculty
Opportunity to study abroad
Faculty involvement with undergraduates
Faculty involvement with graduate students
Distance from home
Acceptance rate
SAT–ACT scores
High school grade point average
Application fee
Application workload–number of essays
Weather at university
Academic reputation
Starting salary of graduates
Career opportunities for graduates
Party school
Attractiveness of campus
Ranking of university
In-state–out-of-state
Average time to graduation
Cleanliness
COVID vaccination situation
Faculty–student ratio
Internship opportunities
Cost of room and board
Faculty reputation research
Applicant selection rate
Personal contact with faculty

Irrelevant Variables

The first step in this process is to recognize the fact that not all variables listed will be applicable to every college applicant. For example, there are rare situations where students from very wealthy families have such huge financial resources that variable of family finances becomes irrelevant. Such fortunate students are likely not concerned about tuition or any other expenses, but this is an uncommon situation. Other students may be uninterested in study abroad programs and that variable may also be ignored. Ignoring and deleting variables may simplify the total selection matrix of college variables; however, most of the items listed in Table 12.3 are relevant to selecting a college. Of course, I doubt that many perspective students go to the trouble of creating an extensive list as in Table 12.3, and so important and relevant variables are simply not included, ignoring the fact they should be included.

Detecting Underlying Identities

Second, we need to identify those variables that are identities, so they then can be reduced to a single variable. For example, a large number of variables relate to finance, but all of these either add or subtract from the total expense of college; therefore, these variables will be reduced to one variable that encompasses total expense. We can see that variables such as tuition, room, and board costs, whether a university is public or private, the area cost of living, in-state or out-of-state college, and scholarship money all are interconnected and with some calculations will reduce to a figure of total college expenses. For example, private universities, usually but not always, have higher costs than public colleges and therefore may have interconnections with the total cost of a college education. At times, some variables may be somewhat deceptive in that a student may value the seeming prestige of a scholarship more than a lesser tuition even if they calculate the same amount; nevertheless, all of these variables reduce to the same identity which we can label finance.

Opposing Variables

The third step in this process is to identify variables that are correlated but opposite to one another. Certain variables on the preceding list fall into this category because they are related but are opposites in function, and so knowledge of one can cancel or significantly modify the importance of another. For example, increasing one will result in a corresponding decrease in another or vice versa, thus eliminating one or more variables and simplifying the matrix. That will allow the cognitive model of college choice much more understandable and manageable.

This can be illustrated by the relationship between opportunity for athletics and the size of a school. Colleges with a smaller student body tend to have smaller athletic departments, so in those schools, nonathletic scholarship students might be able to participate in Division III or club athletics, whereas schools with a large student body are likely to have highly competitive Division I athletic programs and only scholarship athletes will be talented enough to be able to be selected for a team. Another related, but opposing variable is school spirit. Generally, school spirit is higher in large universities where students are involved in attending games and sharing their enthusiasm for their own teams against rivals. As a general rule, attending games and cheering on Division III or club teams are not as important in smaller colleges. Thus, the size of the school is generally going to determine other variables such as athletic participation and involvement in school spirit. As a result, these variables can be eliminated from the confusing and perhaps overwhelming total of variables involved in making a college choice.

Another important set of opposing variables relates to academic characteristics of a university and the type and quality of a student's education. Many universities, especially prestigious ones, have faculty that are heavily involved in their own research and collaboration with their graduate students. Oftentimes, these senior faculties will only teach graduate courses or occasionally large undergraduate lecture classes. Consequently, they have less involvement with undergraduate students. Looking at the list of variables in selecting a college, we can see that faculty involvement with graduate students, ranking of the university, the faculty's involvement with research, and its academic reputation may tend to have an opposite relationship to other variables such as personal contact with faculty members, undergraduate involvement in faculty research, admission acceptance rate, and undergraduate class size. For example, universities that are very selective and have a low admission rate are more likely to be prestigious universities with research-oriented faculty and many graduate programs, and in such universities, the faculty will tend to have little contact with undergraduate students. Prospective college applicants who want smaller classes and personal academic contact with faculty members are wise to choose smaller colleges, and in that, way they can eliminate a number of variables relating to the size of a university and its prestigious research reputation.

In our discussion of cognitive reductive methods concerning how the Wright brothers developed the principles of flight, the relationships between variables involved in the physics of flight could be calculated and therefore were very precise. For example, the relationship between lift and drag was quite exact and could be calculated by a mathematical formula that divided the lift coefficient by the drag coefficient (CL/CD). The formula for lift involves a number of variables such as density, velocity squared, wing area, and a compressibility factor. This formula is very precise and provides a very accurate measurement of lift. The precision of these simple formulas means that an aircraft with higher L/D ratios will be more efficient which not only simplifies the matrix of flight variables, but also provides useful information for aeronautical designers.

In dealing with social situations, such as college selection, we do not have a precise mathematical relationship between opposing variables. For example, the general rule that prestigious universities tend to have faculty that do not have significant contact with their undergraduates is not a precise relationship as in some schools, certain senior faculty might choose to teach advanced undergraduate classes or mentor undergraduate students in an honor program.

Separating Variables into Relevant Groups

The preceding operations have reduced our cognitive matrix through the process of eliminating variables, and in doing so, we have also eliminated the interconnections between these variables. The next step in this cognitive reductive process is to place related variables into relevant groups. This does not eliminate variables, but through the process of inclusion, this creates cognitive models that simplify the decision process. I have organized the original 46 variables minus those we eliminated into eight general categories. These are as follows:

Finance
Life comforts
College size
Classroom learning (positive or negative)
Admission difficulties
Career opportunities
Athletic opportunities
Extra-class learning (internships and study abroad programs)

Each of these categories contains one or more of the original variables; however, this kind of grouping reduces the complexity of the matrix, so there are fewer to deal with, and more importantly these groups in most cases are independent of each other and therefore will have fewer and less connections between them. Of course, we need to remember that though these groups are relatively independent of one another, there may be some variables that may belong more than one grouping, but this should not interfere with process of simplifying the cognitive model of college admissions. Such a grouping will still aid perspective college applicants to better understand the complexity of this important cognitive model and should result in more robust and valid decision making. Obviously, the preceding list of relevant groups demonstrates my own personal way of reducing the complexity of the college admission process, and other individuals (the vast population of young college applicants rather than one fossil of a professor) will generate a completely different set of relevant groups better reflecting their own idiosyncratic approach to developing their own personal cognitive model of the college application process.

Assessing the Importance of Each Group

Once an individual has developed the variable groupings relevant to their own interests and abilities, they will need to assess the importance of each group. Perhaps, the simplest way to reflect the importance of each is to assign them weights on a simple 10- or 20-point Likert scale. I think that is preferable to merely rank the groups since a Likert scale tends to show the degree of differences in importance on a scale of approximately equal intervals. In that way, it will demonstrate which groups might be similar or even equal in importance and which groups will be quite dissimilar. Simply ranking the importance of each group will not have the same precision as giving them weights according to an equal interval Likert scale.

There may be some groups that are so important, either positive or negative, that they may determine the entire cognitive matrix. For example, a student may decide that school admission requirements involved in a large number of essays and so may be too much of a pain and not worth the bother. The importance of that group may effectively negate a number of possible college choices. Similarly, a prospective student may feel that the Life Comforts group including geographic location is very important, and if they believe that their personal and emotional life will be unhappy at other than certain locations, they are likely to eliminate any schools that would not rate very high on this group. This could become a somewhat catastrophic situation because if they were to choose a college where they would be unhappy, they are likely to drop out of such schools and either quit the opportunity for a college education or transfer.

One applicant I know was quite sure he wanted to have a career focused on the business of Internet security, so he sought out colleges with interdisciplinary programs that provided a major focused on computer programing, Internet security, and business economics. Since there were very few such programs within the limited geographic area of his choice, the only relevant group important to him was career opportunities. He was uninterested in athletics, extra-class learning, class enjoyment, and the size of the college.

Another example of a particular group attaining such importance that it eliminates all other considerations was the son of an acquaintance who was only interested in a sports management major. He immediately eliminated any schools that do not have such a program, no matter how well the alternative schools would fit his requirements in other ways and on others college selection groups. That student only recognized groups such as career opportunities and Athletics as important and negated any other considerations. Perhaps, making such career decisions so early in ones' development may not be a cogent decision, but that would not likely dissuade a student who has strong beliefs about their future and does not care about the useful opportunities that a university education provides in terms of being exposed to new educational interests, opportunities, and careers.

Hold All but One Grouping Constant

For most students, all of the groups they identify with will be important to a greater or lesser extent, but attempting to understand the significance of all groups at one time will likely lead to confusion and cognitive overload. Although we have already assessed the importance of each variable, there is another step through which we can simplify the confusion of the college selection process and that is to isolate a single group to determine its significance without the confusion and influence of the other groups. To do this, we need to assume that all the groups with the exception of the one chosen group are of equal importance and therefore can be ignored. In other words, by equalizing and therefore ignoring all other groups, we can manipulate the different states and significance of the group we are focusing on. We can then imagine how the variables in that group would influence the future contentment and satisfaction of our college life. In this process of holding all groups but one constant, we can even vary the influence of that single group by imagining it either higher or lower in its importance. In that way, we can better predict how that variable group will affect our future college experience.

For example, a student who loves a particular sport and wants to be a member of that college team can imagine how excited she or he would feel if selected to join that team. Similarly, he might want to imagine how unhappy she or he would be at college if not selected for the team and had to give up his interest in participation in a sport that he or she loved. By holding all the other relevant groups constant, that student might realize they will be terribly unhappy no matter how satisfied they might be with the other aspects of their college experience. In that situation, our prospective applicant might decide that he or she should reject any college that likely will not provide an engaging and satisfying athletic life. Similarly, an applicant might want small classes and personal involvement with professors and so would be unhappy if they found themselves in large lecture halls with remote faculty members and perhaps an inability to ask questions or make comments on the subject matter. In this situation, they are likely to feel frustrated and not have the academic and intellectual challenge they expect. Such a student might want to assess their happiness or unhappiness with that aspect of their college experience. If they found the proportion of lecture courses is exceeded number of small classes, they might be better off to reject colleges that fit this academic profile.

In using this technique of holding all but one constant, it might be wise to start with the group that they had identified as most important and then work their way down the list of groups to those listed as least important. That sequence is likely to be the most efficient in simplifying this complex evaluation since groups identified as most important will likely identify colleges a prospective student is most likely to reject. That sequencing will also ensure that their most significant concerns are not likely to be overlooked.

Summary

Finding the solution to a complex matrix of multiple interactive variables is difficult and requires an approach that reduces the overall complexity of the matrix. Even with the use of computer solutions, there is still a cognitive component to understanding and developing a solution to the problem. This chapter proposed certain methods that could be used to accomplish a solution whether they are used individually or as a whole. Obviously, these reductive principles provide a generalized approach, and in the real world of science, an investigator must take account of the individual circumstances inherent in that particular scientific problem.

The Wright brothers faced such a situation in 1900 when they began their investigation into the principles of flight and used those principles to build the first viable powered aircraft. An analysis of their approach shows that they used such reductive procedures to cope with the complexity of interactive variables underlying their ultimate discoveries. Certainly, the genius they showed in solving the problem was due to the way they were able to sequentially reduce the problematic variables and the cautious persistence that marked their methodology.

Despite not having an advanced degree, Wilbur and Orville Wright did have certain experiences and aptitudes that helped them. Perhaps most scientists are unaware of the cultural influences and personal experiences that they bring to their work which either helps or hinders them in their investigations. This factor is the most serendipitous and thus the most difficult to understand or predict since at times ones cultural and personal factors may lead to irrelevancies and distractions, and at other times, it may provide an idiosyncratic insight leading to a solution. The fact that the Wright brothers were bicycle racers and mechanics provided them with special cognitive insights. The use of wing warping to roll an aircraft is similar to cycling in that a person turns a bicycle by leaning it in the desired direction. They understood the importance of drag on an aircraft as that is similar to the drag produced by wind resistance in cycling. Similarly, their understanding that an aircraft is inherently unstable and must be controlled by the pilot is analogous to a cyclist who is constantly making small movements to keep the bicycle on a straight path. Like Wilbur and Orville Wright, most scientists develop insights that are influenced by their history in ways that they only occasionally recognize, but this factor is likely an important one in scientific endeavors.

Chapter 13
Understanding Genocides

Abstract This chapter discusses the cognitive models which ordinary humans use to generate rational explanations and intellectual justifications for their most morally horrific behaviors. External events such as political and cultural differences offer explanations for such horrific events, but individuals must create and maintain a personal mode of thinking that can motivate such seemingly rare, but incomprehensible behaviors. A part of the explanation for these distorted cognitive models comes from the egocentrism of childhood development and the need to bond with a person's social clan. Unfortunately, many of the same principles that are utilized in commonplace thinking can be misapplied to create cognitive models that support distorted and erroneous views of our exterior social environment. An in-depth analysis of the developmental sequence of Nazi genocidal cognitive models and other holocausts are utilized as an example to explain this phenomenon.

Keywords Genocide · Clan identification · Milgram experiment · Ego-dystonic belief · Piaget · Self-Corrected Thinking

The twentieth century has been marked by a horrible series of genocides and holocausts such as the genocide of Armenians by the then Turkish government, the Nazi Holocaust of the Jews, the Rwandan genocide of the Tutsis, and unfortunately many others. History is replete with such events, but the twentieth century seems to be as bad as or worse than other periods of time. This presents an interesting, if terrible, conundrum in that one would expect that cultures affected by the ideas of the Age of Enlightenment and possessing modern philosophical concepts and sophisticated scientific technology would be less likely to engage in such horrific behaviors. However, that does not seem to be the case. One common explanation is that such events are mainly caused by external factors such as territorial conflicts between different groups, ideas of conquest, economic differences, long-standing cultural prejudices, and many other factors that have been identified through the work of cultural anthropologists. While external environmental events may account for significant causes of such moral horrors, genocides, and holocausts must be carried out by individual people. In order to develop a full understanding of how such events

R. Leve, *The Complexity of Human Thought*,
https://doi.org/10.1007/978-3-031-09104-9_13

can occur, we also must look at the way in which an individual's cognitive models allow them to engage in behaviors that are reprehensible to the moralities of almost every culture.

History, ancient and modern, has many descriptions of genocides; however, in analyzing genocides, I find it illuminating to use examples of the Nazi genocide toward Jews, Gypsies, Russians, and the homosexuals and mentally deficient of their own nation. Rarely has any other genocide provided insight and data into the thinking of those individuals who carried out these horrors. Analyzing this data in terms of the individual cognitive models of participants will show that the thinking processes used are similar to those used in everyday life and even in high-level scientific thinking. Though the processes may be similar to other horrific genocides, the distortions in terms of cultural assumptions and identification of variables are profoundly different and yield horrifying behaviors.

Rarely do we form cognitive models that lead to genocidal behaviors toward members of our own group. In fact, from an early age, we form cognitive beliefs that identify our own group and discriminate against other groups as different. This type of "clan" identification is easy to acquire as there are so many environmental influences and factors that we become quite attuned to detecting such differences at an early age, and once we discriminate such differences, we tend to see the cognitive model of our own group as positive and others as at best neutral or oftentimes negative. Without even trying to enumerate the host of environmental factors that cause this group identification, just being part of a clan is beneficial in terms of resource sharing, cooperation, dependence, parental affection, and sometimes our very survival. These factors are seldom associated with a different group. In terms of violence, within-group murder seems as an aberrant event and is severely punished by expulsion, incarceration, or execution. Individuals can be made to engage in within-group violence when they are under intense social pressure or stress, but usually this is rare and can cause severe emotional trauma.

This was demonstrated by a series of classic experiments by the social psychologist Stanley Milgram (1963) in his attempts to better understand obedience to authority. Milgram's studies showed that individuals can be led to extreme violence against members of the same group, but only under conditions of extreme social pressure and at the cost of severe emotional trauma. There were different variations on the study, but in the most common research setting, he had an experimenter and two subjects, with one designated as a learner and the other as the teacher. Unknown to the teacher subject, the learner was a confederate and an actor. Before the study began, they met and chatted together and supposedly drew slips of paper to see who would be the teacher and who the learner. Actually, all the slips of paper said teacher, but the confederate claimed that his said learner. Then the confederate was placed in a different room and strapped to an "electric chair"-looking device. The teacher subject was then told that he was to repeat a list of word pairs for the confederate "learner subject" to repeat back and if the "learner" made an error, the teacher was to administer an electric shock in order to "help" the learner better learn the words.

Although the teacher was pressing a button indicating the delivery of the electric shock, this was a ruse, and no shock was actually delivered though the "teacher" believed shocks were being applied. The "teacher" subject could not see the learner, but would hear prerecorded cries of pain when the supposed shocks were delivered. Each time an error was made, the teacher would supposedly increase the voltage in 15 volt increments and press the button administering the shock. With each "mistake," the voltage of the fake shocks increased, the learner's cries would increase until they began to beat on the wall separating them, and ultimately, with the highest voltage, the learner fell silent. If at any time the "teacher subject" asked to halt the experiment, the experimenter gave specific verbal instructions as follows:

1. Please continue.
2. The experiment requires you to continue.
3. It is essential that you continue.
4. You have no choice; you must go on.

If the subject asked to stop after all four verbal prompts, the experiment was halted; otherwise it was only halted after the subject had given the maximum 450 volt shock three times in succession. In his first experiments, over 60% of the participants administered the final 450 volt shock, and all subjects administered shocks of at least 300 volts. Milgram's obvious conclusion was that even ordinary people and members of the same society can be made to engage in reprehensible and cruel acts. He concluded, "When stark authority was pitted against the subject's strongest moral imperatives against hurting others, and with the screams of victims ringing in their ears, authority was obeyed more often than not."

However, there is another conclusion to be drawn from Milgram's experiments. In spite of their obedience to authority, the subjects were very uncomfortable and upset after carrying out the shocks. They showed signs of moderate to severe stress including sweating, stuttering, groaning, biting their lips, and trembling. The effects of the study on the participants were so traumatic that similar and identical experiments can no longer be approved by research boards and are seen as unethical.

This second finding of the Milgram study shows that though exterior factors can force normal individuals into doing horrendous acts to others, they identify as part of their own group (the subject and the confederate were both subjects in the experiment and even chatted amiably before the experiment began); such acts are ego-dystonic in that they violate moral beliefs. In other words, the cognitive models that support their social beliefs are incongruent with the behavior of administering painful or even lethal electric shocks to members of their own social group. Their social belief was developed and is held together by sharing, group cooperation, dependence on familiar others, memories of parental affection, and shared group resistance to threats. Attempting to inflict harm on an emotionally neutral member of one's group does not fit the factors that compose this social cognitive model. Trying to include hatred, violence, and anger toward a liked or even neutral group member will not form a stable association with other positive variables and may even strengthen the cognitive beliefs toward one's own group and strongly reject threats to that dystonic model. In summary, the Milgram experiments tell us that although extreme social pressures can force individuals into committing culturally immoral acts, they do not create stable cognitive models that will motivate them to continue such acts and allow them to logically justify their behavior. We can wonder if the subjects in Milgram's experiment ever silently or actively became angry and hostile with the experimenter for forcing them into immoral acts that conflicted with the positive cognitive model of their own group. That research result was not reported.

In addition to the genocides of the twentieth century, there have been local and world wars in which huge armies of individuals were engaged in the murder of each other. Although such killings were sanctioned by authorities in the form of their respective governments and cultures, they were nevertheless carried out by individual soldiers whose cognitive models allowed behaviors that would have been unthinkable if they were inflicted on members of one's own group. In fact, most soldiers form incredibly strong bonds with their own local group whether it be a squad, platoon, aircrew, or shipmates, which can motivate individuals to sacrifice their lives for their comrades.

Conversely, many soldiers throughout the numerous wars of history believed that the killing of the enemy as a member of a different clan was appropriate. Sometimes this cognitive model is justified as a measure of self-defense. "If I do not kill the enemy, my enemy may kill me." However, history is replete with many instances of warriors killing the innocent, the aged, women, and children of the opposite group who were not combatants and posed no danger. That, among other reasons and prejudices, may form a justification for killing an unknown human who belongs to a different group; nevertheless, both the killer and the victim must have a cognitive model that motivates, allows, and activates their behavior.

Perhaps it is even more surprising and might even seem incomprehensible that one's cognitive models can form beliefs that are so strong that they drive individuals to willingly enter combat and accept the possibility of their own deaths. We might try to explain this by assuming that most soldiers believe that someone else will die, not them, but most soldiers in combat certainly realize that they can be killed and perhaps endure a slow, painful, and often obscene death. Yet in spite of such self-destructive behavior, the millions of soldiers in World War I, World War II, and every other war seem to have generated a cognitive model that accepts the possibility of self-destruction. We might explain this through environmental factors such as sacrifice for one's country, one's ideals, or the brotherhood of one's buddies, but that is not a full explanation of normal, logically thinking soldiers, accepting their own premature deaths when biologically, culturally, and psychologically they should seek self-preservation. Once again, a full understanding of these behaviors is insufficient if it does not attempt to understand the cognitive models of individuals in such situations. Why and how do we develop cognitive models that fly in the face of individual and species preservation when our evolutionary instincts are almost always pushing us in opposite behavioral directions?

In previous chapters, we have discussed the fact that cognitive models are formed through the association and integration of different individual stimuli into cognitive models. In other words, the many individual visual, auditory, tactile, and other stimuli are coordinated through the process of development into models that allow us to understand and react to our environment. Obviously, the formation of cognitive models has important survival advantages because we can better understand and react to our exterior environment, but in addition to survival advantages, most species have developed patterns of positive cognitive models specific to their biology, culture, and common environment. If cognitive models were initially developed by life-forms to maintain a survival advantage and ensure appropriate and efficient psychological and cultural functioning, then it flies in the face of logic and one's survival to develop cognitive models that decrease one's survival and violate efficient and harmonious social and cultural adjustment.

The first thing we must understand is how such immoral cognitive models are formed. In Chap. 4, we saw how different environmental stimuli are associated with each other to form a cognitive model, and such cognitive models must have a purpose in that the individual senses some sort of advantage. We have referred to the overall survival advantage, but as noted, cognitive models are formed that reflect the real and perceived advantages of a local environment and provide that individual with local advantages. These can be an increase in social status, feelings of increased competence, or enhanced opportunities to gain feelings of happiness and pleasure.

Perhaps a concept from complexity science, attractors, can help us to understand how cognitive models form around such advantages. In complexity science, there are a number of types of attractors such as point attractors, periodic attractors, and chaotic attractors. The simplest of these, the point attractor, can help us understand this process. A good example of a point attractor is gravity. Gravity is a force that causes all things on the surface of our planet to be drawn toward a point in the center of the earth. In that sense, it attempts to draw all things together, and as an analogy, cognitive models also draw aspects of the environment that are related to each other into a cognitive model. Thus, a cognitive model is an attractor that attempts to bring together related stimuli and variables in the local environment to support and maintain an integrated cognitive model.

Of course, this is a metaphor; however, once a cognitive model forms around a cognitive concept or belief, it then attempts to accrete related aspects of the environment to it, and the more variables it can include in the cognitive model, the stronger and more robust the model becomes. Thus, a cognitive model becomes a belief about the exterior environment which has a purpose and a tendency to maintain and strengthen itself by seeking out aspects of the environment that harmonize with the initial concept or idea. This is very common human behavior in that we often seek out information, events, and opinions that will bolster our beliefs and tend to ignore or refute those things that are hostile to our beliefs. For example, people have formed different cognitive models concerning the recent explanations for climate change or if climate change really exists. Not surprisingly, those who believe in climate change will tend to seek out evidence (environmental information) that the burning of fossil fuels is the reason that our planet is warming. They will tend to point to long-term trends that show rises in temperature, especially in the Arctic and the oceans. Those who deny climate change will seek out environmental evidence saying the rise in temperature is simply a periodic fluctuation that is a normal part of our planet's climate. Each side will then seek out and accept the evidence that is harmonious with their cognitive model and ignore or reject alternative evidence.

One would hope that this would be a self-correcting process because eventually the negative environmental effects of maintaining erroneous beliefs would force a change toward a more accurate belief, and the recent increase in environmentally friendly actions such as wind turbines and solar panels seems to bear this fact out. We might also expect that a natural process of cognitive logic would bring about a correction; however, this does not occur in many individuals and in many situations. The problem is that our environments are so diverse and complex that we can always find environmental evidence to support even the most illogical and self-injurious beliefs. A contemporary and rather serious example of this phenomenon is the vast cadre of individuals who reject receiving a vaccine to protect themselves against the many variants of the coved virus, even when they are seriously ill and in the ICU unit of a local hospital. Such individuals have little difficulty seeking out and finding environmental information that justifies their cognitive model concerning vaccinations, because the diversity of environmental information is so vast that there is little difficulty finding illogical and obviously false information that will easily become part of any cognitive model, no matter how self-destructive. Once a central belief is established and individual bits of environmental evidence to maintain that belief are integrated through many interactive associations, that belief will tend to be stable and become canalized.

This explanation is easy to accept and understand with an abstract scientific concept like climate change. However, it is less comprehensible when seen against the backdrop of the worst human atrocities inflicted on fellow human beings for minimal short- and long-term personal advantage. In order to understand how such immoral beliefs and behaviors are formed, we must understand an individual's personal history, and that begins in infancy. Infants emerge into a multitudinous environment of colors, objects, sounds, smells, and tactile sensations. If they have any cognitive models, they are simplistic and fleeting because they have a limited ability to detect associations. Thus, they are born into an egocentric state where their only associations are between outside stimuli and their own feelings and sensations. They are unaware of other humans who inhabit the same universe. They are blissfully unaware of the fact that these other humans who inhabit their environment have their own cognitive models that are different from those of our newborn infants. Perhaps the first cognitive model that slowly emerges is that of a maternal object as the shape, color, movements, and sounds of the mother become associated with pleasurable emotions such as being fed and cuddled. This begins the long and slow developmental process of realizing that there are other individuals in the universe and such individuals do not have the same cognitive models of our emerging child and so they may experience that shared environment in a very different way. The famous Swiss psychologist Jean Piaget has documented the stages that children go through in slowly giving up this natural egocentricity. Actually, even at age four or five, they are sufficiently egocentric to believe that if they have a certain thought, then other people will know that thought without their having to tell them.

I experienced this in a terribly traumatic incident concerning my eldest daughter Lauren when she was two years old. We had been playing a father-daughter game at a friend's swimming pool in which she would jump from the side of the pool into the water, I would catch her and put her back on the side of the pool, and we would repeat this fun game. We had stopped playing the game and were now sitting having lunch on the side of the pool when my wife suddenly shouted, "Bob, that child is drowning." I looked and saw a small child drowning on the opposite side of the pool, and in seconds and two strokes, I was across the pool picking this strange child up, putting her against my shoulder, and walking her to the edge of the pool. In the adrenaline excitement of those seconds, I had a fleeting thought, wondering why this strange child was allowing a strange adult to hold her close against my shoulder. By this time, my wife and our friends had run to the other side of the pool; something they said made me realize that this strange child was my daughter Lori. As I put her down on the side of the pool, she looked at me confused and, in a reproving tone, said, "You didn't catch me." What had happened was that she had walked to the opposite side of the pool, seen me, and decided she would resume playing our game, thinking that if she wanted to play the game, I would know what she was thinking.

The process of human development and similarly the development of certain other mammalian species involves the process of slowly realizing that other individuals are different and their thinking processes and cognitive models are also different. Perhaps there is no motivation for children to come to this realization except for the fact that they are socialized within the benefits of a family and extended clan. That is to say, without the attachment to other caring humans, they might continue to see the world in an egotistic fashion as an extension of themselves. It is likely that their first understanding that other people are different and have different thoughts and cognitive models occurs through their interaction with parents or other emotionally bonded members of their extended clan, and such interactions are honed by the increasing demands placed on children by caretakers. Every time a child wants to do something and the parent says, "No," that becomes an unspoken lesson indicating that a parent has a different understanding of the environment from the child. This process of differentiation of other humans that begins with the identification of a maternal figure and continues throughout childhood is crucial to socializing oneself into the security of a clan; however, we never completely give up our egocentric view of our environment. In other words, we create our own personal cognitive universe that will always be, to a greater or lesser extent, different from the personal cognitive universes of others. Perhaps the most surprising fact is not that we always maintain some of our egocentric infancy and constantly disagree, but that our childhood experiences have allowed us to have a reasonably shared view of our external environment that allows us to understand each other, cooperate with each other, and see the overall universe in a similar way.

Understanding the retention of childhood egocentrism will help us understand how individuals can hold beliefs that are so abhorrent and dystonic to our cultural norms. We must remember that each of us has created our own cognitive universe, and while most of the time we see these universes as quite similar, in many cases, we will see them as profoundly different, which will lead to serious disagreements. By the time we mature out of childhood, we have developed strong beliefs about our environment and especially our political and social environments, and these can be strong enough to motivate and activate personal cruelties. Such beliefs become higher-order concepts as described in Chap. 4 and are composed of individual cognitive models that are mutually reinforcing. However, this model is composed of cognitive experiences and information which form a social and political belief system. Sometimes the origin of these beliefs comes from cognitive models that can be identified such as modeling a parental belief system or succumbing to seductive social pressures; in other instances, it may result from an isolated incident or chance encounter which can serve as an emergent phenomenon that reorganizes a person's belief system. Like most emergent phenomena, they can seldom be identified and predicted ahead of time and can only be understood after a significant change has taken place.

For example, this is similar to a person experiencing a semireligious conversion due to involvement with a charismatic leader or like individual German soldiers adopting the beliefs of the Waffen-SS after exposure to the speeches and writings of Adolf Hitler. In most circumstances and for most people, these variables would be ignored and seen as not fitting into an existing belief system. However, as an emergent phenomenon, that kind of chance encounter can interact with other preexisting stimuli and result in a stable and strong belief. One is reminded of the Nazi Waffen-SS soldiers who when severely wounded and bleeding refused to accept a blood transfusion from an American medic when they could not be assured that the needed blood did not come from a Jewish donor. They held rigidly to their belief and died.

Chapter 14
Generating Cognitive Models of Genocide

Abstract Unfortunately, many of the same principles that allow individuals to solve complex scientific problems can be misapplied to create cognitive models that support a distorted and immoral view of the exterior environment. Individuals who participate in genocides do not display pathological symptoms typical of typical emotional disturbance, but they are able to seriously distort their logic and their understanding of their social environment in a way that allows for immoral reasoning. There are five principles that allow individuals to generate cognitive models that will seem to justify the murder of innocent men, women, and children. The first principle is to select erroneous and immoral variables. Another is to force inaccurate identities on different groups. A third principle is erroneously making an unimportant variable salient to other important variables. Fourth is reducing opposing variables to a single identity, and last is creating a sequence of the unethical variables they have included. A study of the developmental distortions used to justify Nazi genocidal cognitive models is analyzed.

Keywords Cognitive reductive principles · Social · Wannasse Conference · Erroneous identification · Social surplus · Final solution · Nierenberg race laws

How do seemingly normal individuals create cognitive models that allow them to perpetrate the horror and seemingly inhuman acts of genocide? This perplexing question arose after World War II when individuals responsible for the Nazi genocide were interviewed. The expectation was that psychologists would find them to be sociopathic monsters with little human qualities. The surprise was that they turned out to be in many ways rather ordinary individuals who seemed to be carrying out atrocities in a rather clerical, perfunctory fashion. However, as noted earlier, they had to have some form of cognitive model to explain and justify their reprehensible activities. In other words, they had created a cognitive model that allowed for and motivated their behavior. This chapter will attempt to analyze how such cognitive models were created.

Surprisingly, the process of forming cognitive models of genocide as a higher-order concept uses many of the same principles that were discussed in the formation

R. Leve, *The Complexity of Human Thought*,
https://doi.org/10.1007/978-3-031-09104-9_14

of many other complex concepts, although it is misapplied as they do not follow the sound logic of a scientific solution. As we shall see, the process consists of finding ways to reduce variables such that a simple, understandable, and robust belief system develops. That belief may be immoral, insensitive, and cruel in most normal situations, but as a personal cognitive model it will seem to be normal and in harmony with the individual's view of their greater personal universe. This means that cognitively sophisticated life-forms, especially humans, are capable of generating horrible atrocities on other humans they define as different, and that is a rather sad and sobering truth.

Principles Used in Generating Immoral Cognitive Models

As with our study of the Wright Brothers, the first step in generating cognitive models in cultural and social situations is to correctly identify the relevant variables. In the case of the Wright brothers, dealing with scientific variables such as lift, drag, angle of attack, and others was reasonably straightforward. However, when dealing with social phenomena, there is a huge universe of human traits and characteristics to consider as variables, and choosing erroneous variables, either through ignorance or purposeful distortion, is not difficult and can easily lead to prejudicial opinions of other groups. In essence, we are dealing with the complexity of a large matrix of interconnected human attributes. Of course, each individual must create a stable cognitive model of different individuals and groups by simplifying the many variables involved. Unfortunately, the process of simplification and creating such a stable cognitive model can easily lead to errors in the form of prejudice.

In addition, social cognitive models are not self-correcting. Scientific models are self-correcting in that either they work or they don't. In the case of the Wright brothers, their glider or airplane either flew or couldn't get off the ground. That kind of discrete feedback and self-correction does not exist in social cultural cognitive models. Individuals can seek out information from many social sources, whether it be other people, commercial radio and TV, or the Internet, that will justify the simple cognitive model they have created. In fact, unlike scientific cognitive models, the social beliefs of an individual can misinterpret or actually distort the reality of the outside environment such that it will not self-correct distorted cognitive models. There are many ways in which an erroneous simplification of social variables can occur, and we will see that some of these are not terribly different than the methods used in generating the cognitive models used to solve complex scientific problems.

Selecting Erroneous Variables

As we have already mentioned, a common method to simplify a complex cognitive model is to exclude variables and their interactions. However, by excluding variables, we often might omit valid variables that accurately describe different individuals or groups and select simpler erroneous variables that are more congruent with a preexisting prejudicial cognitive model. For example, in attempting to accurately understand and react to individuals in any group, the most important personal characteristics are abilities such as practical and social intelligence, kindness, concern for others, loyalty, and other positive attributes. These admirable characteristics are essential for forming an accurate cognitive model and a robust understanding of any individual. However, they often are ignored in favor of negative attributes, and through a process of prejudicial misunderstanding, individuals can create erroneous cognitive models that focus on the negative social attributes of individuals and groups.

Social beliefs are a higher-order concept which is the amalgamation of many individual variables and parcels of information in our cultural environment. As we learned in Chap. 4, in order to avoid the complexity and confusion of including too many variables, we combine the variables and the interactions between them into a higher-order concept. Usually this is done as a way of avoiding overload and falling into cognitive chaos. However, in social situations, we can erroneously include immoral and unethical variables as we create the higher-order concepts of our social and emotional beliefs. Such errors can be congruent with an individual's idiosyncratic beliefs, but they will not be congruent with the morality of the overall cultural group. Perhaps, such cognitive models will seem logical to particular individuals, but they will not be seen as logical to other members of the overall culture. For example, the prejudicial beliefs of the American Nazi Party can seem logical within the erroneous assumptions of that subgroup, but they will be seen as illogical, and abhorrent according to the assumptions and beliefs of the larger American population. Religious groups throughout human history have often developed assumptions that created immoral cognitive models based on selecting erroneous character traits to describe individuals of a divergent group. That model is then used to justify some of the most barbaric behaviors ever inflicted on other human beings.

The European Crusades of the tenth and eleventh centuries are a perfect example of such terrible cognitive models which gave permission for and justified the slaughter of innocent men, women, and children. During the first Crusade when the Christian armies entered Jerusalem, they killed almost every man, woman, and child in the city. In addition to the Moslem inhabitants who by virtue of their religion were seen as infidels and different, they also killed other Christians who belonged to a divergent form of Christianity. We might say that these horrendous acts were carried out by barbaric soldiers with no sense of decency or morality; however, such soldiers had ethical cognitive models of kindness and piety toward members of their own Christian sect. Their cognitive model toward others than themselves was based on a religious idea that the members of a different religious group were infidels who did not deserve to live. Thus, they focused their cognitive model on an immoral assumption that gave great importance to a flawed religious idea and gave little importance to the observation that the Moslems, Jews, and other Christians, were also humans who looked like them, behaved like them, and bled like them when slaughtered. Their ability to disregard the obvious human characteristics of their enemies might seem surprising, but it is all too easy for humans to mistake or purposefully distort the importance of the obvious variables in their environment which can then lead them into such unthinkable behaviors. Once they had formed a cognitive model focused on the variables defining humans in religious terms, they could organize their perception of the world based on their erroneous interpretations of the environmental variables of their worldview.

There are other personality traits that can be used to describe groups of people such as, "They are dirty, they are a cheating bunch, they are sexually immoral, and don't turn your back on them or they will steal you blind." These are often common phrases used to describe a particular group. They might apply to certain isolated individuals in that group, but such sweeping generalizations are unlikely to apply to every member of that group or even to the group as a whole. Because they are labels applied to a group, they are not particularly useful in developing a robust understanding of any particular individual, and in that sense, they are unimportant variables. They can serve to provide a discrete and definite simplistic separation between clans or groups such that it is easy for an individual to dislike all members of the other clan. Thus, they have developed a stable cognitive model based not on the important characteristics of an individual but on less important and often erroneous characteristics that are not accurate in developing an understanding of any individual in the different clans. Generating such a stable, but unpleasant and immoral cognitive model is an important step toward personal behaviors that initiate and maintain the horrors of a genocide. The process of misconstruing important variables and placing importance on erroneous or unimportant variables is a cognitive process which can contribute to individual prejudices or terrible genocides.

A horrifying example of how distorted cognitive models can occur as a result of misplaced importance on the wrong variables was shown by the infamous Wannasse conference held in January 1942 and attended by the highest-ranking Nazi functionaries. This conference laid the groundwork for the "Final Solution" of the Jews in the Nazi geographic sphere of influence. They quickly decided that healthy adults would be worked to death building roads and railroad lines and the rest would be murdered immediately. After easily reaching a unanimous decision on this issue, they then spent a great deal of time on a seemingly minor question, that of the exact legal definition of a "Jew." The participants debated the question of what to do with "half Jews," discussing alternatives such as forced sterilization, deportation, or being sent to a special concentration camp, Theresianstadt, where they would be housed among high profile Jews. The cognitive model that the 15 high-ranking Nazi conference functionaries created, eight of whom held academic degrees, emphasized the importance of legal definitions and minor differences among groups of Jews rather than on the overriding issue of the horror of planning the murder of millions of innocent people (Rees, 2005). Obviously, intellectual and academic achievement is not a protection against creating distorted cognitive models.

Oftentimes sophisticated intellectual thinking can produce the same kinds of errors in misunderstanding the importance of cognitive variables. In 1941, Nazi economic planners tried to work out a theory of optimum population size for the areas they had or planned to conquer. A German economist, Helmut Meinhold, calculated that 5.83 million poles were surplus to the requirements of the Third Reich. These people constituted what he referred to as Ballastexistenzen or a waste of space which would result in a surplus to Nazi population planning. As a result, millions of Polish people, Jews and Gentiles, were exterminated based on a mathematical calculation that ignored obvious ethical variables. History provides many examples of how erroneous and immoral cognitive models are created by over focusing on calculations and bureaucratic minutia and minimizing the immoral variables of the murder and genocide of millions of innocent people. When through intellectual exercises we can reduce the human and emotional aspects of people to a series of numbers and mathematical calculations, we can easily fall into this kind of cognitive error.

Constructing Erroneous Identities

Another method of developing cognitive models which can lead to prejudicial thoughts and actions is by erroneously constructing underlying identities. For example, we can force our understanding of individuals into cultural, religious, and racial groups, thus losing the obvious diversity that separates us one from another as individuals. History is replete with such examples. Before and after the Civil War many white people in the South and especially slaveowners saw all African Americans as ignorant and unable to be educated. Of course, this view was contradicted by such people as Frederick Douglass, Charles Reason, Ida B. Wells, W. E. B. Du Bois, and a multitude of other African-American men and women. However, if we are able to ignore individual differences, we are then able to lump people together into a single group and affix a negative identity to the group. Of course, this erroneous belief was maintained by not providing or allowing African Americans access to education and refusing to recognize any intellectual capabilities. This method allows us to have a single variable that is easily formed and then incorporated into a belief. It provides the individual with cognitive simplicity by lumping a number of different human characteristics together as if they are identical. Describing a number of individuals exhibiting huge diversity with a single trait allows a prejudiced individual to deal with one cognitive variable rather than attempt to understand their individual differences.

This type of simplistic grouping is common human behavior, but it can be self-correcting by the reality of its obvious erroneous conclusion. In other words, our exterior social environment may self-correct those erroneous beliefs with some sort of social punishment such as rejection or isolation. White supremacy groups may be reinforced within their small social circle and by similar internet sites, but they can be corrected by the social conscience of larger national beliefs, and when taken to its extreme, by engaging in illegal behaviors, they risk incurring severe judicial punishments involving fines or incarceration. The belief that a limited number of subgroups of the Caucasian race are intellectually, behaviorally, and emotionally superior to all other races forms a coherent cognitive model for such individuals. However, that cognitive model can only exist in a limited social universe of other white supremacists who seek out and reinforce information congruent with this limited cognitive belief. Such individuals are able to maintain such culturally aberrant cognitive models by carefully screening and accepting internal aberrant information and rejecting all other informational variables. They are able to reject this universe of conflicting information by assuming it is all the same kind of false information and in that way, they reduce all conflicting information to an identity which they believe is false and of no consequence. Oftentimes, they can find labels that summarize diverse information which is labeled as "fake news," which then simplifies through negation a host of valid information variables.

Reduce Opposite Variables to an Identity

In our analysis of the way in which the Wright Brothers used this principle to simplify the many complex interacting flight variables they needed to understand, they realized that lift and drag were identical in that if you changed one you would change the other. They recognized this identity between these concepts in spite of the fact that on the surface, they seem to be quite different. Many social, cultural, and individual characteristics also have an identity type of relationship although these usually will not have the same precision as scientific relationships. White supremacists often try to use this cognitive principle, but in a distorted way so that it serves to bolster their erroneous conclusions. For example, there is a general, but far from perfect, correlation between education and income in that the higher the educational level, the higher an individual's income. This identity relationship can be distorted to assume that, as a group, Hispanic Americans and African Americans are uneducated and thus poor (they also assume that they then rip off the government by needing food stamps and welfare checks). In that way, they can assume that the imperfect link between educational level and income means that racial groups other than Caucasians are uneducated and poor. This forms a simplistic cognitive model that reduces a complex relationship between two important variables into one simple erroneous and prejudicial belief that Hispanic Americans and African Americans are ignorant in general. Thus, such groups develop simple beliefs based on imperfect or erroneous identities rather than understanding the complexities of a less-than-perfect correlation. Once this connection is established, such prejudiced individuals can apply this simple identity belief to all Hispanic Americans and African Americans instead of trying to understand the individual differences between members of such often hated groups. They have simplified education level, income, skin color, and perhaps knowledge of English into a single variable such as ignorance; they can then generalize that into a single negative attribute of inferiority.

Interestingly, this useful principle can be distorted so that there need not be any identity relationship between two or more variables. Individuals can assume that an identity exists and then use that to further some prejudicial and erroneous conclusion. This type of cognitive distortion was commonly used in Nazi state propaganda where Jews were blamed as being both lazy and industrious. They were seen as industrious because they built up successful businesses, but at the same time, they were seen as lazy because they never worked. Creating an identity out of these two opposites is logically difficult, but this was justified by saying they did not do any real work like farming but were simply shopkeepers (Rees, 2005). Of course, in many European nations, Jews could not become farmers because they were barred from owning land, and in other places where they were allowed to own land, they did engage in farming. However, ignoring the illogical contradiction allowed Nazi propagandists to simplify all Jews into one variable. Inferior! That cognitive simplification justified their elimination. Such cognitive distortions are not unusual human behaviors and are commonly used to create cognitive models that are horribly destructive and can motivate and justify genocides. Such cognitive models can exist even when there has been no actual experience with Jews. Lawrence Rees in his treatise, *Auschwitz, A New History,* tells the story of Michal Kabac, a Slovakian guard who sent Jews to their deaths. He reported that there were no Jews living in his village and he never had any problems with them. Nevertheless, he adopted violent anti-Semitism and had little difficulty sending Jews off to their deaths. Once this kind of cognitive model was created, it had an existence separate from real experience and created emotions such as hatred and revenge, which enabled this Slovakian guard to have little problems participating in the killing of his Jewish prisoners.

Making One Variable Salient and Ignoring Others

Another method which is used to solve scientific problems, but can be used to distort cognitive models is using irrelevant variables in attempting to solve social problems. As is often the case in complex cognitive situations, there are too many variables to understand and integrate a solution within a given period of time, and individuals must have a technique to reduce the complexity of multivariate interactive situations. Aside from the principles we have already discussed, there is another principal which is useful when attempting to resolve a problem composed of a large number of variables. That principle is to hold all the interacting variables constant and then identify one relevant variable and only manipulate that one variable to see how that affects the solution of a problem. However, the variable that is selected must be relevant to the solution, and this can be especially problematic in problems that have many complex interacting variables. Remembering how the Wright brothers used this principle in solving the scientific problem of flight is useful in understanding how this principle can be misused in social and cultural situations. In their attempts to understand the effects of the shape of different airfoils on lift, the Wright brothers focused on one variable, the angle of attack, and then they were able to test their airfoils without the confounding and interacting effects of other variables such as wind speed, wind direction, wing area, and wing weight. In that way, they were able to reduce a complex interactive matrix of variables to manageable proportions. The utility of this technique is that it reduces and simplifies many interacting variables into just two variables and a single interaction between them. That is a much more manageable cognitive situation than attempting to understand many variables and many interactions at the same time. If we are able to hold all the variables except the identified one constant, we are in essence freezing those variables and their interactions.

This technique, which is useful in solving scientific problems, can lead to distortions and errors in attempting to understand social situations. By their very nature, social situations are composed of many complex interacting variables, and trying to ignore and hold constant variables is much more difficult in social as compared to scientific situations. In addition, selecting the important variable to manipulate is likely to be influenced by one's personal and cultural biases. Using the principle of holding all variables constant while manipulating only one is like solving a mathematical equation by disregarding all but two variables (x and y); however, social variables and their interactions can be very difficult to hold constant because unlike scientific variables, they constantly change and cannot be frozen in time. Whenever we have a cognitive model of another individual, that cognitive model is constantly changing due to the diverse speech and behaviors of that person. We often end up defining that person by one social or cultural attribute rather than dealing with the multitude of changing behaviors, reactions, and emotions of that individual.

Seeing groups of people as a single identity without assessing their many differences is a very common cognitive process. People often attribute all sorts of cultural misperceptions to groups because we usually do not see or focus on the personal idiosyncrasies and abilities of individuals in a group. Trying to focus on the different and varied behaviors of the many individuals comprising a group is just too complex and difficult a task. For example, we have a much simpler task when we think of the Irish as a group. As a group, we can describe them as liking whiskey, poetry, and singing. That is a much simpler and less complex cognitive model than trying to understand the differences and idiosyncrasies of all individual Irish. In that sense, we can focus on one or two chosen variables about the Irish and hold all the myriad differences among the many people of Irish identity constant by ignoring them.

Applying this principle in scientific situations allows an investigator to manipulate one variable to better understand the influences and effects of that variable. However, in social situations, this cognitive reductive principle allows us to over focus on the one identified variable and ignore the many other variables that distinguish both individuals and groups; as a result, we then form erroneous and destructive attitudes toward any group that is different, and once that erroneous cognitive model is formed, we can then use it to justify our behavioral reactions to this group. There are many examples of this cognitive principle being used to create immoral and unethical cognitive models that justify and motivate genocidal acts of violence toward individuals throughout history and into our present times. Eliminating all the diverse and complex information that provides an accurate description of other human beings is an unfortunate, but all too common, human cognitive process. Oftentimes, labels are used in this cognitive simplification which eliminates the complex attributes and developmental history of every human being. Words such as Welfare Queen, Cheap Jew, Stupid Pollack, and Lazy Mexican, work by holding constant through elimination all the many relevant social attributes of an individual.

That particular individual is then erroneously and often immorally simplified into one negative social variable.

This phenomenon was used among German soldiers who were ordered to execute groups of men, women, and children during the Nazi Holocaust. As soldiers of the Third Reich, they accepted such social simplification and developed individual cognitive models based on the salient idea that Jews and Slavic peoples were an inferior race that ought to be eliminated. This was done by holding constant and eliminating all individual aspects of these peoples, so they could only deal with the hated and negative aspects of these groups. By seizing upon what they felt was the important salient variable describing Jews and Slavs, they only had to deal with the simple interaction between the negativity of these groups and their extermination. That provided them with a very simple cognitive relationship, but that did not always protect them from the consequences of their murder.

Such social simplification often does not work when faced with reality. Initially, special groups of German soldiers called Einsatzgruppen and members of the dreaded SS executed men, women, and children, by lining them up before a pit and individually shooting them. However, the strength of their simple immoral cognitive model was eroded by the fact that they had to see the individuals they were executing, and it became difficult not to see the individual differences inherent in the faces of their victims. This created a serious problem for the Nazi program of ethnic and cultural extermination. A German officer, Walter Frentz, who witnessed one of these executions, reported that he was shaken by the killings. Not only was he affected, but also he reported the following.

> I went along to the site of the execution, and afterwards the commander of the auxiliary police approached me…. "Lieutenant," he said. "I can't take it anymore. Can you get me out of here?" I said, "Well I don't have any influence over the police. I'm in the Air Force. What am I supposed to do?" "Well," he said, "I can't take it anymore. It's terrible."

An SS Obergruppenfuhrer (a lieutenant general) who witnessed the same execution complained to his superior, Reichsfuhrer Himmler, that the men carrying out the killings were deeply shaken. "These men are finished for the rest of their lives." Later that same Obergruppenfuhrer became psychologically ill and experienced visions of the killings he had watched.

These reports demonstrate that German soldiers were not able to hold the individuality of their victims constant and eliminate those differences, and as a result, many complained about being asked to individually shoot their victims. Their military superiors soon realized that asking these soldiers, who were easily hardened to kill their military enemies, to kill innocent civilians was a serious problem. As a result, this type of execution was stopped, and the more impersonal methods of gassing people in concentration camps were adopted as this eliminated the need for individual soldiers to be involved.

Once the system of mass killings using Zykon B was adopted, there was little need for individual soldiers to be involved in the shooting of other humans. Now the killings were carried out in an impersonal, almost industrial fashion. However, this still required some direct contact with the killings and the disposal of the multitude of dead bodies. For the most part, the German concentration camp staff, the SS, kept a level of separation from the multitudes that they were killing, and almost all the direct work was forced to be carried out by other prisoners, called "Sonderkommandos" and "Kapos." One SS officer, Oskar Groening, described his work at the Auschwitz concentration camp as routine. His job was to sort out the various currencies that had been taken from the prisoners, count the money, and send it off to Berlin. He describes his time at Auschwitz as follows.

> Auschwitz main camp was like a small town. It had its gossip; it had a vegetable shop where you could buy bones to make broth. There was a canteen, a cinema, and a theater with regular performances. There was a sports club of which I was a member. There were dances, all fun and entertainment. (Rees, 2005)

For the most part, Groening stayed in his office and was insulated from the brutality. When he walked about the camp, he could easily choose not to look at anything that was upsetting. Ironically, in an immoral contradiction of the work of the SS at concentration camps, stealing any money or possessions of the prisoners was considered to be a serious crime, whereas killing other humans was not.

A terrible, but all too common example of this cognitive principle shows that most of the dictators, politicians, and bureaucratic functionaries who initiate and carry out genocides usually separate themselves from contact with the individuals they are eliminating. In order to reduce a group of humans to a single cognitive entity, they need to distance themselves from those humans. If not, they run the risk of seeing that they are killing people like themselves; people who have emotions and feel pain. That allows them to maintain a simple salient view of their victims. However, no matter how distorted their motivations are by hatred, they are usually unable to directly deal with the many individual aspects of their horrible acts. The visual, auditory, and olfactory horrors are too direct an assault on their senses.

In that way, they develop a simplistic and salient cognitive model which holds constant (and likely eliminates) the individuality of humans and then only focuses on one culturally distorted cognitive belief such as Jews are animals, Slavs are sub-human beings, or the mentally deficient are useless consumers of food, and therefore all these groups can be eliminated (Rees, 2005). Perhaps, if they had to directly participate in the human horror of their "work," they would not be able to so easily live with their simplistic cognitive model, a flawed and falsely salient model that held the individual human aspects of innocent men, women, and children as something to be ignored.

Creating a Sequence of Immoral Variables

As with our discussion of other principles used in problem solving, this principle can also be distorted and misapplied to achieve an immoral solution to a social problem. As we saw with the Wright Brothers finding the solution of manned flight, they realized that the correct sequence of aircraft balance, lift, and propulsion power, in that order, was necessary to develop a viable aircraft. However, solving social problems is quite different, and in many situations, there need not be any particular sequence to reach a solution. I must point out that the solution of a scientific problem is usually advantageous to humankind; however, in social situations, the solution to a problem might be useful, but as in our present discussion, it may describe a reprehensible and immoral genocide. We humans are very creative in generating cognitive concepts to justify the genocide of another group, but four major reasons are paramount:

1. We need the land and resources of the other group.
2. The other group is a subhuman form of humanity.
3. The other group is our enemy and wants to destroy us.
4. Social Darwinism holds that we are superior and should control other groups.

Each of these concepts forms a cognitive model that allows for the killing of other human beings. These are simple cognitive models that are easily formed and easily understood, and taken separately or in combination, they have motivated the genocides of countless previous generations. Because they are simple cognitive models, they do not require the complicated principle of correct sequential development. However, the modern genocides of the twentieth century are quite different and do require a sophisticated cognitive approach.

Once again, the example of the Nazi genocide provides a useful illustration of how this cognitive principle of sequential problem solving can be utilized to understand the creation of genocide. Analyzing, such bestial behaviors is an emotionally difficult task, but a necessary one if we are to understand how the Nazis created such an efficient genocide. As we have previously discussed, there have been many human genocides, but none that reached the number of deaths or the efficiency of what was created by the Nazi Reich. The authors of the Nazi Holocaust used the four cognitive concepts we listed to justify their behaviors. The first was Lebensraum (living space), meaning that Germany needed to increase their living space to survive. That required the expulsion or destruction of the peoples of Eastern Europe to make way for German settlers. The second concept was to assume that Jews, Slavs, Gypsies, homosexuals, and enemies of the Third Reich were subhuman and therefore expendable. The third concept was that groups such as the Jews and communists were politically dangerous and would try to destroy the Third Reich. The fourth concept was a belief in Social Darwinism which dictated that Aryans were a master race that should control all others (Friedlander, 2007).

Each or any combination of these concepts can and often were used to kill other groups not just by the Nazi regime, but throughout many groups in our history. Each of these concepts, taken individually or together, is powerful enough to justify the murder of individuals, religious groups, or entire races. In addition, these concepts can be used in any sequence or order, and so this cognitive situation is different from solving complex scientific problems. The murder of others, different from ourselves, is sadly a common enough historical event, and as such, it does not require a sophisticated cognitive-scientific approach. However, the holocaust of World War Two was a very different situation; simply killing people was not the ultimate solution to this social problem. The real problem was how to kill people on such a massive scale and so efficiently, and that needed an industrial and engineering solution. Using science to carry out a genocide did require a particularly logical sequence of steps to achieve a solution, and if any of these steps were taken out of order, the Nazi "Final Solution" could not have occurred as it did.

The sequence of steps the leaders of the Third Reich used was as follows:

1. Identify the groups to be eliminated
2. Justify the need for killings
3. Maintain secrecy
4. Generate a killing process
5. Organize and industrialize the process

I will explain each of these steps in detail, how they occurred, and the emergence of the sequential relationship between them. At times, the steps and the sequence were carefully planned and in other instances seemed to be the result of accidental occurrences. Perhaps the first step, the identification of a particular population, was the easiest and most obvious. Pervasive European anti-Semitism and the dislike of the Roma (Gypsies) made these groups an obvious target. Certainly, the Nazi planners could have selected other groups, but in selecting, these they were building on a common historical aversion and a preexisting prejudice. Later, in the progression of the Nazi war efforts, they identified the Slavs of Poland, Czechoslovakia, and Russia as peoples who could be enslaved and perhaps eliminated. Here, they used existing cultural prejudices describing the Slavs as poorly educated slaves and thought they should best be seen as a leaderless laboring class. Of course, this was a grievous error and costly error since ironically, it was Polish intelligence experts who were the first to crack Germany's secret military Enigma code, which became instrumental in the defeat of Germany in World War II.

The second step, justifying the need to eliminate such groups, required an extensive propaganda campaign associating them with negative attributes. In one form or another, words such as lazy, thieving, filthy, greedy, sneaky, rodent-like, dangerous, illiterate, and many others could create a permanent cognitive association inducing the emotions of hatred, disgust, and loathing. This was a methodical and well thought out plan, mainly the work of Dr. Josef Goebbels, perhaps the most effective propagandist of the twentieth century (Rees, 2005). His approach was always to reinforce existing prejudices rather than trying to change people's minds, and his methods have been described as a "cumulative radicalization." Goebbels himself described his methods as being sure to always move at the speed of the slowest ship in the convoy. Certainly, the process of justifying persecution of the Jews proceeded slowly. The first step was the 1933 boycott of Jewish businesses and professionals, followed by the 1935 Nierenberg race laws. Overt government-sanctioned violence against the Jews did not begin until 1938 during Kristallnacht and the beginnings of the deportation of Jews into concentration camps (Steinhoff et al., 1994). Using such sophisticated propaganda, it was but a series of small steps to justify the elimination of the Jews, Gypsies, Slavs, and any others that they had identified.

There are many indications that secrecy about the Nazi genocide was essential for the "Final Solution." If secrecy was not maintained, there are strong indications that the process of genocide could not have begun, or once attempted, it would have been severely compromised as it would be seen as "uncivilized." Hitler even before his ascension as Chancellor of Germany publicly proclaimed in *Mein Kampf* his anti-Semitism, stating that 10,000 to 20,000 Jews should have been killed by using poison gas as they were destroyers of the nation. The constant anti-Semitic propaganda diatribes continued throughout the 1930s, but these, the Nuremberg laws, and even Kristallnacht were not as alarming to the greater world as an open announcement that Jews, Gypsies, mentally defectives, and Slavs were being systematically murdered.

There were three different aspects to the Nazi secret of open genocide. The first concerned the reaction of other Western nations as in the late 1930s, Germany responded to international pressures from the outside world and at one point they even released prisoners from the Auschwitz concentration camp when the Red Cross formally complained. Their concern for secrecy was so important that they forced the released prisoners to sign a form saying that they were satisfied with their stay in the camp and had no complaints. A rather ludicrous procedure! It strains credulity to imagine that one would not have complaints about life in a concentration camp. On another occasion, they were forced to release professors from the University of Kraków who had been sent to a variety of concentration camps including Dachau after receiving complaints from representations of the Pope.

A second purpose of the secrecy was to make the killings more efficient. The SS early on realized that if their victims knew they were going to be murdered, the victims were likely to revolt, attack the guards, or try to escape. As a result, they used many forms of deception to make the prisoners believe that they were being transported to a safe work location rather than a death camp and that they would be simply employed as industrial workers. In that way, the innocents could be marched directly from the arriving freight cars to the gas chambers. They were instructed to take off their clothes so they could be bathed in group showers, and the SS were even reported to be polite with their instructions. To maintain the deception, the gas chambers were even fitted with false showerheads to maintain the secrecy. Of course, the Nazis made sure that information about the purpose of the camps was a closely held secret, and not until the rare escape of a few prisoners did news of the mass killings emerge. This secrecy was aided by the fact that few outsiders could believe that a country as seemingly cultured as Germany could possibly participate in such a humanitarian abomination.

The third purpose of the secrecy was to maintain the cognitive model that the camp staff and the SS troopers held to justify their "work." No matter how fervent their beliefs in the mass murders they were perpetrating, this gross and pervasive violation of humanities rules had to emotionally affect many, if not most, of these individuals, and there is much historical data to indicate this fact. Attempting to hold onto a cognitive model that allows and justifies the murder of other humans while also maintaining a cognitive model of morality toward members of one's own group is a contradictory cognitive activity which can only be preserved by extreme forms of cognitive dissonance and distorted justifications. For example, in 1941, thousands of Jews were collected into the Lodz ghetto, where they faced a slow death from disease and starvation. The Nazi officer in charge of the ghetto stated that it would be more humane to kill them rather than let them suffer their slow deaths. This is an example of a "humane" attempt to justify the deaths of the thousands in the ghetto; of course, ignoring the fact that it was the Nazis that had created the ghetto and its starvation in the first place. There is one report concerning the deaths of thousands upon thousands of Soviet POWs who had been registered at Auschwitz in the camp death books. Their average survival time was two weeks. The Auschwitz staff attempted to explain these deaths by making up a variety of different diseases including reporting 600 of the prisoners as having died of heart attacks. This type of secrecy and deception long predated the establishment of the concentration camps. In December 1941, Hitler authorized the incarceration of any citizen deemed dangerous to the state security. Such individuals were not publicly executed, but simply vanished "into the night and fog," a euphemism for those who suddenly disappeared (Steinhoff et. al., 1994). The same sort of "disappearance" occurred with mentally and physically defective children who were supposedly sent to special institutions. In fact, they were murdered because Hitler stated that he did not want such children reproducing other defective individuals.

The fourth step in this sequence was to generate a killing process, and sadly the development of this process can be described in complexity science as a complex adaptive system. The "Final Solution" was not the immediate and well-formulated answer to the problem of getting rid of Jews and other undesirables, but rather the final step in an evolving series of attempts to solve the problem of the elimination of these unwanted people. The first step in this process was the idea of a large-scale emigration of Jews to the former African colonies of the French, especially Madagascar. The unrealistic idea of a large-scale emigration of millions of Jews to African colonies was taken seriously by Nazi leaders. Initially, this idea would have removed all Jews from Germany, but later it was expanded to include the millions of Jews in Poland, Czechoslovakia, Hungary, and other nations. As we have previously noted, Heidrich Himmler, a Nazi leader and architect of the plan, preferred this forced migration because he thought "physically exterminating a people" was fundamentally "un-German" (Rees, 2005). We will never know whether this unrealistic plan could have been initiated because Germany was unable to defeat Britain and the vastly superior British Navy would have intercepted the ships needed for this massive undertaking and prevented such a plan.

The next attempt at ridding Germany and its newly conquered nations of the "Jewish Problem" was to establish ghettos and house those people within their borders. There were many ghettos such as Warsaw, Vilnius, Lodz, and many others; interestingly, there were none in Germany. Rapidly, these ghettos became places where Jews, Gypsies, and Slavs were slowly starved to death or killed by disease. Of course, this was not a satisfactory solution for extermination because the deaths occurred slowly and unpredictably. The next step in this process was to take prisoners from ghettos, local villages, and surrounding areas, force them to dig a large ditch, and have soldiers execute them individually by shooting them. As we have already noted, this was undesirable because of the emotional affect that it had on the soldier executioners, and this method went at too slow a pace for the Nazi administrators in charge of this method of execution. In addition, the shootings of innocent people compromised secrecy, as the large ditches filled with bodies provided evidence of these mass murders.

The next steps seem to progress almost by accident. Dr. Albert Widmann, an SS Untersturmfuhrer, attempted to improve the extermination process by using explosives. He placed a number of mentally ill patients in a bunker with packets of explosives. This experiment was unsatisfactory as some of the victims were wounded but not killed and body parts were scattered about the area. Widmann then learned about an acquaintance, Artur Nebe, who had nearly died after returning drunk from a party and falling asleep in his auto while the engine was running. Widman decided to use this method on mentally ill Russian patients. He first hooked up the exhaust of a car to the locked room containing these patients; however, this did not work as planned. Next, he tried using the exhaust of a large truck, and the carbon monoxide killed all inside. Widmann had found an efficient method of extermination which was first used in Germany's conquered Eastern European countries; however, this method of mass murder was still too slow and complicated.

The final and efficiently industrialized method was developed at the Auschwitz concentration camp by the deputy commandant, Karl Fritzsch, who noticed a chemical, Zyklon B, used to remove insect infestations around the camp. He thought that if Zyklon B could be used to kill lice, perhaps it could be used to kill "human pests." Dropped into a sealed room filled with prisoners, the chemical caused almost instantaneous death. It was but a short step to placing Zyklon B into sealed death chambers filled with innocent people and designed to look like benign shower rooms. Now the dead bodies could be taken by Sonderkommandos to nearby crematoriums where they could be made to disappear. This, "Final Solution," avoided the problem of concentration camp staff having direct contact with their victims and seem to provide some secrecy to their genocide. Finally, they had found a rapid and efficiently industrious method to murder millions of innocent people.

There was a significant cognitive difference for the people carrying out this genocide. In most situation, the person doing the killing has a cognitive model of the person they are killing, no matter how immoral and distorted. This process did not require a personal cognitive model of those carrying out the genocide because they were removed from the murders, and the only cognitive model required was ordinary clerical duties similar to maintaining an elementary assembly line. Of course, the planners such as Hitler, Himmler, Goering, etc. had a cognitive model that was devoid of personal contact (except in rare instances of experimentation) and their cognitive model had to do with a remote group process, not with the actual individual experience, and that is a much less difficult and complex intellectual process than dealing with the far greater diversity and complexity of a dying individual.

In order to understand how individual humans can inflict a genocide on the other individual humans, we need to understand the role of industrialization and mathematics. By seeing individual people as a single group, we simplify vast numbers of individual complexities into a simple equation. Once we allow X to represent the genocidal group, we can treat that X as if it is a mathematical variable, and if we include process Y, we have a simple equation of $X - Y = 0$ with 0 being the number of X individuals remaining alive after their elimination. Even if we add values to the X variable such as 100,000X indicating the 100,000 individuals, the equation still simplifies and eliminates a cognitive matrix of human beings, their appearance, their characteristics, their feelings, and their histories. Now the process of genocide is nothing more than solving an equation and an accounting ledger. The equation and the ledger are now devoid of humanity.

In many ways the Nazi concentration camps functioned as a complex adaptive system in that they constantly adapted to the changing requirements of their genocide. As the system needed faster killing methods due to increased victims, they stopped using bullets and adapted using Zyklon B. As the allies began approaching camps in Poland and Czechoslovakia, they were able to further speed the killing process. Eventually, when the allies approached certain camps, they marched their victims to killing camps further away. Whether through psychological isolation of the camp personnel, changing killing methods, or many other changed efficiencies, the Nazis were able to adapt so that the death camps functioned until the very arrival of the Allied armies.

American slavery used all of these misapplied principles to create the cognitive models that justified this abhorrent social institution. There are similarities between slavery and the prisoners of a concentration camp in that all were used as instruments of work. However, the inmates of a concentration camp eventually were killed, and/or they were worked to death. American slavery was an economic enterprise, and a slave was too valuable to be killed. In addition, American slavery maintained a kind of individuality as opposed to industrialization. To a greater or lesser extent, slave owners had individual contacts with African-American slaves, whereas the Nazi authors of their genocide and their staff tried to avoid such individual contact. States such as Georgia and Louisiana had laws protecting aged slaves and saying masters had to maintain them (but not always followed). This was an industrial endeavor different than the Nazi system. In the early years of the American Colonies, we imported indentured servants, but even that system had laws to protect these servants who were mainly children taken from their families in England. Their bondage ended after a fixed period of time after which the individual who imported a servant had to provide their indentured individual with a monetary grant to begin their new life as a free person. That system of time-limited bondage was not maintained for African slaves as they were too valuable an economic resource. Humans have had a long history of poor treatment of each other but not systematic and industrial genocide. In the Nazi system, the I.G. Farben company bought the work of prisoners they never knew or cared to know. When people become an economic commodity, they can be treated like an economic commodity and are expendable when loss exceeds profit.

Chapter 15
The Complexity of Kindness and Selfishness

Abstract Organized in three sections, this chapter demonstrates the developmental origins of kindness and selfishness and how these develop into constantly changing cognitive models. Kindness is a pervasive behavior that develops very early in childhood and is an elementary $k = 2$ cognitive model. Basically, it is a complex adaptive system of reciprocal interactions between parent and child that utilizes social reinforcement and modeling. Selfishness, which emerges later in childhood, is a complex cognitive model where $k > 2$. It is motivated by the initial perception that children will lose their caregivers and eventually generalizes into a loss of needed resources. Selfishness requires an understanding of the future and is maintained by a sense of generalized anxiety. The third section of this chapter discusses the role of social belonging and clans as a way of ensuring the giving and receiving of kindness. It also illustrates the creation of various types of social groups and claims as a natural form of self-organization. Like other forms of self-organization in complexity science, rules naturally emerge to guide the behavior of individuals. Such rules determine whether such behaviors will emerge in the form of kindness or selfishness.

Keywords Kindness · Selfishness · Loss of resources · Lord of the flies · Developmental selfishness · Developmental kindness

Kindness

If you found the preceding chapter to be upsetting, you are correct. One cannot easily discuss the worst aberrations of human behavior without some feeling of revulsion and disgust. However, such unpleasant feelings show us that the murder and violence of a genocide or holocaust are not the normal state of human thinking or behavior. In fact, quite the opposite is true; the normal state of human behavior is one of kindness and concern for others, and in this chapter, we will attempt to answer the question of which we are: are we a kind and thoughtful species or a

R. Leve, *The Complexity of Human Thought*,
https://doi.org/10.1007/978-3-031-09104-9_15

species that can engage in the genocidal murder of our fellow humans. The obvious answer is that we are both, and the problem lies in our need for simplicity in the types of cognitive models that we construct about our social universe. For the most part, I believe it is obvious that the vast majority of human thinking and emotions reflect cognitive models of kindness and concern for others, and though murder and violence are an infrequent aberration, we have the potential to construct cognitive models that justify our most abhorrent behaviors.

In writing this chapter and the preceding one, I was in a quandary as to the order in which they should be presented. I ultimately decided that the chapter explaining genocide should come first as that details a relatively minor aspect of human behavior, whereas this chapter on kindness explains our most common behaviors. I also felt that from an emotional viewpoint, I would rather end such a discussion on a positive note.

There is so much evidence that humans are kind species, I hardly know where to begin. So much of human behavior revolves around the many deep and casual friendships that we create, and without such friendships, our emotional world would seem quite empty. Of course, we seek out long-term relationships with spouses and significant others, and some of the most painful episodes in one's life occur as a result of the death or loss of that person. The same holds true for our children upon whom we lavish our most tender feelings of concern. But aside from these relationships, we often have a natural attitude of kindness toward strangers. Most of us have a desire to help someone we do not know if we see they are hurt or in danger, and we have entire professions such as physicians, nurses, psychologists, social workers, and a host of others that are devoted to the health and healing of people who at least initially were unknown strangers. If we had no concern for others in need, we would not have created our many charities to help them or in the age of the Internet, Go Fund Me sites. And we reserve our highest honors in the form of the military Medal of Honor or the Victoria Cross for soldiers who often sacrifice their lives for their comrades or even military strangers (it is telling that such honors are reserved for sacrifices made for the preservation of other humans and not for the preservation of valuable military property or wealth). Human kindness and concern for others is so ordinary in human social behavior that most of the time we do not recognize it. Such behaviors fill the entire spectrum of human interactions ranging from a casual friendly wave to acknowledge another individual, to holding the door for a stranger, to the formal rules of polite conversation expected at a state dinner.

How human kindness emerged and become such a pervasive mode of behavior is a useful question to consider. Many theorists have proposed genetic and biological factors to explain kindness (Ballat & Campling, 2011; Titmuss R, 1977; Kogan et al., 2017), and these are accurate explanations within those dimensions. However, there is an obvious explanation inherent in the psychosocial development of humans as children. Infants and young children do not survive unless they are cared for by parents or other adults. Thankfully, most children are born into loving and caring families who provide these young children with not only food and sustenance but also physical and emotional warmth and pleasant tactile contact. The definition of family may vary from a single parent to different forms of surrogate parents;

nevertheless, there must be a loving, concerned, and kind adult(s) at the center of every child's life, or they will not survive. I doubt that I need to list all of the different kinds of parenting behaviors that children experience because they are obvious to any observant individual. If we can just picture the life of a week-old infant, we can imagine the constant pleasant and often unpleasant tasks that parents provide ranging from feeding to changing diapers, to simply watching and reacting to the simple behaviors of a baby. Being a parent is such an ordinary and usually sought-after situation that we seldom realize that it is the ultimate form of kindness and responsibility. In other words, the basic environment of infants and young children is one of care and kindness.

As a result of the immersion in such an environment, a child cannot avoid learning the complex and intricate social thoughts, emotions, and behaviors of human kindness, and they do that by simply modeling the behaviors of their caregivers. Most of what children and infants learn is through imitation and who are they more likely to imitate, but the most important and continuously present adults surrounding them: their parents and other significant caregivers. In addition, when they model these behaviors, their efforts are likely to be reinforced and rewarded by those around them with responsive attention. Of course, the behaviors they learn from their caregivers are not going to be sophisticated and complex acts of kindness, but rather simple behaviors of recognition and response to parental attention. In infants, this may be making eye contact with the caregiver or moving their body in response to parental touching. While this may not resemble cognitive acts of kindness, it is the simple physical and sensory recognition of another individual, and certainly the most elementary form of kindness is recognition of another person's existence. If we view this in terms of complexity science, parental caregivers set up an initial condition that will generate behaviors even in the behavioral simplicity of a newborn infant, and that situation creates a simple yet complex adaptive system in which the infant and the parental caregiver are constantly adapting their behaviors to one another. This adaptive system may involve a host of complex little behaviors but is so pervasive in the life of an infant that it can scarcely be avoided.

The development of such a complicated and complex social behavior as kindness might seem impossible given the initial simplicity of infant behaviors. Infants emerge into an undifferentiated and terribly confusing environment of sounds, sights, touches, smells, and other stimuli. They have no conception of time, no past or future, so they live in a form of extended present. In this simple world, nothing is permanent. The parent that cares for this infant will seem as if he or she is a new object each time that person appears. Eventually and after a period of approximately 8 to 12 months (Piaget, 1969), the infant will develop object permanence and slowly come to realize that the mother who feeds the child from a bottle or breast is the same person each time. Once this parent and other people in the infant's life become permanent, they can and do become associated with pleasurable feelings. Our infant's behaviors and ability to respond are still very elementary, but slowly they develop an ability to influence this environment of caring people.

As an example, imagine an infant scanning its environment, and at some point, the infant randomly makes eye contact with the parent. Attentive parents are likely to make a loving sound, touch the infant, or in some idiosyncratic way to respond. Now the infant is likely to respond to the parent perhaps by maintaining longer eye contact or shaking some part of their body or making an infantile sound. This may generate further responses from the parent which will continue this interaction with the infant. There are likely thousands of these brief scenarios occurring throughout infancy through which the infant learns that the recognition of another individual, by some simple behavior, is reinforcing because it elicits pleasurable responses from the caregiver and creates a changing and more interesting environment for the child. In the case of infants, they learn that simple reciprocal recognition is important and that recognition of other people is a basic step in developing kindness. In fact, nonrecognition of other humans as different from objects is a serious cognitive and emotional deficit. It is a type of severe autism and indicates a serious inability to engage in normal human relationships and often impairs the understanding of kindness. In each of these many developmental episodes, the infant and their caregiver are engaged in a reciprocal complex adaptive system, and this social system is complex as it is always changing in accordance with the developmental stage of the infant and is adaptive because both parent and child are adapting their behaviors to the other. Infants and preverbal children will respond to the many caring parental behaviors by responding through movements or preverbal sounds, and this is reinforcing to parents. Once again, this adaptive system is composed of many kinds of caregiving behaviors and child responses and will continuously repeat itself. As our infants get older, we will see that in addition to recognizing their caregivers, more cognitively sophisticated forms of actual kindness will emerge. As children develop simple verbal skills, they may say, "I love you mommy," or some other pleasant words. Children who are raised in such a caring environment can hardly avoid developing the cognitive concepts and behaviors of kindness and concern for others, and through this process of modeling and reinforcement, they realize that the expression of altruism, in its many forms, is a pleasant feeling.

Of course, there are situations where infants are not born into and are not raised in caring environments, and as might be expected, such children do not develop the cognitive and behavioral attributes of kindness. There are many examples in the child development literature of such situations, and such children do not develop feelings of emotional closeness or even recognition toward other individuals (Dennis, 1960; Werner, 1972). Of course, such psychologically damaged children will have an impaired ability to show kindness. Thankfully, most children are not raised in such an impaired environment, and so our social world is characterized overall by pervasive kindness.

In terms of complexity theory, the cognitive model that determines kindly behaviors toward others is rather simple because it is composed of only two variables, the giver of the kindness and its recipient. Thus, kindness tends to describe a $k = 1$ matrix. Perhaps its inherent simplicity is one reason why kindness is such a common human behavior. There may be some exterior stimulus that triggers the behavior such as the sight of someone with a disability or someone asking for aid, but most kindness behaviors are generated by a kind, giving individual. Also, most kind behaviors and thoughts are emotional in nature, which means they tend to be binary in that either they are absent or they emerge full-blown. For example, holding a door for a stranger, offering a helping hand to someone who has fallen, or even administering first aid to an injured individual is an act given in its entirety. The helping individual is hardly likely to half open the door or only administer a little first aid. Because of their emotional nature, kind thoughts and behaviors tend to be self-reinforcing because the individual offering the kind thoughts, words, and behaviors usually feels a sense of pleasure from their actions. Feeling a sense of pleasure from giving something to another individual may seem contradictory, but the self-reinforcing action has deep roots in our early developmental years through receiving and modeling the caretaking of our parents. As we shall see in the next section, the cognitive models underlying selfish behaviors are much more complex.

I'm sure some people would disagree with the notion that kindness describes the great majority of human behavior and thinking, and certainly they can point to the many instances of every day news reports of all types of malicious and malevolent behaviors. Local newspapers and cable TV will provide a daily list of murders. Nevertheless, we are more likely to hear about these behaviors because they are rare and salient, whereas the everyday simple kind behaviors are not noted or reported because they are too common. Holding an open door for someone, offering a hand to someone who's fallen, giving money to a homeless person or a charity, or offering soothing words to an upset child is not likely to be reported on the evening news because they have little salience.

William Golding's novel, "The Lord of the Flies" is a classic work which won him the Nobel Prize, but it is only a work of fiction and a terribly depressing work of fiction. We might wonder how such a depressing work of fiction achieved such literary prominence. Likely, it is because it describes a very unusual situation and one that casts doubt on the goodness of humanity. Its theme says that if children are left without the trappings of civilization, we would become murderous barbarians as did the boys in his novel. Golding describes a marooned group of boys who slowly deteriorate into barbaric behaviors and even toward cannibalism. Amazingly, an actual event similar to Golding's story has been unearthed and identified by historians and journalists, and as will be discussed in the next chapter, we will see that marooned children do not become barbarians, but rather they create a kind and caring society.

Selfishness

Now that we have seen that the development of kindness and concern toward others is a very simple, natural, and inherent group of behaviors resulting from infant and child social development, we need to answer the other question: why are humans inherently selfish, and why does this selfishness sometimes result in violence, murder, and even genocide? In discussing selfish behaviors, we need to include behaviors such as greed, possessiveness, and envy. An attitude of selfishness means that we do not want to share or give up our own possessions and we may feel that we need or want the possessions of others. We have already recognized the fact that both kindness and selfishness are an integral part of human thinking, feeling, and behaving, and in spite of the individual differences among us, they exist in us all and will emerge in different ways in accordance with different environmental situations. In order to understand why humans are inherently selfish, we need to understand how thoughts, emotions, and behaviors of selfishness emerge as a natural part of our human development and how those behaviors, like kind behaviors, will come to form a complex adaptive system which will generate many different selfish cognitive models.

If we investigate the cognitive models of infants and very young children, the term selfishness does not accurately describe their motivations and thoughts. True selfishness arises gradually throughout childhood and of course varies with each individual. Just as infants and young children learn caretaking skills from their parents, they also develop a realization of their inherent vulnerability. As they gradually differentiate their parents as the caregiving objects of their environment they also slowly, but increasingly, realize that without these caregiving individuals they cannot survive and that naturally generates a form of simple infantile anxiety and a possessiveness toward their caregivers.

We have mentioned that infants live in a kind of extended present in their understanding of time; however, as they mature (Piaget, 1969) and their understanding of time develops, they begin to realize that there is a future and they begin to anticipate what might happen to them in this unknown future. When infants live in their extended present and they are unhappy because they are hungry, or their diapers are soiled, or they feel a minor pain, they react by immediately expressing their displeasure through some form of crying. However, when they can anticipate the future, they now can imagine unpleasant events that may occur and become anxious about such future problems. The most common scenario for this anxiety is separation from their parents or other caregivers. Depending upon the child's personality and circumstances, they become afraid that even a brief separation means that their parents are gone forever, and that is terrifying. In fact, many children's fairytales such as Hansel and Gretel, Snow White, and the Little Match Girl are illustrative of the sadness and danger of children separated from their parents. Being an orphan is a frequent theme in children's literature because it is so terrifying to a child.

One of the most traumatic events of childhood is being lost, and the emotional power of that experience is illustrated by the pitiful sobbing of children who cannot find their parents. The experience of being lost is one of catastrophic fear because they come to believe that this temporary parental separation will become permanent. Thus, even though these lost children do not usually develop direct scenarios of a dismal and frightening future, they can and do anticipate a generalized future of abandonment.

I experienced such scenarios with children in the years I was a lifeguard on the New Jersey ocean beaches. Commonly, some children would become separated from their parents on a crowded beach, and a caring stranger would find the crying child and bring the child to the lifeguards. Some children were sobbing and terrified, while others stoically held in their fear. Taking the child by the hand, we would walk them through the beach area in an effort to find their parents. The emotional relief on being reunited with their parent(s) was so intense that every child, stoic or not, burst into tears at seeing that parent. Depending upon their age, they tried to cognitively understand what had happened to them. Some of the younger children would say, "Where did you go?" whereas older children would say, "I couldn't find our blanket." This was their attempt to try to understand what happened to them, but their main emotional reaction was one of profound relief at being united with their parents. I mention these incidents to illustrate how terrifying it is to children and how that fear ultimately leads all of us into a form of selfish possessiveness. If you are terribly afraid of losing someone, the obvious solution is to hold onto that person as tightly as you can.

This situation becomes more complicated as children grow older. Infants and very young children live in a restricted environment centered around their parental caregivers, but as they mature, their environment slowly but surely expands to include many other people and objects. Just as they are selfishly possessive of their parents and fearful of losing that security, they now become selfishly attached to other people and even familiar objects in this new expanded and enriched environment. Of course, children will not become attached to every new person or object in the environment, and trying to predict what particular people and objects children become attached to is very difficult to predict as it is an idiosyncratic choice related to the life of each child. However, the general principle underlying such attachments is that in some form or another, they will feel the loss of these special people and objects as some manifestation of the early infantile anxiety around parental loss. Perhaps it is an overgeneralization to say that all selfishness and possessiveness come from a basic fear that we will lose the early parental resources we need to survive, but this situation generates many of the early anxieties of childhood, and many of our adult anxieties and selfish and possessive thoughts have their genesis in our long forgotten childhood.

There is an inherent relationship between these early childhood worries and selfishness and possessiveness. If one is worried about losing parental care or a valued personal possession, then one is likely to be possessive about such things. This is not likely to be a perfect relationship, but in general, the more one worries about losing something, the more one is likely to be selfish and possessive about that person, object, or relationship. Some authors have postulated that we humans have a selfish gene (Dawkins, 1976), but this is not a convincing concept since no particular gene or combination of genes has ever been identified, nor is there an explanation as to how this gene exerts its selfish motivation on the rest of our biological system. However, we need not look for genetic explanations when a more obvious explanation is a natural childish reaction to the anticipation of dramatic loss within their environment. Of course, most people are unlikely to recognize or accept that their selfish behaviors relate to their early childhood experiences; nevertheless, many people feel intense emotions and often powerful anger toward even the most benign situations associated with loss. We face many situations in our environment that are certainly not life-threatening, yet we react as if they do involve the profound loss of life-sustaining resources similar to the reactions of infants and young children fearful of the loss of their parents. Much of the time, our imaginations project into the future the perception that a situation involving the possibility of loss seems catastrophic, and that can generate very powerful and unpleasant emotions.

In order to understand the selfishness and possessiveness of adults, we need to analyze the developmental progression of these behaviors. Just as children are possessive of their parents in infancy and early childhood, as they mature and become adults, they become possessive of the resources needed for their perceived survival. I doubt that children have a cognitive model sophisticated enough to realize that their parents and the resources provided by their parents ensure their survival, but this must occur on some emotional level or they wouldn't become so terrified of a future without their parents. As cognitive and emotional maturation continue through childhood, we become less attached to our parents directly, and we assume more and more of our own care. That means that we must assume control of the resources we need to survive and thrive, and any threat to these resources is likely to generate aggressive and selfish reactions. Usually, these reactions are not necessarily directly related to survival, but generalize to the many possessions in the child's environment. I refer to this concept as a form of anticipatory survival because the child will react to the loss of a possession that is not related to actual survival as if it is. Most children really don't have to worry about the food and shelter required to survive; however, because they can anticipate the future, they often overestimate the actual aspects of their environment that they will need to survive. In that sense, we become very sensitive to loss and often react as if the loss of a possession is life-threatening and generates a deep sense of anxiety and sadness.

The concept of selfishness has a negative connotation in most cultures and societies; however, if an individual existed in a nonsocial environment or a social environment that had no social interactions between its members, then selfishness is a useful attribute as it helps an individual gain needed resources and ensure survival. However, in an interactive social environment, selfishness has important limitations because impinging on the resources of others or trying to acquire too many resources is likely to bring social resistance, rejection, and anger. Therefore, this potentially useful attribute of selfishness may in fact lead to acquiring fewer resources because of the resistance of other group members, and children need to learn such limitations and balance selfishness against the attitudes and needs of others. As children develop a selfishly oriented cognitive model concerning their environment, that cognitive model will become increasingly complex because it needs to reflect the interactions between others in that environment at that time. Generally learning such a complex interactive cognitive model takes time for children, and an emotional descent into a temper tantrum when children do not get what they want illustrates the difficulty in understanding and mastering such a complex cognitive model.

Another aspect of anticipatory survival is the worry a child may feel anticipating the loss of needed personal resources when, in fact, this has not occurred. Because children are now able to understand there is a future, they can imagine many different futures, and now they are able to imagine a future loss of resources. This can be generated by some incident in their environment or even by hearing a chance comment that can be either true or misinterpreted, but this may initiate the child to generate an unpleasant future of loss. Trying to predict what environmental stimulus might provoke a child to imagine some dismal future situation will not be obvious and will depend upon the particular sensitivities and personalities of each child. In terms of complexity science, this is similar to an emergent phenomenon where a relatively minor stimulus or incident can produce a cognitive model of a frightening future. Obviously, any such a future projection will cause the child to become anxious, and most children at one time or another will experience such worrisome future situations. Like most emergent phenomena, they are very difficult to predict ahead of time and sometimes are difficult to densify even after the emergence of an emotionally distressing cognitive model.

The term "loss of resources" is a very general concept, and though it does not describe the idiosyncratic desires and fears of any individual child, it is the basis for the emergence of selfishness. In actuality, each child will define that term according to their own perception of the things and people that they need to survive and, hence, are afraid to lose. Anticipating a future loss of resources will be different according to the past developmental history of each child and the past deprivations and losses they have experienced. Often this behavior will be difficult to predict ahead of time but will be easily identified by the child's emotional reactions and behaviors when it occurs. Usually, children are not sophisticated enough or have enough control over their lives to engage in future planning concerning available food or protection from realistic dangers in their environment, such as illnesses or lack of a safe place to live. These resources have been planned for and provided by their parents or other caretakers and are of no concern in a healthy childhood environment. Perhaps, the most frightening loss that can occur in a child's life is the loss of a parent as that means not only the loss of their caring but also the loss of the love and affection of that parent. Of course, children commonly develop anticipatory anxieties concerning the loss or death of a parent even if there is no realistic or imminent parental death. A large number of children's stories and even films focus on this theme of losing one's parents or being taken away by strangers. As mentioned earlier, being an orphan is a terrifying situation for a child.

In addition to fearing the loss and death of their parents, children begin the natural developmental process of fearing their own death. Very young children, around age one through two, do not have an understanding of death, but they still may associate death with a terrible kind of sadness. Preschool children become very interested in death although they believe that it is something that is reversible and like a broken object can be fixed. By the early school years, a child's conception of death is similar to that of adults in that they understand it is not reversible, and is a frightening and sad occurrence. Whatever their age or cognitive understanding, children sense that death is a terrible loss, whether it is their own death or the death of a parent. Both mean the absence of needed love and caring. The natural reaction is to want to hold on to their own life or the life of their parents.

The loss of parental resources easily generalizes to an overall sense of loss, and the reaction to that is to attempt to hold onto their resources in whatever form and acquire new ones. A common example of this is the transitional objects that children hold onto such as cuddly blankets or soft stuffed animals. Whatever other meaning and symbolism such objects have to children (and sometimes to adults), they symbolize something about parental love and caring and the loss of these objects can be very difficult emotionally. These feelings are easily transferred to any other person or object that a child develops an attachment to, and both children and adults will respond to any loss with a possessive selfishness. Thus, we all learn to be selfish as one part of a natural developmental process.

As children emerge from infancy and continue to mature into later childhood, they face an increasingly complex environment across many social dimensions. Learning social behaviors while also mastering the complex vocabularies and grammars of language is a very difficult task since language and social behaviors are intertwined. Imagine the myriad instances and events that a child faces every day. There is no way that any child or even an adult could deal with such a complex and interacting environment without learning how to organize all of those individual events into some sort of cohesive intellectual grouping. As was discussed earlier, children need to form cognitive models that represent the individual aspects of this seemingly infinite environment in order not to be cognitively overwhelmed, and that is the beginning of the cognitive simplification process that will continue throughout the rest of their lives. Of course, that is a difficult task since so many aspects and variables in the environment have interconnections with each other. The major task of childhood maturation is to simplify their environment, especially the social aspects of the environment, so it becomes understandable, and children learn to do this by developing idiosyncratic cognitive models. Perhaps we can get some glimpse into the difficulty of this problem by realizing that as children mature in age, the environment which was simple in infancy is constantly becoming more diverse. Of course, learning the social and personal aspects of their environment is a very daunting task because the people they relate to are not only different one from another but also the same person may seem different from one time to another.

Kindness, Selfishness, and Clans

The major way in which children slowly come to simplify their social environment is to develop cognitive models that emphasize or even create similarities between people and social events. In other words, children tend to form a dichotomy among the many individuals in their lives such that some individuals become part of their group or clan and others become strangers. In reality each person in their life is an individual with individual characteristics, however attempting to cognitively remember and react to such an overwhelming number of individual differences among individual people is impossible and so children begin a task that continues into adulthood; that of organizing people into groups. Most of this social organization is done without awareness and is a natural developmental process.

The formation of social groups is a self-organizing phenomenon that is inherent in all higher life-forms and may be a property characteristic of almost all, but the most simple organisms. This may take many different forms depending upon the individual species and the environment, but every individual's behavior will self-organize into some variation of social interaction. This important concept of complexity science allows individuals to organize and recognize the organization of their social environment; if this self-organization did not naturally occur, we humans would need to spend great amounts of time and energy on organizing both important and banal aspects of the world we live in. Just as birds organize their migration formations and ants organize their body constructed bridges, so too do we humans use this process to simplify the complexity of our social environment.

There are many advantages to self-organized social behaviors such as increased access to reproduction, increasing acquisition of resources, emotional security and satisfaction, individual survival, and many others; however, whatever the advantages or disadvantages, self-organization into social groups in some form or another will occur, and this is a process that will continue throughout the rest of that individual's life. As I have previously mentioned, the process of simplifying an environment composed of different individuals with many different idiosyncratic characteristics means that in this effort to develop simpler cognitive models, we give up and ignore a great deal of detailed and often useful information. However, that is the price we pay to simplify our social environment and avoid becoming cognitively overloaded with social information. Unfortunately, in terms of individual and cultural human interactions, this simplification and the formation of cognitive groups can exacerbate human selfishness and result in terrible human behaviors including racism and genocide.

How do we humans form into groups? In trying to understand how social groups or clans form, I am somewhat baffled by the simplicity and obviousness of the question. We humans form and need to be part of one or more social groups, and this is a behavior that starts in infancy and continues throughout most people's lives. I suppose there are unusual individuals such as hermits who do not participate in social groups, but these are rare individuals. A number of social isolation studies such as those of long-distance solo sailors show that after a period of time, many of these individuals begin to hallucinate that there are other people on the boat with them. The lack of social stimulation seems to cause these individuals to hallucinate a fantasy social network because they need the interactions of others (Goldberger, 1966).

We have already discussed that joining groups is a self-organizing phenomenon that is natural in all life-forms and can be seen in the flocking behavior of migrating geese and the schooling of fish. Of course, the behavior of fish and geese can only serve as metaphors for the complexity of human social groupings. In the case of humans, self-organization means that people will spontaneously form groups without any authoritarian influence. In other words, this is a bottoms-up phenomenon. In addition to forming into groups, basic rules governing the behavior of each individual will spontaneously emerge. The most basic rules that emerge for any group are that members must feel an affinity for the group, they must agree with the group's purpose, whether social or other, and they must feel some degree of emotional or intellectual closeness to other members. Of course, there are a myriad of different groups in human society and each of these groups will create specific rules beyond the basic rules that arise as a result of self-organization. Such individual and detailed rules can range from Robert's Rules of Order, which governs the structure and behavior of organizational meetings, to the tattoos required by members of the Nazi SS. These group-based idiosyncratic rules will reflect the identity and purpose of the group, but the essence of group formation comes from the self-organization of long-standing child developmental needs to belong.

Just as we self-organize into similar groups to simplify our complex interactive social environment, humans have a tendency to simplify foreign groups (any group we are not part of). They will view such groups as either neutral if they are irrelevant to the values of our group or negative if they seem in some way to be opposing to our group.As discussed earlier, in the process of this cognitive simplification, we eliminate the individual differences among members of those opposing groups. In that way, we can form a simple binary cognitive model of that group which protects us from being overwhelmed by the diversity and complexity of the individuals in that group. However, there is a serious consequence of this simplification of groups, both positive and negative, and that is that we will generally behave in a kind way toward members of our own group, and we are likely to behave in a selfish way toward members of an opposing group. In other words, we tend to see all groups as binary, either positive or negative. Throughout childhood development, humans become aware of and sensitive to the loss of resources, and now we are likely to see members of an opposing group as competitors for these resources, and this is likely to generate selfish thoughts and behaviors. Thus, we can understand that the same process of cognitive simplification is likely to produce a global kindness toward members of our own group and a global selfishness toward other groups. As an example, members of one political party are likely to have a positive attitude toward members of their party even though they know nothing of the individual characteristics of such individuals and may never have had personal contact with them. Nevertheless, in many behavioral circumstances, they are likely to be seen in a very positive light and thought of with kindness. Members of the opposite political party are likely to be seen as people who not only differ in political beliefs but ultimately are competitors for resources as a result of those beliefs, and although they likely don't know and have never met such individuals, they will apply the same negative attitudes toward such individuals as they hold toward the entire group. Thus, they will see such individuals as competitors and will behave in a selfish fashion toward them even when they know nothing about that particular individual.

Chapter 16
The Interconnection of Kindness and Selfishness

Abstract Kindness and selfishness are reciprocally related opposite attitudes; however, that relationship is quite complex and unstable since it is easily changed by many environmental variables. Kindness is the default attitude of humans, but it can rapidly change to selfishness when resource allocation is believed to be scarce or unequally distributed. Because selfishness, unlike kindness, also includes objects, the cognitive models of selfishness do not have an upper limit in terms of the number of variables coveted or the complexity of the interactions between them. In addition, kindness tends to occur in the present, whereas selfishness is easily projected into future situations of resource inadequacy. As a result, anxiety about the need for resources is easily and often overestimated, leading to cognitive models of possession. The historical introduction of money is discussed as a factor that tends to increase selfishness by making human relationships more impersonal compared to a human barter system where the bartering individuals were likely local and knew one another. Concern and kindness would have been common in such a system. Money also introduced a precision allowing for the comparison of objects (and sometimes people), which has created a vast array of rules which further contribute to impersonal relationships. The many economic systems generated by the introduction of money cause individuals to create and attempt to understand cognitive models of great complexity devoid of personal kindness.

Keywords Simple kindness matrix · Complex selfishness matrix · Loss aversion · Barter economy · Money · Future resource inadequacy

Kindness and selfishness may seem opposite aspects of human behavior, but in reality they are closely connected because each is a normal cognitive reaction to appropriate, if different and changing, aspects of every individual's environment. We have discussed how an individual is born into and learns to model human kindness, but that individual also needs to secure and protect the resources needed for survival and comfort. The complex interaction between these two basic aspects of human understanding and behavior underlies and defines most human activity. Since the development of kindness is one of the earliest learned behaviors and it occurs more

R. Leve, *The Complexity of Human Thought*,
https://doi.org/10.1007/978-3-031-09104-9_16

frequently in our thoughts and behaviors than selfishness, we need to think of kindness as the default cognitive activity and selfishness as a less frequent behavior that exists as a cognitive interference to kindness. Kindness is almost solely a social behavior in that is initiated by and directed toward other people, other living organisms such as pets, birds, and sometimes even animals that we have no direct contact with such as dolphins, whales, and elephants. This is documented by the affection we have for such creatures and the fact that there are many organizations that try to protect animals and preserve them from extinction, and these organizations rely on the inherent kindness of human beings. It doesn't make much sense to be kind toward inanimate objects such as hammers, screwdrivers, and electric drills, although at times, we may become attached to objects such as a favorite boat, automobile, or in my case my bicycle, and provide that with human characteristics. However, this is a relatively rare phenomenon in most people's lives, and we reserve expressions of kindness mainly toward other humans and pets.

As we noted in our earlier discussion, kindness tends to be a simple phenomenon in terms of complexity theory because it is mainly an interaction between an individual and one other person in that individual's environment. At times, there may be more than one individual in the environment or even a group of other individuals; nevertheless, it is still a cognitive situation with few interacting variables, in this case, people. I refer to this as a simple cognitive model because it has only two variables, ourselves and the person who is the recipient of our kindly feelings. This is illustrated in Fig. 16.1.

It is also simple because there is only one interaction, that between the two variables. For example, encountering a good friend or even thinking about that person is likely to engender pleasant thoughts, and we may display a kind demeanor toward that person. Whether or not we initiate overtly kindly behavior toward that person is irrelevant because our cognitive model is one of kindly thoughts. In this situation, the interactive relationship between us and our friend are connected through reciprocal feelings. Some kindly words on our part may engender kind feelings and kindly words from a friend, and thus, our cognitive model is a simple one of kindly feelings between two people.

Given that kindness is the more basic cognitive model of human behavior, we need to analyze how selfishness at times can come to predominate kindness. Selfishness is different in that it is more instrumental and pragmatic. It also can be composed of many environmental variables and so tends to generate complex cognitive models as opposed to the simple cognitive models of kindness. We have discussed the fact that selfishness is motivated by the actual or anticipatory loss of resources. In other words, selfishness describes a kind of thinking that is motivated

Fig. 16.1 Simple interaction between two persons

by actual events in our environment or our perception of events or future events in our environment. We might describe this as the interjection of foreign events into the status quo of human kindness. In that sense, selfishness is motivated by the anxiety we feel when we face loss or the inability to obtain what we perceive as necessary resources.

Of course, the words "necessary resources" are idiosyncratic to every individual as each of us will have different degrees of what we see as our needed resources, and this will vary across the multitudinous dimensions of our exterior environment. For example, in our modern world, one individual may be quite content with a $90,000-a-year income, whereas someone else may feel that $1 billion a year does not satisfy their needs. Many people are quite happy using a simple paddleboard for water recreation, whereas a select few others might feel quite wretched because they don't have a 40-meter-long motor yacht and a paddleboard. This instrumental selfishness also occurs as a result of the personal goals we desire. A recreational jogger may be quite happy just to complete her goal of a five-mile run, whereas an Olympic athlete may be quite disappointed by coming in third in an Olympic marathon. All of these situations can potentially produce selfish thinking and behaviors because our environment has not provided the needed actual or social resources we desire. Looking at these examples, it may seem that selfishness is a very simple concept; however, it is quite complex, and we need to understand it through the lens of complexity theory.

Remember, a cognitive model is an intellectual thought or understanding composed of two or more variables or environmental stimuli, and these are connected by interactions such that a change in one may result in a change in all the others. Since we live in a vast and ever-changing personal environment, there are many social and nonsocial variables in that environment that can be identified as needed resources. To cope with such a complex personal environment, we need to construct cognitive models that are mental and neurological representations of the exterior environment. A cognitive model can include a host of resources in our immediate and distant environment that we have or want to obtain, and we will feel deprived if we do not have these things. There is hardly any limit to the number of objects we can desire and feel deprived of if we don't have them; thus, cognitive models of selfishness are likely to have many variables with interconnections between them because there can be or is a host of environmental resources that we desire.

In analyzing the structure of a selfish cognitive model, we see that it can be quite confusing because it can contain many variables with many additive and multiplicative interactions between them, as shown in Fig. 16.2.

As we have already noted, there is almost no limit to the number of variables that will be seen by any given individual as needed resources. We humans seem to have a boundless ability to possess almost anything in our environment, whether it is an object, a person, geography, free time, currency, or even information. Of course, our need to selfishly possess these things is enhanced by the fact that many of the things we want to possess have associations with other things, which means that cognitive models reflecting possession will tend to be complex in nature. In other words, possessing or wanting to obtain one variable will likely have associations with other

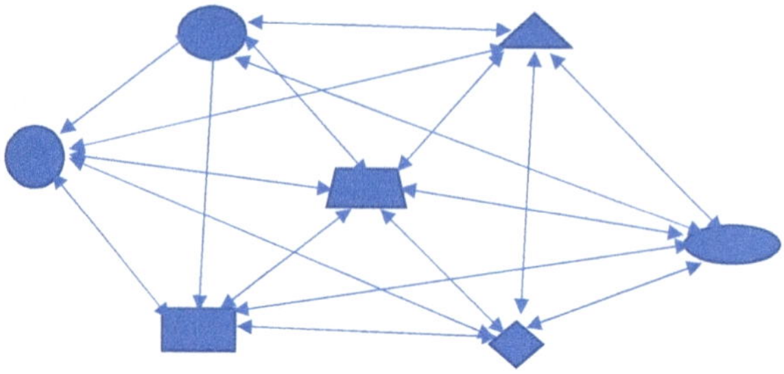

Fig. 16.2 Cognitive interactions among possessiveness variables

variables that will lead an individual to want to possess those variables also. Perhaps this is a bit of a cognitive chain reaction of acquisition and results in creating a complex interaction comprising a cognitive matrix as previously shown in Fig. 16.2. For example, a workman might need a flathead screwdriver, but on going to the hardware store, he will often buy a set of different screwdrivers and then realize he may need a power drill, which will lead him to buy a tool chest to house his tools. Thinking ahead to a bigger construction project, he may decide he will need a pickup truck to transport supplies from the local lumber yard. These kinds of associations are common in everyday life and oftentimes characterize individuals shopping for most any kind of object. Such acquisitional associations are common among authors and researchers where the discovery of one piece of information will lead to another and another. Although academics are usually keen to share their information, they may desire such sharing to be accompanied by some sort of selfish professional recognition in the form of a book or other publication, bringing attention to the author in terms of career advancement or payment. This not only occurs in adults but also is characteristic of children. I am reminded of the old saying, "like a kid in a candy store," where children become confused by which of the many multitudes of sweets they want to possess. Perhaps a more realistic example is watching children fill their bags with candies when they are trick-or-treating on Halloween. They are not likely to turn down any candy gifts even though there is a limit to how many Hershey Bars they can eat before they become sick.

Another important factor that initiates and maintains selfishness is the fact that we live in a universe in which the environment is constantly changing, and that introduces less stability and less predictability to the environment we inhabit. Humans and other higher-level organisms are obviously attuned to such unpredictability, and they are likely to change their behaviors so that they can cope with and endure negative environmental changes that can potentially affect their functioning and survival. An obvious way to do that is to try to obtain and hold on to more and more resources as a way of protecting themselves from adverse environmental changes. In addition to actual changes in the exterior environment, there is also the perception, correct or incorrect, that future adverse changes and instability may occur. In other words, individuals are constantly creating future cognitive models of their universe, and such future cognitive models may reflect the reality of a future lack of resources or the perception of such a situation, but either situation is likely to result in possessive and selfish behaviors. This can be generated by present information about adverse resource availability through contemporary news or an individual's personal sensitivity to anxiety and worries.

Changes in the environment not only decrease the stability of cognitive models and future cognitive models but also change the interaction between the sense of available resources and the perceived need for different resources, thus creating models of increasing complexity. One can hardly feel secure if the relationship between the availability of different resources is changing as this is likely to affect how we go about planning for the resources we need. Obviously, one rather selfish and likely flawed way is to try to possess every conceivable needed resource and likely a good bit more. Of course, attempting to acquire an excess of resources as previously mentioned increases the complexity of cognitive models. This is exacerbated by a sense that the matrix of needed resources when it becomes more complex may tend to become more chaotic, and people sensing this pre-chaotic situation are likely to become anxious. Individuals may react to such anxious feelings by continuing to acquire more perceived needed resources, but this is likely to introduce even greater complexity in the cognitive model of the universe and may result in more selfish behaviors. The resulting cognitive model may become so complex that it becomes chaotic and generates even more anxiety, sometimes resulting in a repetitive cycle of chaos, anxiety, and more acquisition.

At this point in our discussion, we need to question why we try to obtain more "needed resources" than we actually need since it makes no sense and can add negative burdens to our human functioning and is likely to generate unnecessary complex cognitive models. We might try to answer this question by looking at genetics, cultural, or developmental explanations; however, I think there is also a logical explanation generated by the often unstable and changing environment we inhabit.

Since the cognitive model of possession can contain an overwhelming number of interactions among "needed resource" variables, the complexity of such a cognitive model can exceed an individual's ability to effectively use such a model in the realistic pursuit of valid needed resources. Thus, like other complex cognitive models, it must be simplified in some fashion. The usual way to simplify such a complex cognitive model is to focus on one variable within a given time span and ignore all others. For example, a child may desire a particular toy seen in a store, on the Internet, or possessed by a friend, and at that time interval, the child will want that particular toy and not focus on the many others that fall within the child's repertoire of desired toys which may emerge at a later time when the child sees a new toy. So for that limited period of time, the child has ignored or held all other possible possessions constant while only focusing on the particular toy being attended to. This cognitive reductive principle applies just as well to adults as to children. As mentioned earlier, an individual may want a new expensive sports car and focus solely on that object rather than many others that individual may also desire. Perhaps possessiveness is a better description of this process; nevertheless, there is still the selfish impulse to obtain an object and not to share it or give it to another individual. In the real world, individuals commonly simplify a vast matrix of obtained and desired objects into a small and realistic number, and that becomes their solution to dealing with the overwhelming difficulty of a multiple cognitive matrix of selfishly desired resources. In a later section, we will discuss the development and influence of money and how that generates the interactions between desired objects and also becomes a desired possession in and of itself.

The natural concern over the loss of needed resources often can lead to an increasing level of complexity in generating cognitive models of selfishness. This increasing complexity is caused by the concern over what constitutes an adequate amount of needed resources. In a sense, this is the classic human problem of how much is enough. Since we humans can predict into the future, we can also anticipate facing a lack of resources at some future time, and this is likely to create some sense of concern and potential inadequacy. Thus, we introduce a sense of anxious complexity between a cognitive matrix of time, existing resources, and projection of needed future resources. As a general rule, the cognitive models we develop toward the future are more likely to focus on a future inadequacy of resources and not an overabundance efficiency of resources. This seems to be a natural human tendency, and we might speculate that it is related to a more general and historical survival behavior.

Obviously, when we are attentive to future cognitive models concerning resources, we are not likely to tolerate the loss of the resources we already possess to others unless those others are intimate members of our family or clan. In most situations, we humans selfishly try to hold on to our valued possessions. Interestingly, there are a large number of studies in behavioral economics showing that humans are more upset by losing existing resources they possess compared to gaining new resources even if the amount lost and gained is the same. This phenomenon known as loss aversion is a common human behavior and indicates that we feel quite selfish toward the resources we have even when we are compensated for the same amount of our loss (Thaler, 2015) (Angner, 2016). There are many theoretical explanations for this seemingly illogical behavior, but we need to consider the fact that our developmental selfishness can often overcome rational and mathematical logic.

The ability of humans to predict the future often seems to increase our anxiety and our possessiveness. We have discussed in previous chapters the errors in predicting the future increase with the expansion of time and we humans have some awareness that we may incorrectly estimate our needed future resources. Obviously, we will believe we are better off overestimating those needs rather than underestimating them. Of course, the word "resources" covers a wide variety of present and future objects, people, land, dwellings, and currency, which tends to generate a rather complex future cognitive model. One way of dealing with the complexity of this future model is to focus on possessing and acquiring more and more resources, often far beyond what we can actually use, certainly much more than we need to ensure our survival and to maintain our happiness and contentment. Perhaps driven by our anxiety of the future, the acquisition and possessiveness of resources become compulsive in thoughts and behavior as that is a way of simplifying the complex projective cognitive model and the anxiety caused by a possible future inadequacy.

There are many ways to explain compulsive acquisition and possessiveness of resources according to different theoretical orientations including personality traits, psychopathology, behavioral economics, and societal and cultural expectations. These theories provide useful explanations of selfish over hoarding; however, complexity science may help us to understand and analyze the cognitive models that underlie such selfish behaviors. As we have already noted, attempting to predict the number of future resources that we need is very difficult because the environment we live in is very complex and constantly changing. Of course, this not only applies to ourselves, but we often expand this future model to provide for a social-familial network of individuals, present, absent, and even unborn, with needed and unnecessary objects and currency in an unknown future economy.

As we have discussed in previous chapters, the primary purpose of human cognition is to simplify the many variables of our complex environments, so we avoid cognitive overload and mental chaos. Although selfishness is motivated by the need for actual environmental resources, it often becomes a social activity because we associate selfishness with particular people or groups of people. Rarely do we associate selfishness solely with inanimate objects we desire. When we anticipate the loss or absence of needed resources, we usually believe that the loss of those resources is due to other people, and we may realize or imagine that other people have the resources that we feel deprived of. In that sense, though the resources we desire may be inanimate objects or money, we usually associate other people with having these inanimate resources to our own detriment. Usually, we are not aware of our own selfishness as we are likely to engage in egocentric thinking, which justifies our needing the resources possessed by others. Thus, we are likely to develop a cognitive model of our universe that projects the attitude of selfishness onto others while remaining ignorant of that attitude in ourselves. In that way, we likely form a cognitive association between those people who have the resources and our deprivation of those resources. Our cognitive model of selfishness in others can quickly become very stable because we are likely to take in environmental data that justifies and affirms our selfish needs while ignoring any reason or justification for other people possessing the resources that they need. Of course, this situation may involve not only particular individuals and groups of people but also unknown individuals and groups.

For example, hearing that a business associate has received a generous salary increase may engender selfish feelings toward that individual, or reading about an academic colleague receiving a large research grant or praise and recognition for a new book may create a similar feeling of envy. When we read that a rich corporation has used legal or illegal tax favors to avoid paying any income tax, we are likely to feel a self-justified selfish anger toward the unknown group of individuals who are the board members and corporate officers of that corporation.

Of course, we can attempt to develop an adaptive cognitive model identifying the resources we desire and how we might go about obtaining them. This is likely to be a complex cognitive model composed of the desired resources, difficulties obtaining such resources, the psychological, energy, and financial cost of these resources, and various problem-solving methods involved in obtaining our resources. This involves the creation of a multifaceted and interconnected cognitive model. However, we might find it easier, if less adaptive, to just create a less complex cognitive model of selfishness toward perceived individuals or groups that have our desired resources. Usually such a cognitive model based on selfishness does not require a great deal of cognitive effort since it has only two variables, ourselves and the other person or people who have or who we believe controls our resources.

At its most fundamental level, the term "necessary resources" reduces to what is needed for survival, what gives us pleasure and comfort, and what allows us to eliminate or minimize physical and emotional pain. Perhaps in a simpler hunter gatherer society, there is a limited number of things that fit into these categories, and so our ancestors created simpler cognitive models that had fewer items (variables), and there were also fewer and less changeable interactions between the variables. For example, finding food resources required simple interactions based on environmental memories of the geographic and seasonal locations of food sources. However, these cognitive models involved interactions with the food environment and likely had minimal interactions between individuals other than in cooperating to obtain the food through hunting and gathering and the preparation of the food. If the food supply was adequate, I doubt there was much selfishness involved in the sharing, and certainly that was the case within members of the same clan. At best, this simple sharing of goods involved an elementary social economy of favors, and the cognitive models in this simple economy involved reciprocity. Such a reciprocity of favors and obligations is more characteristic of social kindness, which would have been quite common. Thus, sophisticated and extensive cognitive models of selfishness were likely not predominant as a method of personal interaction. In terms of complexity, hunter gatherer societies were rather simple in that there were fewer variables, and reacting to these variables was reasonably immediate. Our hunter gatherer individuals did not likely project cognitive models of their environment into the distant future, but rather they reacted to things that tended to be immediate. For example, our hunter gatherer individuals were not concerned about laying in enough money for their retirement. Perhaps early patriarchal and subjugating societies found pleasure and comfort in obtaining an especially desired woman or the accumulation of slaves to carry out unpleasant work, and desiring such individuals is a form of selfishness. Of course, we can only speculate about such early relationships, but it seems likely that reciprocal human interactions and kindness characterized the thinking and behaviors of clan members.

Aside from bartering for resources, our hunter gatherers also need to find pleasure and comfort and avoid physical pain. These needs were also obtained through simple cognitive models involving relationships with other clan members just as we later *Homo sapiens sapiens* still do. Such cognitive models are simple interactions between an individual and one or more other individuals in their group. In terms of avoiding physical and emotional pain, our unhappy hunter gatherer would likely consult and submit to the local tribal healer. There seems to be little need for selfish interactions in the healer-client relationship, certainly no more so than in a typical modern doctor patient relationship (Of course, that doesn't mean that a social relationship only generates kindly feelings because if the treatment becomes rather painful, I imagine our patient might become very unhappy and angry with his healer; nevertheless, this is still a simple non-selfish two-person cognitive model.).

As our early societies began to coalesce into farming communities and individuals began to specialize in certain skills, the number of tangible items and social benefits that could be obtained increased exponentially (Harari, 2015). Instead of going barefoot, one could barter your food for shoes made by the local shoemaker, a bowl from the local potter, or honey from the local beekeeper. This increase in specialization likely had an effect on individual selfishness in two ways. First and most obviously, there was an increase in the number of items that might be desired. If there were more available items, there were more things to want and generate a sense of selfishness. Secondly, the process of obtaining a desired item became more complex because one now had to find the shoemaker who made the best fitting and most long-lasting shoes and the beekeeper who had the tastiest and cleanest honey. An added complication was having to calculate how much of your resources such as wheat, barley, or potatoes might be fairly bartered for the item that you desired. Thus, there were interactions between suppliers of the desired goods, the assessment of what one needed, and the relationship of one's own resources to what was desired, and a change in one likely produced an interactive change in the others.

This cognitive model is far different and much more complex compared to the simple hunter gatherer model in that each individual in the trading would want to maximize what they were obtaining compared to what they were giving up. Thus, they would likely initiate a selfish cognitive model through which they would maximize their profit by taking advantage of the other individual. Obviously, such barter-based cognitive models are more complex compared to the more limited environment of a hunter gatherer, but they are still limited by the number of things that are available, needed, or desired within the confines of a small farming community. Another limitation of the cognitive models of a barter economy is that the individuals trading with each other are engaging in a personal relationship and are likely to be members of the same clan. In such a situation, selfish interactions that take unfair advantage of another person are likely to be problematic as they may sour future barter relationships and create social difficulties within the clan. This situation creates a complex cognitive model involving present and anticipated future social interactions. For example, one might be selfishly tempted to cheat or in some way take advantage of the other trading individual; however, such dishonest behavior might engender an angry reaction from that individual or a refusal to engage in future trades. In a closed clan society, people are likely to avoid selfish trading interactions because of the present and future consequences, and this places a limitation on selfish behaviors.

The simple cognitive models of the hunter gatherer and the within-community bartering became much more complex with the invention of money. Any discussion of selfishness needs to understand the concept of money and how money expanded the accessibility of resources in an environment and in the process increased opportunities to generate complex cognitive models of selfishness. There is little point in trying to assess whether the introduction of money has been beneficial or detrimental as it will depend on one's circumstances, environment, and sense of morality. However, we cannot doubt that there is a relationship between the emergence of money, in its many forms and cognitive models of selfishness.

Money was created in many places over our history, and it took many forms. In addition to the government currency bills and coins which are familiar in our modern economy, money existed in the form of shells, cattle, grain, beads, cloth, and ounces of silver called the Shekel. The first coins with a standard weight of gold and silver were struck around 640 BC by the king of Lydia in western Anatolia. The invention of money meant that these coins could represent any needed or desired resources. In other words, a certain number of coins could represent a tool, a weapon, an article of clothing, a house, land, or even a person in the form of a slave. The utility of money meant that it could represent anything in one's environment because it placed a value on any resource, and it provided an individual with a comparison value between disparate resources as measured by the amount of coins required to obtain the resources. As we shall see, the simple fact of comparing the value of one resource to another has the ability to bring about complex models of selfishness and greed.

The concept of money emerged as a kind of social phenomenon of convenience, and in that sense, it is a mutual agreement between groups of people. However, as a social phenomenon, it has little to do with human kindness but rather depends upon a form of impersonal convenience. The use of money does require personal trust and cooperation, because the trust is in the concept of money per se and not in people, and it requires that everyone in the economy participates in the system. Of course, the system is so powerful, universal, and convenient that no one can decide not to participate. The concept and practice of money quickly become entrenched in political and governmental structures. Governments have institutionalized the money systems in their countries such that they can hardly become separated, because each government guarantees the value of the currency, and in addition to putting guarantees on their currency, they use it to extract taxes from their citizens. Obviously, the emergence of the simple concept of money has generated layers of complexity in terms of stock markets, treasury departments, governmental forms of taxation, and the many various and different types of banks. These institutions and the seemingly simple concept of money now depend on supply and demand. Any system so complex and universal which changes according to the vicissitudes of supply and demand will naturally introduce selfishness into the thinking and behavior of individuals who have an opportunity to manipulate this economic system for their personal greed and to the detriment of others. By creating a complex economy with so many interactive variables, they create unpredictability in that economy. For example, many individuals have spent a great deal of time and effort trying to accurately predict the price of individual stocks from day to day in an attempt to accumulate personal wealth, and many have lost their personal wealth in this selfish attempt to predict a relatively unpredictable complex economic system (most economists recognize the fact that they can observe and record economic factors but have limited ability to predict the economic future. I suppose if they could, economists would be the wealthiest people in society).

Money has also introduced impersonality and social distance, and that is quite different from a community barter system. In that system, usually one has personal contact with the producer of the goods that you are trading for, whereas a money economy introduces social separation between the individual producing the resource and the person desiring it. This lack of personal contact decreases any opportunity for kindness between the individuals because often we are interacting with members outside of our clan. For example, unless I am buying vegetables at my local farmers' market, I have no contact with the many individuals who produced the myriad of foodstuffs lining the shelves of my local supermarket. I suppose my schedule or anyone else's would hardly allow me to meet all those individuals growing the food I eat, the clothing I wear, and the carpentry tools I use, but that creates a loss of emotional contact, friendliness, and the opportunity for kindness toward others.

We can see the complexity of the money system in terms of a historical anecdote and its confusion in cultures that did not have concepts of money (Harari, 2015). When Hernan Cortez began his conquest of the Aztec empire in the 1500s, the natives noticed that the Spaniards had an extraordinary interest in gold. To the Aztecs, gold was just an unusual, soft, malleable metal useful in making jewelry and statues because it did not tarnish. The Spanish interest in gold was confusing because of its limited usefulness. When the natives questioned Cortez about their desire for gold, he answered, "Because I and my companions suffer from a disease of the heart which can only be cured with gold." Perhaps that statement more than any other captures the selfishness that money in the form of gold, silver, or any other scarce commodity can induce. Sadly, and tragically, that disease of the heart resulted in the countless deaths and enslavement of those native peoples and the destruction of their empire.

In some ways, the emergence of money introduced a form of simplicity into an individual's environment, and in other ways, it introduced many new and unique levels of complexity. Money simplifies the resources of an environment because the relative value of resources can be reduced to simple arithmetic calculations which can show the relationships between resources. This avoids the need to understand other relationships between completely different and unrelated objects like how many pots of honey are equivalent to a sack of potatoes. Of course, the arithmetic relationship as measured by money may appear to be perfectly objective, but the underlying relationships may not be accurately measured by arithmetic calculations as they are often imprecise and likely to differ according to individual perceptions, particular circumstances, and social changes over time. In spite of relative inaccuracies, money does reduce the plethora of environmental resources and objects to a simple arithmetic code. Money also simplifies a complex environment because it forms a universal language that everyone can understand. It hardly matters whether one speaks Sanskrit, Proto-European, Gothic, or modern Chinese and English; everyone in these ancient or modern cultures can understand the value of their many environmental resources through this simple arithmetic code. Another advantage of the arithmetic code is its ability to transform differences in local currencies. I have little trouble transforming American dollars into British pounds or the European euro, and I can obtain a Spanish cappuccino, a Viennese pastry, or a new Italian Ferrari (I wish) in spite of the fact that each of these depends on the currency of the local government.

However, the emergence of money has also introduced many new layers of environmental complexity, and this has had a profound effect toward introducing selfishness into the cognitive models of our social world. As we have noted before, there is a relationship, if imperfect, between complexity and selfishness. The more complicated one's environment is, the more variables exist which allows an individual to find variables that support anxieties about losing needed resources or feeling that one has less resources than one's neighbors. Perhaps, money started out as a simple arithmetic code that facilitated people buying or selling things among themselves, but it quickly evolved into a complex economic system that created new institutions and relationships that never existed in a barter economy. Many of these institutions such as banks, stock markets, currency exchanges, government treasury departments, and others are emergent phenomena that would not have been predicted to arise from the early use of coinage; however, they are now institutions that can significantly affect human behavior and cognition. Individuals can now use these institutions to store money in the form of accounts and to trade and manipulate monies and accounts so that additional monies can be accumulated in the form of profits or monies can be lost. For the most part, profits and losses in a moneyed economy are a zero-sum game in that usually the accumulation of one individual's profits comes from the losses of another individual. Both of these situations have the potential to generate selfish behaviors because people may want to accumulate the resources of others through greedy behaviors, and those people who have lost money may selfishly attempt to recover their losses at the expense of others, motivated by fear and anxiety. Greedy behaviors are so common in every modern society that one hardly needs to provide an example of these behaviors. The effect of money is so pervasive that it affects social and cultural relationships. My kind neighbor, Joanne, is likely to occasionally stop by to bring me a container of her delicious seafood chowder; however, she is unlikely to ever stop by to offer me the monetary equivalent of that same seafood chowder. That is not a socially appropriate behavior.

Another important phenomenon created by these many and complicated institutions is the concept of debt. Now individuals can now be financially indebted to other individuals and institutions, while others may be the lenders who can claim the resources of the debtor whether it be money, their goods in the form of food, dwellings, or land, or their services in the form of labor, or their children as slaves or concubines. In the laws of modern countries, individuals can escape debt through bankruptcy, which often places an individual in a different social and financial status. The arithmetic code resulting from money and money-based financial accounts introduces a precision in terms of how much is owed, so a lender or borrower can put a calculation on their selfishness. Of course, this is not only true in terms of debtor relationships but is generally true for selfish cognitive models in all situations because one can now place a numerical value on how much they desire of someone else's resources or to what degree they need to protect their resources from the predatory behaviors of others.

Being able to calculate the exact financial obligations of an individual is quite different from the communal favors and obligations that exist between members of a community barter society. In a communal barter economy, social concepts such as loyalty, honor, and morality are very important; however, in a money-based economy, these are foreign concepts that lie outside of the system. Concepts such as loyalty, honor, and morality depend upon social interactions; however, in a money-based system, these have been replaced by numbers on impersonal ledgers and financial computer programs. Now, individuals may take satisfaction in the accumulation of profits without being troubled about whether such profits have resulted in losses to others because they have no social contact in such a system.

The Interactive Balance of Kindness and Selfishness

If we lived in a world of perfect economic efficiency, it would make no sense to give away any of our resources, and the concept of charity becomes self-defeating. That economic belief creates a very simple cognitive model of never parting with any resources. This is perfect selfishness. Similarly, perfect kindness would cause us to happily share any and all of our resources needed by other people. However, at this point in our discussion, most people will have realized that there is a relationship between cognitive models of kindness and selfishness. This is not a simple binary relationship, but is quite complex with many idiosyncratic variables that interact with each other. I think it is obvious that an individual that is perfectly kind and selfless runs the serious risk of not retaining even the most elementary resources needed for happiness and survival. Similarly, maintaining a cognitive model of utter selfishness and viewing other people only as competitors for resources does not lead to a life of happiness and contentment and in the long run may decrease opportunities to attain desired and needed resources due to the reactions of others in social situations. In fact, there is a complex balance between these two modes of thinking such that we are likely to obtain many tangible and social resources by being kindly to others, and if we behave in too selfish a manner, we are likely to shut access to tangible and social resources.

However, just recognizing this relationship and that there is a balance between these two human attributes does not adequately describe what is in fact a very complex situation. People do not exist in a stable state of homeostatic balance somewhere on this kindness to selfishness continuum, but as noted earlier, this is a changing situation that varies within and between all individuals. In that sense, the kindness-selfishness relationship will self-organize according to different environmental situations. For example, a non-compromising capitalist may selfishly make cruel and inordinate demands upon employees, customers, and associates, whereas that same individual may act in a loving and kindly way toward his children and may make generous charitable contributions to his or her house of worship. That individual's cognitive models are likely to be quite different in their understanding of each situation such that they likely harbor a series of politically conservative views toward employees and associates. Our capitalists may believe people are poor because they are lazy, people who aren't smart should be cheated, capitalist leaders deserve their high salaries due to their rare and valuable talents, and many other similar beliefs. Each of these cognitive models may have developed as a result of some of the myriad of conscious and unconscious experiences in childhood or later life. They may have come from emergent situations that at the time were unpredictable in forming those particular cognitive models. Once such cognitive models form, they likely self-organize into default behaviors that will characterize general tendencies toward kindness or selfishness in particular situations. In other words, different cognitive models on the kindness and selfishness spectrum are created for many different environmental situations. These situations are likely to be composed of many different interacting variables; however, the cognitive models will tend toward cognitive simplification as always.

Even the simple act of deciding whether or not to give a homeless beggar money may be very complex, yet it is often simplified into binary types of simple reasoning. One individual may react to a beggar by thinking he or she is probably too lazy to work or they probably do not need any money because they aren't really homeless or poor, whereas another individual may see the beggar as a needy person who through no fault of their own has fallen on hard times and needs help. In reality, this simple situation of giving money to a beggar is quite complex. Some of the cognitive variables involved are as follows: does the beggar really need the money, is this beggar really a cheat, can we, the giver, really be the judge of the needs of others, will the money we give seriously deplete our own resources, what is the state of homelessness for this individual in our region, and will we feel cheated or happy that we have helped another individual? Another factor that may influence our behavior is the clan identity of the unfortunate individual. We may feel more kindly and therefore are more likely to donate to an individual that seems to be from our own clan, but this reaction may be quite idiosyncratic as some people may feel less kindly and more suspicious toward members of their own clan. These are just some of the confusing variables that interact with each other in this complex situation and as in many multivariable interactive situations, predicting what beliefs and behaviors will emerge will be very difficult. We might assume that we humans develop personality characteristics and beliefs such that some of us will act kindly toward a beggar, whereas others will be selfish and choose not to donate any of their resources, and as such, general personality characteristics likely do exist. The main point is that donating to a needy beggar is so complex that rather than trying to resolve the many variables and their interactions, in some fashion, both the kindly and selfish individuals are likely to ignore or reject consideration of those variables and focus on one or two, thus utilizing cognitive simplification to guide their beliefs. Certainly, certain factors will become more salient and so become important. Perhaps, there is something about the appearance of the beggar or a particularly sad facial expression that may affect us and determine our behavior in that instant. Obviously, the season of the year may become salient in our thinking, and so we may be more likely to donate during the Christmas season. Charles Dickens popular story, "A Christmas Carol," perfectly captures the extremes of interaction between kindness and selfishness. Ebenezer Scrooge starts out as a perfectly selfish individual, but after salient experiences of great power in the form of three rather frightening ghosts, he is transformed into a perfectly kind individual. In his wonderful heartwarming tale, Dickens has found a way to simplify this situation into a classic story and, in its simplicity, likely makes even the most selfish of us feel kind. Our world would be a much better place if the transformation from selfishness to kindness could be as simple as we see in Dickens' story, but alas our real world is rather short on terrifying Christmas ghosts.

In summary, kindness and selfishness are complex human behaviors because they involve so many cognitive models associated with different learned reactions to social situations. However, there is a basic emotional simplicity underlying these human reactions. Selfishness relates to the external environment in that it seeks to accumulate the resources in that environment and is motivated by anxiety and fears. Acquiring environmental resources produces a form of temporary pleasure because it reduces anxieties. Selfishness is also motivated by anticipatory anxiety in which although we have adequate or more than adequate environmental resources, we anticipate that we will not have these things in the future.

By contrast, kindness is related to our positive inner emotions such as affection, pleasure, and attention from others. Although these emotions may come from our social interactions with others, they ultimately are forms of our positive inner feelings and provide us with those necessary but difficult-to-define emotions, happiness, and contentment. Our cognitive models for kindness are easily triggered by the helplessness and unhappiness we might see in an unhappy child, an abused pet, a friend in distress, or even the face of a sad stranger. These initiate cognitive models and behaviors that may cause us to give that person or animal a comforting touch, our reassurance, or we may happily part with our resources as an act of charity. Usually these behaviors are self-rewarded by our own feelings of satisfaction and happiness.

Chapter 17
Rational Human Thought

Abstract This chapter demonstrates the process of how rational and valid cognitive models are created and then describes the inherent environmental factors that place limits on human cognitive abilities. We inhabit environments composed of such a vast array of variables that we could never know all of them and the many interactions between them, unless we were omnipotent beings. Even the huge neurological universe of our brains is still inadequate to comprehend our entire changing exterior universe, and therefore we live in a continual state of partial ignorance. In addition, as individuals, we bring historical, cultural, and neurological differences to our interpretation of that universe, so we develop different rational cognitive models. Such differences in rational thinking mean that we will negate information that does not fit with our cognitive beliefs. Negating information means that we can create models that are so extreme that they may defy reality and logic. Unfortunately, such a situation can self-organize around limited and negated information that will generate distorted cognitive models that are erroneous representations of our universe. This is often further exacerbated by the development of rigid habits that crystalize distorted thinking and behavior. These processes are discussed through examples from military, medical, and political events.

Keywords Informational ignorance · Cognitive habits · Cognitive flywheel · Cognitive energy · Negating information · Complexity and individual differences · Self-organization and ignorance

Through much of this book, we have been analyzing how complexity science affects cognition and especially how complexity imposes limitations on thinking. While this has been somewhat of an academic and theoretical study, complexity science does have pragmatic implications for how we use cognition to understand our environment in a logical and accurate way. Obviously, such implications must be somewhat general in their application in order to be useful, because trying to develop a specific application for every situation, stimulus, and phenomenon within the incredibly vast environment of our universe would be an impossible task.

R. Leve, *The Complexity of Human Thought*,
https://doi.org/10.1007/978-3-031-09104-9_17

Complexity and Informational Ignorance

The basic problem is that we live in such an information rich exterior environment that we can never know all the information that surrounds us and the interactions between the many bits of that information. Thus, we do not know all the relevant information that would provide a robust and valid cognitive model of our environment. Of course, this situation is compounded by the fact that relevant environmental information is constantly changing due to changes in the environment and changes in our daily human needs and functioning. In other words, we live in an environmental ocean of ignorance such that we create cognitive models based on limited information. This may seem to be an unfortunate state of affairs, but it is the reality of our situation, and there is little that can be done about it. Only an omnipotent and all-knowing deity can cope with this situation, and of course, such a being is a fanciful and perhaps wishful construction of our own cognitive model. However, even a godlike being still might not survive the chaos of so much information and so many associations, but I'm better off leaving such cogitations to theologians.

Accepting that we can never know all the environmental information surrounding us seems so obvious that one might wonder why one might even bother reflecting on something so self-evident. However, accepting our ignorance is inevitable can be a useful piece of knowledge as it reminds us of the complexity of the informational space we inhabit. That should inflict an intellectual humility concerning the cognitive models we create, and a sense of cognitive humility is a beneficial state of affairs as it can never allow us to be content with our existing cognitive models and will motivate us to be open to recognizing and accepting new information. But even dealing with the information that we can access still leaves us in a cognitive state in which we can easily become overwhelmed. As we have pointed out previously, the concepts of complexity science describe a situation in which people inherently avoid integrating too many variables and the changing interactions between them in an effort to make our universe and our personal external environment understandable. However, this useful and valuable cognitive process has an unintended consequence. That consequence is that we necessarily disregard many important aspects of our environment, and oftentimes, that simplification process leads us into cognitive errors and intellectual misunderstandings.

We have already noted that trying to take in too much environmental data results in the unpleasant state of cognitive chaos, and we humans and likely all other cognitive life-forms are programmed through evolution to unconsciously avoid such an intellectual situation. Since this process is a very natural and protective state of affairs, there is likely little we can do to overcome this form of environmental ignorance. I suppose if we maintain awareness of the fact that we are ignorant of vast parts of our environment because of our inherent tendency toward simplifying our cognitive models, that knowledge in itself will be helpful. Accepting that we are in a constant state of partial environmental ignorance might be useful in that we might then make greater attempts to search out new environmental variables and test their relevance to our concepts and beliefs. Of course, detecting which variables are truly irrelevant and which might have a valid cognitive relationship is not an easy task. In a sense, this is like searching for an emergent phenomenon before we can detect the significant consequences of that seemingly minor emergent phenomenon. As we have already noted, predicting emergent phenomenon in a complex environment is quite difficult and might involve a good bit of logic, luck, intuition, and a determined attempt to seek out and test seeming irrelevant variables in our environment.

Perhaps a useful example is the Covid-19 pandemic occurring as I write these words. With the exception of a few viral researchers, the mutation of viruses in bats or other species (or even in laboratory blunders) was irrelevant to most of the world's population. That particular viral evolution had little to no significance for humans and had no cognitive associations with our everyday cognitive models. Certainly, few people would have predicted a relationship between an unknown and seemingly unimportant virus and the precipitous decline of national economies across the world. This situation underwent a drastic change when one of the mutating viruses was able to jump onto humans and become highly transmissible. That seemingly unimportant virus turned out to be closely associated with countries closing their borders, near universal mask wearing, social distancing, a rapidly spreading serious illness, death, and the frenzied and fortuitous development of a vaccine. Thus, an unimportant virus that seemed to have little to no significance turned out to have significant associations with many seemingly diverse things of terrible importance. Of course, trying to predict and attain knowledge of what we are by definition ignorant of is a difficult state of affairs. However, there were some very wise people who did anticipate the general possibility of a pandemic even if they were unable to specify all of its effects in terms of the number of deaths, population migrations, economic disruptions, the rapid creation of many vaccines, and other effects.

A study of history across all fields of knowledge shows us many examples of unknown variables that had important effects once they emerged. No one would have expected the invasion of Europe by the Mongols in the thirteenth century since Europeans didn't know that such a warlike people even existed. Similarly, there were very few physicians before 1982 and the pioneering work of Drs. Marshall and Warren, who predicted the role of *H. pylori* bacterium as the main causal effect of gastritis and peptic ulcers. Perhaps an even better example of the difficulty in identifying and understanding the emergence of variables in a complex environment is what is referred to as the fog of war. Most military technicians realize that in spite of the best preparations, once a battle or war begins, it is very difficult to predict what will happen and how it will end.

For example, the military planners of the World War II Normandy invasion were counting on airborne troops to seize specific German military objectives before the main invasion. But instead of landing near these objectives, the paratroopers were scattered randomly all over the Normandy Peninsula due to enemy flak and navigational errors. Thus, the carefully drawn military plans were disrupted by the navigational difficulties, adverse weather, and pilot errors of the C-47 troop-carrying aircraft. As a result, the cohesion of units was fractured, the timing of attacks on objectives was delayed, navigational signals to guide succeeding units were missing, needed weapon such as explosives and antitank guns went missing, and some soldiers wandered about ignorant of their location. Thus, the crucial interconnections between these and many other variables were shattered. Fortunately, the destruction of the complex interconnections between these parts of the invasion plan was compensated for by the flexibility and excellent training of the airborne soldiers. Individuals that were separated from their units spontaneously joined together to form new units. Missing weapons were improvised, and captured enemy weapons were used. If planned enemy objectives could not be found, the scattered units attacked any and all German soldiers. In essence, the Allied airborne units self-organized into a complex adaptive system that was able to accomplish three things: capturing their objectives, eliminating occupying German troops, and allowing the second seaborne part of the normative invasion to be successful. Paradoxically, this confusion had a fortuitous effect as it confused the German military who seemed to think that there were allied invasion soldiers all over the Normandy Peninsula and not in the places anticipated by German military planners. Thus, the fog of war introduced unknown variables that had unpredicted positive and negative effects.

One might wonder if ignorance of important environmental variables might not sometimes be a fortuitous situation. As occurred in the Normandy D-Day invasion, when the meticulous top-down planning of generals failed, a bottoms-up solution was generated by the tens of thousands of individual soldiers. They simply responded to a chaotic situation by self-organizing themselves into effective, if random, military units who cobbled together the necessary material from any source at hand. If the most important function of a cognitive model is to avoid chaos as the result of overload and confusion, then a bottoms-up solution in the case of the Normandy invasion might have been as effective as any complex plan by their military superiors, perhaps better.

However, it's useful to imagine the situation of the American paratroopers basically lost behind German lines. They had lost the cohesion of the units, their friends, and often their weapons and equipment. Fear and perhaps panic would not have been an unexpected reaction, and the alternative to self-organizing themselves was a form of chaotic wandering about trying to avoid capture and accomplishing nothing. In this situation, as in most others, self-organization is an inherent and basic human reaction. Just as we avoid chaos in our cognitive models, the Allied soldiers of the Normandy invasion inherently avoided chaos and self-organized themselves into new groups and continued on, creating many individual mission tasks that prevented the German defenders from defeating the invasion. Cognitively, they formed new battlefield models that generated a new and effective self-organized force.

Of course, the military planners were facing a situation of immense complexity and could not have known about all the important variables and their interconnections. Even the best intelligence and reconnaissance could not have made them aware of all of the problems created by the German defenses, and the best maps still did not completely capture the natural hydrography and geology of the Normandy Peninsula. Given the immense complexity of coordinating over 5000 naval vessels, countless aircraft and gliders, tens of thousands of landing troops, and supplying an immense number of vehicles, tanks, artillery, and munitions, there was little hope that all these variables could be perfectly sequenced and connected. Ultimately it was the individual soldiers who created individual cognitive models of their constantly changing precarious situations that made the invasion successful.

Even after the beachheads were secured, the individual soldiers faced obstacles that were missed by the military planners in their environmental ignorance. In their efforts to break out of the Normandy Peninsula, soldiers were faced with Norman hedgerows that surrounded all of the small farming fields, which made for excellent German defensive positions. This should have been obvious to the general staff planning the invasion, but it was missed. Once again, the individual soldiers in their small groups developed cognitive models of coordinating flanking movements and artillery strikes which were independent of any overall plan, and eventually they were able to successfully defeat the German defenders and breakout into central France.

Complexity and Negating Information

In addition to variables and associations that we are unaware of, higher life-forms, and especially humans, have to deal with very complex multivariable exterior environments, and so we, of necessity, often resort to eliminating and negating the many variables that we are aware of. This occurs as a natural attempt to simplify the complexity of the environment. As we noted in Chap. 12 on the processes underlying scientific thinking, this can be a fortuitous process that can untangle difficult scientific problems; however, it can also serve to distort the validity of cognitive models and maintain erroneous cognitive models. Deleting variables may be satisfactory if we are willing to live in a limited universe, but any time we limit our cognitive models, we develop a skewed and incomplete understanding of our exterior universe, and any time we eliminate a variable, we are eliminating associations with other variables. This process means that rather than exploring the universe around us and then forming our cognitive models on that information, we are creating an imperfect universe and likely erroneous beliefs. The problem is not only that we may delete or negate informational variables but also that those variables may conflict with a preexisting cognitive model, and that does not allow an individual to correct errors in that cognitive model.

This situation is especially likely in understanding social environments. Obviously, deleting variables can lead to imperfect cognitive representations of the social universe and may maintain the perpetuation of an erroneous cognitive model. For example, people who only watch one news television channel such as CNN or Fox will develop a highly skewed and limited cognitive model of national and international politics. Thus, an attempt to minimize the complexity of our social environment can cause us to make errors by disregarding or negating valid observations, and once we have constructed an imperfect and erroneous cognitive model, there is a tendency to try to maintain that cognitive model as a way of maintaining cognitive simplicity. Obviously, when dealing with a complex environment, we will expend less cognitive effort by maintaining an existing model, even if it is erroneous and invalid, since maintaining an existing cognitive model requires less energy than creating a new one. Constructing a new cognitive model requires the identification of new variables and understanding the complex associations between them, and that is much more difficult than simply being content with the model we already have. Once a belief in the form of a cognitive model is established, it is usually quite difficult to change because it begins to self-organize. If we think of a cognitive model as consisting of a few interacting variables, that cognitive model is likely to only seek out informational aspects of the environment that are in harmony with that core belief, and once such self-organized models are created, they will be very difficult to change.

Political beliefs are especially sensitive to self-organization as they will tend to self-organize around a central belief system. In other words, as a cognitive belief system is exposed to new environmental information, information that has a positive association with the belief system will be incorporated, whereas information that seems to contradict the belief system will be eliminated or negated. This all has to do with associations, in that it is simpler and requires less effort to only develop associations with complementary information. Developing associations with contradictory or opposing information is quite difficult intellectually and may require the cognitive model to be changed or completely discarded. That might even require the creation of a completely new cognitive model. As we have previously noted, that requires not only developing new associations and a new complex cognitive model matrix but also the destruction of an existing self-organized cognitive system. Most individuals will tend to avoid giving up an existing cognitive model because it requires too much cognitive energy.

The extent to which humans will go to avoid such a situation is quite remarkable, and this process can lead to the creation of outlandish cognitive models which disregard obvious valid facts about their environment. Complexity concepts serve to explain how intelligent individuals can often hold on to irrational beliefs that lead to errors and misunderstandings in the life space we inhabit. This is especially true of individuals who hold on to irrational religious, political, and cultural beliefs in spite of obvious and compelling information that should easily dispel such erroneous beliefs. A contemporary example of this phenomenon is the present political belief in the Q-Anon conspiracy ideas. This irrational belief briefly states that Satan-worshiping pedophiles, mainly consisting of elitist Democrats, politicians, journalists, and entertainment moguls, have controlled what they call the deep state government. Q-Anon followers believe individuals meet to carry out their activities in a Washington DC pizzeria and that former President Trump was elected to destroy this evil cabal. They also believe that Q is a high-ranking government insider who often sends signals about his or her existence using the number 17, the letter Q's placement in the alphabet. The central part of this belief is that the current government is evil and a danger and must be overthrown. Once that central theme is adopted, much of the other irrational information about Satan and pedophiles forms an association with that central belief, thus enhancing it with supportive evidence. Other irrational information will tend to self-organize around that central belief, whereas valid information conflicting with that belief will be negated. The fact that there has been no evidence of child abuse or Satan worshiping among those individuals will be refuted.

A further irrational belief is that a mythical beast called the Kraken would be released to show the evidence of widespread voter fraud. In spite of the fact that no Kraken of any mythical beast has appeared, maintaining this well-integrated if irrational cognitive model is easier and requires less effort than creating an entirely new cognitive model with new variables and new interactions between those variables. That would require the creation of a completely new self-organizational model centered around complex democratic ideals as written in the US Constitution. Creating this kind of cognitive model is quite complex, involving a great many variables which must be associated with each other. Maintaining the belief that there are evil pedophiles running the US government is much simpler and requires little cognitive effort. This is a good example of the extent individuals can go to hold on to absurd ideas rather than invest in the energy to create valid cognitive models. It shows that by using one's imagination, there are few limits to the invalid cognitive models that can be created and maintained. Perhaps Mark Twin captured this human trait best by his quote from Pudd"nhead Wilson's New Calendar, "Faith is believing what you know ain't so,"

Complexity and Individual Cognitive Differences

Human beings differ from one another, and we are likely to differ on almost any topic or belief even in the face of similar environmental information. Logic would tell us that if there were no environmental differences, we should all agree, but we do not live in a perfectly logical world. The obvious answer is that we interpret the same information differently, so the question is why and how do we do that. As I am writing this, the United States is going through a time of major political and cultural differences. Some of the major political and cultural identities are centrist Democrats who support President Biden, progressive Democrats who support politicians such as Bernie Sanders, Republicans who support ex-president Trump, more traditional Republicans who support the Lincoln project, and radical conservatives who support organizations such as the Proud Boys, the Three Percenters, and Q-Anon.

Each individual has many historical, developmental, and even genetic differences that will cause us to interpret information differently; however, in terms of available information, we all live in a reasonably similar environment and could have access to the same environmental information. Nevertheless, we still differ in our thoughts, beliefs, and conclusions, and commonly we select environmental information that supports our existing cognitive models and ignore those that conflict with our models. This is true in almost every aspect of our lives, and the ideas of complexity science help to provide an explanation for how we go about creating and maintaining these differences.

As a general rule, the more complex an environment, in terms of the number of variables and the interactions between those variables, the more likely individuals are to develop differences from one another. Beliefs in the form of cognitive models are composed of a matrix of cognitive variables that have strong relationships with each other. They will also have little or usually no relationships with informational variables that are likely to conflict with the variables of a given cognitive model. Obviously, if the number of informational variables increases in an overall environment, there is more opportunity for an individual to include certain variables in their cognitive models, whereas other individuals may focus on and include different variables. Thus, as the number of informational variables increases, it is likely that the number and extent of differences between individuals will also increase, and since we live in rather complex social, cultural, and political environments, we should expect to find that differences within individuals and between cultures will be common. For example, there are likely to be greater individual differences in the political allocation of governmental funding among different government agencies and social groups, whereas there will be fewer differences among individuals on the best calendar date to plant corn in a given region. The political and economic consequences of governmental funding have a huge number of economic and social variables compared to the few variables involved in planting corn, and there are a greater number of differences in the extent of interactions between political economic variables. I suppose in terms of semantics, there really is little difference between the word "differences" and the word "complexity," and the more complex the environment, the more opportunity for differences. Thus, even though we may live in similar environments, the increased complexity of an environment is likely to increase individual differences. This is a general rule defining the relationship between environmental complexity and individual differences.

The preceding discussion shows that although we may share differences in history, development, and even genetics, the main reason why people develop the many and profound differences between us has to do with the complexity of our exterior environment in terms of the number of variables and the number of interactions between them. In reality, the environment we all live in may not be terribly dissimilar, especially in terms of obvious natural phenomena. There would certainly be general agreement on the times of sunrise and sunset in any given location and the fact that the earth is round, not flat (it's not exactly round as its rotation makes it bulge in the center, so technically it is an oblate spheroid). However, our environment in terms of social, cultural, and economic aspects is much more complex, and in these areas, we will find great differences between individuals and between cultures. Actually, the data and information in social, cultural, and economic environments may not be all that different, but the great complexity of these areas in terms of the number of variables and interrelationships is such that there will be a great number of differences that will emerge. Thus, the main driver of our differences is the inherent complexity of our environment.

Of course, having individual differences between our cognitive models may be a fortuitous state of affairs because if we all agreed on the same thing, perhaps humans would not have made much progress in the way of exploration or science. As a general rule, scientific research is constantly searching for differences between things in our universe while scientific theory seems to search for similarities in that universe. We might also wonder if there is a similar relationship between individual differences among scientists and scientific exploration in that the greater the number of individual differences, the greater progress is made in the understanding and exploration of the universe. And, of course, if there were no human differences, I think life would be very, very dull.

Another important question is how individuals maintain their erroneous cognitive models in spite of the potential of being attacked by the contradictory arguments and logical explanations of other individuals. To answer this, the concept of self-organization offers a likely explanation. Self-organization occurs in the physical world as a way of avoiding chaos and confusion, and a similar type of self-organization occurs in the cognitive realm. Attempting to form a cognitive model composed of diverse and conflicting informational variables is likely to produce an uncomfortable sense of cognitive confusion and requires a good bit of cognitive energy. It is far simpler to organize a cognitive model composed of similar informational variables even if these variables ignore other relevant pieces of information or conflict with the obvious reality of an individual's environment. In other words, we would rather hold onto a cognitive model that self-organizes around related pieces of information. It is a natural phenomenon that occurs by forming associations between similar agents, entities, and variables.

Self-organization in biological and social situations occurs when a pattern arises from an initial disordered system such as ants forming a bridge over a water obstacle, or the students in my classes almost always taking the same seat week after week without being prompted. If the ants never formed a bridge of their bodies, the alternative is for random groups of ants to chaotically walk about the obstacle, never achieving the goal of crossing it. Thus, the pattern of forming a bridge reduces chaos and achieves the goal of perhaps finding food on the other side of the obstacle in a faster and more secure way. Similarly, it is easier for a student to always return to the same seat rather than risk displacing another student or having to adjust to a different seat location. If they did not take the same seat, then we would have a semi-chaotic group of students walking about the aisles in their attempt to find a free seat. Taking the same seat each time is likely faster, more efficient, and might even provide a sense of classroom comfort.

In terms of cognitive thought, self-organization serves to limit cognitive effort. As we noted in the previous section, cognitive models form through finding or creating associations between variables. In that sense, such a cognitive model is commonly generated by the natural process of making a very complex environment easier to understand by simplifying it to only a limited number of variables. Once these variables are identified, the associations between them are strengthened, and variables outside this cognitive model are negated by eliminating their associative relationships with variables within the cognitive model. Thus, a simple and understandable cognitive model is self-organized and will be used to represent and understand the exterior environment in spite of the fact that many variables within that cognitive model may be excluded and thus will not provide a complete and accurate model of the environment.

Once this self-organization among the limited number of variables in the cognitive matrix is established, there is little reason to change it as it is maintained by cognitive simplification, which requires less intellectual energy. I suppose this is an abstract way of saying people do not like to change their minds; they would rather hang on to their beliefs often in the face of compelling factual evidence.

The social world is replete with examples of self-organized and factually incomplete cognitive models, and an excellent example is the group of individuals opposed to vaccinations. In spite of overwhelming evidence of the benefit of many different vaccines, there have always been individuals from the 1800s who used cowpox to protect themselves from smallpox, to more recent individuals who believe that present day children's vaccines will cause autism or other neurological disorders. In spite of overwhelming medical evidence that vaccines are effective and have almost no danger other than minimal side effects, people opposed to vaccines will form a cognitive matrix composed of variables such as the following: pharmaceutical companies can't be trusted, governments use vaccines to control the population, vaccines violate certain religious beliefs, vaccines are really ineffective, and many other specious ideas. Variables such as these become associated together in an anti-vaccine cognitive model, whereas a relevant variable such as data showing that diseases such as measles and smallpox are virtually eradicated is negated. Certainly, the scientific evidence showing the efficacy of a vaccine and its minimal side effects by well-respected scientists is also ignored and will not be integrated into the anti-vaccine cognitive matrix.

The same situation exists in many everyday activities. For example, the act of purchasing an automobile involves a large number of complex variables including the cost, whether it is new or used, anticipated mileage, engine size, type (such as sedan, SUV, or mini), foreign or domestic brand, anticipated usage in terms of climate, anticipated reliability, and a host of other variables. Of course, all of these variables interact with each other such that, for example, cost is related to brand and model, mileage is related to engine size, and so on. In other words, the environment of choosing an automobile is very complex composed of many interacting variables. To simplify the situation, some individuals will focus on certain variables and their interactions, whereas other individuals will focus on different ones. Once they have identified a few variables that they deem to be important, they are likely to negate other variables; otherwise, they risk cognitive confusion and chaos. As soon as they have developed a limited cognitive matrix, this will self-organize and become stable in that they will only consider automobiles that fit the characteristics of their cognitive model. I suppose automakers count on these self-organized differences among individuals because in that way they can build and sell many different types of cars. If people had not developed these different and stable cognitive models, I suppose we would all be driving exactly the same automobile in the same color.

A likely consequence of self-organization is the emergence of habits as part of human behavior. When a cognitive model becomes stabilized, that cognitive model will produce the same behavioral reactions to environmental stimuli, especially if the environment tends to be simple with little variation. In other words, using the same simple behavior as with a habit is energy efficient as the cognitive model remains the same and the behavior can become quite repetitive. William James, in his beautifully written chapter, describes habits as the enormous flywheel of society in that "habit simplifies the movements required to achieve a given result, makes them more accurate, and diminishes fatigue." James notes that habits increase our efficiency because they diminish the need for conscious attention when we are engaged in a behavior. In his description of the strength of habits, James writes:

> It alone prevents the hardest and most repulsive walks of life from being deserted by those brought up to tread therein. It keeps the fishermen and the deckhand at sea through the winter; it holds the miner in his darkness and nails the countrymen to his log cabin and his lonely farm through all the months of snow; it protects us from invasion by the natives of the desert and the frozen zone. It dooms us all to fight out the battle of life upon the lines of our nurture or are early choice, and to make the best of a pursuit that disagrees, because there is no other for which we are fitted, and it is too late to begin again. It keeps different social strata from mixing. Already at the age of 25 you see the professional mannerisms settling down on the young commercial traveler, on the young doctor, on the young minister, on the young counselor at law. You see the little lines of cleavage running through the character, the tricks of thought, the prejudices, the ways of the 'shop' in a word, from which the man can by-and-by no more escape than his coat-sleeve can suddenly fall into a new set of folds. On the whole it is best he should not escape. It is well for the world that in most of us, by the age of 30, the character has set like plaster, and will never soften again.

In terms of complexity theory, James is describing that self-organization once established is permanently maintained and cannot be changed or can only be changed with great intellectual effort. However, habits, as behavior, are based on cognitive models, and if an individual is to guide the development of habits into a useful path, it must occur in the initial formation of the cognitive model. James recognizes this in his discussion of the initial plasticity of habits.

This process of creating cognitive models based on a limited number of variables can lead to generating erroneous and even outlandish cognitive models which disregard valid facts about the universe. Unfortunately, this is not an uncommon process in human thinking. As any study of human behavior will show, many individuals have little problem with disregarding facts or put another way disregarding valid variables. As we shall see in the next section, human imagination is so flexible that it can create models of an exterior environment that does not or even cannot exist. I suppose this is a formal way of stating the simple fact that we can allow our beliefs to color or even disregard our understanding of our environment rather than having environmental information guide our beliefs.

Chapter 18
Predicting the Future

Abstract Prediction of the future in the long or short term is an essential survival skill for most higher life-forms. For humans, prediction requires a sound understanding of the interconnections between the past, present, and future because the prediction of future models requires both past and present information. The future predictions we humans construct are actually cognitive creations that do not exist in reality and therefore are very sensitive to errors. Generally, the accuracy of any future prediction decreases at a geometric rate with time because the complexity of future variables and their interactions also increases geometrically. In addition, the accuracy of any human prediction is affected by a number of factors. The stability of the environment is crucial because predictions in stable environments are likely to be more accurate than predicting events in a changing environment. Also, the prediction of events in a bottom-up environment will be more accurate than in a top-down environment. Similarly, prediction in a complex adaptive system is likely to be more accurate than prediction in a chaotic nonadaptive environment. The explanations for these general principles are discussed as well as predictions in large- and small-scale environments. Also discussed is the fact that predictions of social environments can be especially inaccurate due to the fact that social environments can be especially unstable. Knowledge of these principles can be a useful guide to making accurate predictions and knowing when to avoid making predictions.

Keywords Predictive ignorance · Compound and complex prediction · Additive prediction · Geometric prediction · Top-down prediction

Up to this point in our discussion, we have mainly dealt with cognitive models as static entities in the present time dimension. We have discussed the fact that although cognitive models are constantly changing, they still describe an environment as it presently exists. However, humans and other higher functioning organisms are continually involved in the process of creating future cognitive models of their environment because the ability to predict what is going to happen either in the immediate future or in the long term is essential. In that respect, we are creatures of constant prediction. Clark (2019) has an excellent discussion of human prediction in his text,

R. Leve, *The Complexity of Human Thought*,
https://doi.org/10.1007/978-3-031-09104-9_18

Surfing Uncertainty, in which he describes some of the neurological relationships in prediction and the top-down and bottom-up aspects of this crucial cognitive ability. Clark also points out that prediction, even in its most primitive form, is not only an ability possessed by all life-forms but also a necessary function if life-forms are going to survive.

Human cognition, and likely the thinking skills of many higher order organisms, usually incorporate some level of understanding of the past and the future. Obviously, the past, present, and future are time dimensions that are interconnected, and we are able to go back and forth between them in our thinking. Our ability to predict the future is particularly crucial for our functioning and even our very survival because thinking about the future and developing cognitive models that can or may exist allows for the cognitive skill of prediction. In Chap. 5, we discussed how children develop a sense of time including past and future and how the skill of future prediction tends to develop early in a child's developmental life. However, this cognitive skill involves a great deal of complexity which needs to be understood.

As verbal concepts, the notions of past, present, and future appear to be quite distinct, but from the point of view of human cognition, they are so closely interrelated that such distinctions may be meaningless. Obviously, in order to predict the future, that prediction needs to be based on environmental situations occurring presently or having occurred in the past or both. However, the anticipation of what is predicted to occur in the future will modify what is occurring in the present here and now. Since the arrow of time only moves in one direction, present or future behavior cannot affect what has occurred in the past, but the memory of past environments will no doubt determine the cognitive models of our present and future behavior. I suppose many memories and recollections of the past can be changed by what is occurring in the present and what we anticipate will occur in the future. That does not change the past, but it can change our recollection of the past. If this seems rather confusing, we only need to remember that in terms of cognition, we simply function in a closely interrelated matrix of time and events, and our predictions of our future will be determined by past and present events.

From this point on in our discussion of prediction, we need to understand future cognitive models as opposed to present cognitive models. Future cognitive models are creations, creations that don't yet exist; they are creations of what we anticipate a future environment will be, and our prediction will be based on present and past cognitive models. Perhaps, now we can see some of the complexity involved in creating future cognitive models. They depend upon and are related to the complexity of our past and present environments and the cognitive models that we created to understand those past and present environments. Based on those cognitive models of our existing environments, we can predict future environments with greater or lesser accuracy, and we can predict how we will understand and also be part of that future environment. Of course, our ordinary physical and social functioning as well as our very survival depends upon how accurately we can predict future cognitive models in spite of the fact that these future cognitive models do not exist in reality. Obviously, this ability to predict future cognitive models depends upon our understanding of time. Usually, most mature humans have a more than adequate grasp of the passage of time since we have divided it into convenient daily intervals based on the rotation of our planet and even yearly intervals based on our planet's rotation around our sun. At this point, I might be tempted to discuss the concept of time in terms of Einstein's special and general theory of relativity, but we need to limit our focus to a cognitive understanding of time.

Our cognitive processes provide us with a great deal of flexibility in understanding and manipulating time and the prediction of future events. We can speed up the dimension of time, slow it down, or even stop it in our thinking as if we were controlling the frame of a movie film. Our concept of cognitive time is closely related to our environment since time can seem to go very quickly or very slowly depending upon our situation. Perhaps this gives some hint as to the complexity and flexibility of future thinking and the creation of future cognitive models.

In an earlier discussion, we recognized the importance of the law of unintended consequences as a useful concept concerning unexpected errors in human prediction, but we need to understand the complexity principle underlying this law. Whenever we construct a predictive cognitive model, time is a crucial factor. The farther into the future we try to predict, the greater our chance of invoking the law of unintended consequences because there is likely to be an increase in the diversity of the environment. (I suppose there were few rats in the Parisian subway system the day after they removed the trash barrels, but by the time a month or two went by, I imagine the well-fed resident rats were having healthy babies and they may have even invited their rodent relatives into this wonderful garbage feast.) In addition, as the time span of our attempted prediction increases, the accuracy of that prediction is more likely to err because we are constructing future models based on a present environment. As a general rule, the greater the time span, the more opportunity for errors in our predictive models, and this may tend to follow a geometric rather than an arithmetic function. That means that as time increases arithmetically, the errors and irrelevance of a predictive model will increase exponentially (Fig. 18.1).

To provide an explanation of the exponential nature of this graph, we need to look at the relationship between variables, their interactions, and time. Since we live in a changing environment, we are likely to encounter more and more environmental variables with the increase in time. In other words, we can more accurately predict what we will be doing at 3:45 PM today than what we will be doing at 3:45 PM a month from now. If we try to predict what we will be doing at 3:45 PM five years from now, we certainly will have introduced even more errors in our prediction. The number of determinant variables within the same day will be much less than the number of determinant variables that can affect our behavior and schedule a month or five years into our future. As our expanse of time increases, the number of variables we encounter will increase and certainly will make predictions increasingly more inaccurate. In essence, we are dealing with an increasingly complex predictive situation with an increasing number of variables. For the most part, the number of variables that increase over time will tend to increase at an additive rate. In other words, the different variables in terms of experiences and other environmental stimuli will likely be the same from one day to the next, or from one time period to the

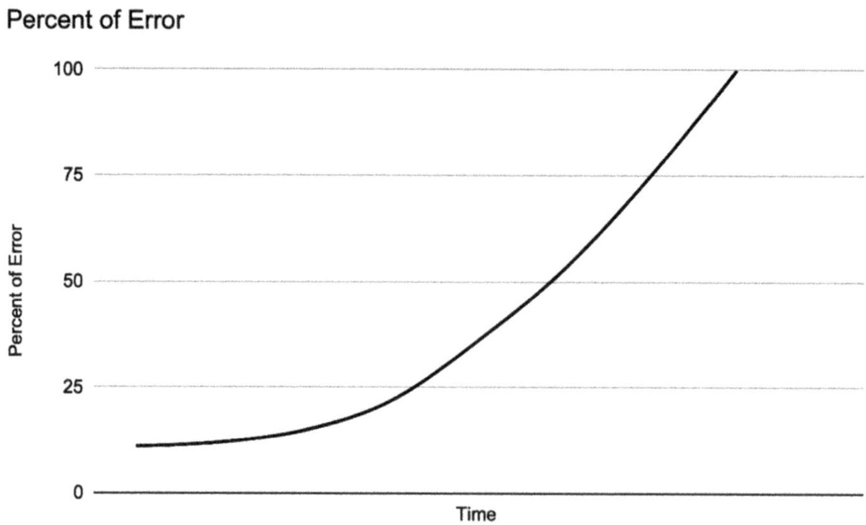

Fig. 18.1 This graph demonstrates how prediction error increases geometrically with time

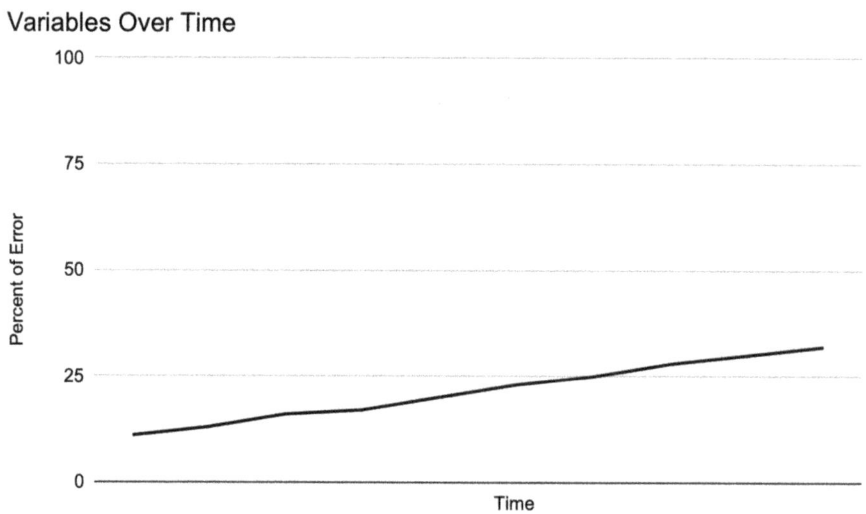

Fig. 18.2 This graph demonstrates the arithmetic increase in prediction errors as the number of environmental variables increases over time

next. Of course, there will be variations from one day to the next, but these will even out to an average number (Fig. 18.2).

Unless one inhabits a stable, unchanging exterior environment or one possesses a functioning crystal ball, human prediction is going to be flawed and increasingly error-prone as time increases. The situation becomes even more complex when we include the interactions between environmental variables. As diagramed in our earlier chapters, we are generating a dynamic matrix of variables where the change in one can produce changes in others, and this matrix becomes increasingly complex over time since the addition of more variables will greatly increase the number of interactions between those variables and these interactions will increase at an exponential rate (Fig. 18.3).

There are many examples of the fact that the farther we try to predict into the future, the more likely we are to incur the law of unintended consequences and a host of other prediction errors due to the many variables and variable interactions encountered. Looking at changes on a geological scale, most geologists would have a difficult time explaining the future movements of tectonic plates in any great detail. For example, trying to predict the size and location of mountains resulting from the collision of the North American and European plates in Nova Scotia 100 million years from now would be quite imprecise. Political proclamations over the course of history seem to document this phenomenon. Most political scientists would be hard-pressed to predict who would be elected president of the United States in 2044, and a sizable majority of US citizens were amazed at their error in assuming Donald Trump would not win the Presidency in 2016. Perhaps, one of the most erroneous political predictions was Adolf Hitler proclaiming that his Third Reich would last 1000 years. It fell woefully short of that prediction (thankfully) and only lasted 12 years. Hitler did not realize how drastically the world environment would change within four short years. Over that time span, the USA entered the war, bringing with it an increase in sophisticated technology including improved nautical sonar, better use of radar, more sophisticated and lethal airplanes, and finally, the development of the atomic bomb. These technological advances also

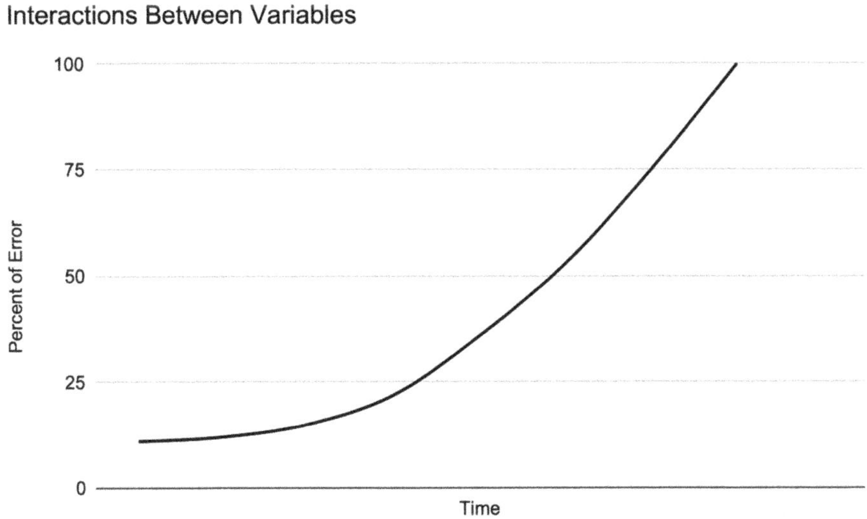

Fig. 18.3 This graph demonstrates the geometric increase in prediction error as variable interactions increase over time

interacted with one another. For example, radar and the advanced B-52 bomber enabled the delivery of the two atom bombs dropped on Japan.

Accurate prediction in social environments is especially difficult and fraught with errors because of the complexity of social environments. Social environments not only contain many interacting variables, but those variables are other people whose behavior is constantly changing. To truly understand the complexity of social environments, we need to realize that each human agent in this matrix of social variables is also engaged in creating future cognitive models which contain the errors of that agent's predictions. Thus, in order to make any accurate future predictions, we need to accurately understand our environment to minimize our future predicted errors and then be able to understand and correct the errors inherent in the future cognitive models of those human agents who inhabit or will inhabit our social environment. Understanding the predictive complexity of one's own environment is a difficult enough task, but to then understand the total social environment well enough to understand and analyze the predictive errors of others is exceedingly difficult and requires an unusual talent in understanding others. In essence, we are dealing with the complexity of our own social environment compounded by the complexity of the social environments of others, which introduces a huge degree of complexity.

To better understand predictive cognitive models, we need to recognize the fact that in this situation, time and complexity are related and there is a general but imprecise relationship between them. Thus, as a general rule, the complexity of an interactive variable matrix will increase with the passage of time. However, depending upon the situation, predictive errors can also occur in a reasonably short period of absolute time so long as the complexity of the interactive variable matrix increases exponentially within that period of time. That means that in terms of prediction time is a relative concept and is determined by the rate at which our complex matrix changes. Thus, even in short-time span situations, the rate at which variables and their interactions can change is quite rapid, and attempting to accurately predict the future will result in many errors.

An excellent example is the stock market and currency trading. Trying to predict the value of stocks or currency even within a day or a week is very difficult, and attempts to do so have often resulted in the financial deterioration of many brokers. The obvious problem with this kind of prediction is that the stock market and currency trading are related to a host of economic, political, and even weather variables that are constantly changing and interacting with each other even though these changes occur within a relatively short period of time. In that respect, our graph indicating the exponential relationship between prediction errors and time is accurate so long as we realize that time is a function that tends to increase the interactive variables in any exterior environment.

To summarize, we need to recognize that the accuracy of future prediction is seldom perfect because we are dealing with complex past, present, and future interactive environments. As a rather general rule, we can say that the accuracy of future predictions depends upon the complexity of the future environment, the number of interactive associations in that future environment, and the length of time in the prediction. In other words, the accuracy of future predictions decreases as the number of variables and associations in an environment increases and the predicted passage of time increases. A simple way of stating this is to say that the more inherent complexity in an environment, the poorer our ability to predict that environment. In more prosaic terms, don't bet a lot of money when you are trying to make predictions in a very complex environment into a distant future. Of course, that is not likely to stop us egocentric humans from such predictive speculation, but we had better be careful if we try to rely on such predictions, especially if money or romance is involved.

Predictions in Compound and Complex Environments

In an earlier chapter, we identified the differences between compound and complex environments and the unique properties of each. By way of a quick review, in compound environments there are no associations or interactions between variables, whereas in complex environments there are interactions between the variables such that a change in one variable will cause a change in one or more other variables. In this section, we need to look at how each of these situations affects our ability to predict the future. Coping with complex environments requires first a recognition that they are complex and then an understanding that they must be simplified in order to be understood and not understanding the properties of a complex environment is likely to result in cognitive chaos. A complex environment is something that exists in the exterior world, but for us humans and other highly cognitively functioning organisms to understand that complex exterior environment, it must become a complex cognitive model. Perhaps it would be more accurate to describe such models as complex cognitive environments. Basically, complex cognitive environments will have a number of variables, but most importantly, they will have many interactions between the variables such that changes in one or any can result in changes in the others, sometimes including catastrophic changes. The degree of complexity of an environment does not depend on the number of variables in the environment but rather on the number of interactions between those variables. An environment that has a number of variables without any interactions between them is not really a complex environment but might be best described as a compound environment. Compound cognitive environments might have a number of variables, but compound environments are much simpler, will tend to be static, and will be resistant to change. Algebraically, this is a simple additive situation where the complexity of the environment is equal to the sum of the number of variables; however, if these variables have interconnections, then this is a geometric situation, and the complexity of the cognitive environment can far exceed the number of discrete variables. It is the existence of interactions between variables that allows for the more confusing properties of complexity to occur.

In one sense, complexity science depends upon and is a study of interactions. In order to understand some of the concepts of complexity science, one must be aware of and study the interactions between variables in a complex environment. For example, self-organization is only going to occur in an interactive environment where the effect of variables can be changed because interactions are a form of communication between variables. In that way, a change in the external environment can bring about a new self-organized pattern. This can be seen by looking at a line of ants building a bridge composed of ant bodies when it contacts a water obstacle. This self-organized bridge building can only occur if the ants have some form of interactive communication among themselves. In other words, any ant approaching the bridge under construction must know the position of other ants in order to accurately and successfully place their body to a position which will result in a useful and completed bridge of ants. If they were not able to interact with each other, they would likely form a random pattern of individual ants wandering about near the start of the obstacle. This kind of interaction means that the ants must be able to predict the future by knowing or anticipating the position of other ants. The time period of prediction for an ant may be quite short, but it still requires a predictive model of the location of other ants and an anticipation, however primitive, of the location of the bridge in relation to the obstacle.

A similar situation occurs when agents such as geese fly in a V pattern or baitfish form a tight ball flocking together according to simple rules. If the geese had no interaction or a fixed unchanging interaction with one another, they are likely to form a random and disorganized flight pattern. In actuality, the flocking behavior of migratory geese shows that the interaction between them changes within the overall V-shaped pattern of the flock. The V-shaped pattern of the flock may be stable, but there is movement between individual geese such that each individual goose will be in a different position in the flock over time. To do that, the geese must have some sort of visual communication so that they respond to the differing flight positions of their neighbors. If a flock of geese never changed so that each individual goose stayed in the same place, that would be a compound flock of geese, but it would be a very inefficient form of migration. The few lead geese would quickly get tired and, likely, quite irritated with the laggard geese who were cruising along in the beneficial helpful air currents. As with our busy bridge-building ants, the geese need to be sensitive to the interactions between other geese and have a short-term prediction of the future location of the other geese in their V pattern.

Similarly, the concept of emergence also depends on interactions between variables and is unlikely to occur if there is no opportunity for the variables to interact over time. Although I am not a great fan of the meteorological butterfly example, it will serve as a useful metaphor to explain this point. The butterfly effect postulates that wind created by a butterfly flapping its wings in the Amazon can create a hurricane that eventually devastates the Caribbean Islands and coastal American cities. Obviously, for this to happen, the butterflies flapping must interact with another air current, which then must interact with moisture differences, air mass heat differentials, weather fronts, and so on and on until it finally generates a hurricane. In other words, there must be a series of interactions between different meteorological variables to finally produce the hurricane. If our heroic butterfly flaps its wings and the minuscule wind created does not interact with any other weather variable, then it is just an isolated variable with no interconnections and will never produce a hurricane. The interaction between variables in this situation is likely to be critical in terms of its values. We might speculate that the butterfly needs to flap its wings to create the perfect wind current, neither too fast nor too slow, which must interact with a certain humidity level, again neither too humid nor not humid enough, and so on to generate our hurricane. We can describe this situation in another way by saying that the butterfly effect requires a large number of variables with many interactions over some period of time. In other words, we are dealing with a very complex interactive environment which will be extraordinarily difficult to predict. Predicting the hurricane would mean creating a future cognitive model, and accurately predicting such an occurrence from our heroic little butterfly is well-nigh impossible.

We have already discussed the fact that cognitive models are mental representations of environmental variables, and such models must also contain the interactions between the cognitive variables that represent the interactions of the exterior environment. Thus, cognitive models are composed of the many variables that represent the exterior environment; however, it is the number of interactions between those environmental variables that determines the complexity of our cognitive model and whether it will fall into a state of chaos. Obviously, this also applies to the future cognitive models that we create to predict and anticipate our future environments. As already noted, predicting future cognitive models of our environment can be quite problematic in terms of accuracy, especially if we are trying to predict a future environment that has many changing interactions. That's because the cognitive model we predict for the future is likely to deviate from the actual future environment, which is another way of saying, "predicting the future is dicey at best." I suppose this discussion is rather obtuse in dealing with existing environments, future environments, and the cognitive model of what we predict to be the future environment, but that is what we are constantly doing, either consciously or unconsciously, whether trying to solve a scientific problem or just going about our daily activities.

As a general rule, people tend to overestimate the accuracy with which they can predict the future. As we have seen, the accuracy of our future predictions declines geometrically as the number of variables, interactions, and time span increases. Much of the time, we humans are trying to make predictions in political, social, and economic spheres which contain too many variables and interactions and which are likely to change over even short time spans. Attempting to predict a future economy or any part of it is fraught with dangerous inaccuracies because there are so many variables including many that can't even be identified. Even small national economies are likely to have a huge number of interactive economic variables. I imagine prediction would be better in a simple barter economy over a short time span, but the complexity of variables and interactions in a modern national economy is mind-boggling. There are many individuals attempting to predict the future of the US stock market including financial analysts, stockbrokers, and day traders, and all of them are willing to offer encouraging financial predictions, but those who have made accurate predictions are likely equaled by those whose predictions did not work out, contributing to the financial detriment of their clients. The only prediction that seems reliable is that if the overall national economy expands, the overall stock market will also expand, but only over long periods of time that cancel out short-term variations, and even this principle of prediction does not hold in the face of great political, social, and natural upheavals.

Perhaps physicians are in the most difficult social situation in terms of the predictions they need to make for the health of their patients. The accuracy of a physician's diagnosis is crucial to the prediction of what treatment will result in the best outcome. What we are describing is a medical situation involving a number of symptom variables, many of which will interact with each other, resulting in a diagnosis which will hopefully predict one or more treatments which will also interact with each other. That is a very complex interactive situation! The ICD-10, the international physicians' guide to diagnoses, lists over 70,000 different codes, which means that physicians are dealing with a universe of over 70,000 diagnoses. Thankfully, this universe of variables will be greatly limited to a subset that is related to the presenting problems, lab information, and intuition of the physician. However, the physician must generate a present cognitive model concerning the patient's present situation and a future cognitive model based on a proposed treatment and prognosis. This can be a simple situation where the symptoms are such that a diagnosis and treatment are closely related, so there are few interactions between related diagnoses. If the treatment protocol is also obvious, then there will be few interactions between different diagnoses and different treatments. However, most medical situations are more complex and require the skill of an experienced and knowledgeable physician. Oftentimes, they will be interactions between diagnoses such that the choice of one will have a relationship or connection with others. Similarly, there will be interactions between different treatments such that the use of one will affect or may preclude the use of another, and of course, there are interactions between diagnoses and treatments. Obviously, both medical diagnoses and treatment are complex interactive medical situations which need to generate an accurate future cognitive model. There is little wonder that the training of a physician involves years of study and many more years of residencies and clinical practice. I am reminded of the words of a close friend and very competent and caring physician, "I try my best but many times its nature that cures and I get the recognition".

Ignorance of the Environment and Prediction

Throughout our previous discussions on cognition, we have focused on how our cognitive models and future cognitive models allow us to understand the complex exterior environments we inhabit by reducing the number of variables and associated interactions that are relevant to our functioning. However, there are situations in which our attempt to understand a complex exterior environment fails and we accept ignorance for that particular complex exterior environment. There are two general situations where this occurs. The first is when we cannot identify any variables that are relevant to generating a cognitive model. The second situation is when there are so many variables and interactions between them that any attempt to generate a future cognitive model would result in cognitive chaos. There seems to be no complexity in the first situation, and in the second situation, the complexity is so overwhelming that it cannot be understood. In that situation, we are likely to delay or give up any attempt at creating a relevant future cognitive model, and that may be the best decision. These two situations are not as disparate as they might seem, especially since both result in ignorance of the exterior environment and an inability to create a predictive cognitive model that allows us to understand and cope with changes in our environment. Neither of these situations are unnecessarily as negative as they might seem because accepting ignorance of our environment may be quite functional. Accepting that there are aspects of an environment that cannot be understood may prevent us from attempting a dysfunctional and impulsive solution, and perhaps simply allowing time to pass or for the environment to change may result in our ability to eventually better understand the environmen and generate an accurate future prediction.

Choosing to do nothing and avoiding any prediction means that we have decreased the number of variables and their interactions to zero, which greatly simplifies our future cognitive model. In that situation, we have a frozen predictive cognitive model with one variable and no interactions. At best, that is a simple additive model rather than a geometric model. That means that patience in the face of ignorance is often the best solution. Unfortunately, we humans are not terribly accepting of ignorance, and so we may insist that we do understand the variables and interactions in our environment even when such an understanding is flawed or completely irrelevant. A common but usually flawed attempt to deal with a situation of environmental ignorance is to focus on one or a few irrelevant or erroneous variables in an attempt to create a cognitive model. In other words, we might choose variables that are irrelevant, or we might misconstrue or ignore interactions between variables, and these will result in a dysfunctional future cognitive model. Accepting ignorance of our exterior environment is often a better solution than the choice of some erroneous solution because accepting what we do not understand leaves open the possibility of future efforts of understanding, whereas accepting an erroneous solution stops any further investigation of the environment, perhaps permanently or at least until the effects of utilizing an erroneous cognitive model are detected often because of unpleasant consequences.

Complex Cognitive Factors Affecting Prediction

Prediction in Stable Environments

There are two general categories that affect an individual's ability to predict the future; the individual's environment and the individual's cognitive abilities, and these are interrelated. Obviously, prediction in an environment that is stable and has few changes will be more accurate. I certainly would have little difficulty predicting the shape of the granite boulder resting alongside my driveway 10 years in the future. It is a single variable in my domestic environment, has little to no interactions with anything else, and would hardly tax the accuracy of my future cognitive model concerning that boulder. As a general rule, the more stable the environment, the more accurate one's prediction of the future. Obviously, the opposite is also true. Attempting to make accurate predictions in an unstable, changing, and interactive environment will be quite difficult, and as already has been mentioned, attempting predictions in a social environment can be especially problematic.

Prediction in Self-Organized Systems

Many of the concepts in complexity science can be quite useful in determining whether a future cognitive model will make accurate predictions or poor ones. For example, phenomena that are self-organized are easier to predict for the obvious reason that there had to be a purpose or cause for the self-organization to occur, and as long as that purpose remains, the self-organization is likely to continue. That is another way of saying self-organization has created a stable environment and so predicting that environment will be more accurate. Earlier, we discussed how Antarctica penguins self-organize into a large group facing into the wind with each individual penguin remaining huddled within the group, but slowly moving forward until any individual penguin had moved to the front of the group and was now facing the full force of the wind. Of course, at that point, our penguin peeled off, walked to the rear of the group, and once again was sheltered from the cold winds. So long as the freezing Antarctic winds continued to blow, the huddled mass of penguins would remain, and we could safely predict the general location and existence of the huddled mass of penguins. Within some degree of error, we might even be able to predict the position of individual penguins within the flock. Our group of penguins formed as a reaction to the bitter Antarctic wind, and so long as the wind creates a purpose for their self-organized huddling behavior, this social phenomenon of penguin huddling will be easily and accurately predicted.

As I mentioned earlier every semester, my students present me with an example of almost perfect predictability. I do not assign classroom seats; however, by the second class, the students take the same seats, and this self-organized seating pattern never varies. With rare exceptions, I can predict the future seating behavior of every student in my class perfectly. I've often wondered if that perfectly predictable seating pattern would continue indefinitely across many semesters. I think it would, which makes me muse on the cognitive similarity of university students and penguins. Of course, I likely did the same when I was a student.

Prediction in Complex Adaptive Systems

Predicting the behavior of complex adaptive systems will also tend to be accurate since such systems are also inherently stable. Complex adaptive systems tend to be self-perpetuating because they are adapting to the specific requirements of their environmental system. In a complex adaptive system, the different parts of the system will remain in balance within certain parameters. In other words, there are reciprocal interactions between all the variables of the overall system. As a simple example, we might look at the food and waste requirements in large cities or small towns. The food consumption of their citizens might vary from one week to the next but only within limited bounds. As food consumption varies, supermarkets and other local stores might increase or decrease their food orders. This bounded increase in food orders might also affect the amount of garbage generated and will increase or decrease the work of the local sanitation workers. In this adaptive system, predicting the amount of food imported, the amount of waste produced, the amount of time and energy of local sanitation workers, and perhaps any increase or decrease in the number of food delivery trucks should be fairly accurate.

Of course, the adaptive interactions of this system could be interrupted by the arrival of a significant snowstorm which would certainly affect the accuracy of predicting any of these variables. However, if we were to include the severity of the snowstorm as part of our complex adaptive system, we might accurately predict the number of food trucks on the road or the number of bread loaves on store shelves. So long as the system remains in an adaptive balance, it will help us increase the accuracy of our prediction. Thus, recognizing that we are predicting the elements of a complex adaptive system should provide more confidence in our predictions. The opposite is also true. Attempting prediction in a random system will always be inaccurate because such systems are unstable, and they can change rapidly due to unexpected emergent influences and random changes in variables. The problem with attempting to predict in such a chaotic system is that changes can occur in one or more variables and because those variables interact with other variables the system may not adapt to such changes causing the system to fall apart and become unpredictable.

Prediction in "Bottom-Up" and "Top-Down" Systems

As a general rule, predicting the future behavior and decisions in bottom-up social systems will be more accurate than predicting the behavior and decisions in top-down systems. The accuracy of prediction is improved because bottom-up systems are likely more stable than top-down systems. Bottom-up systems are the creation of a large number of individuals and will tend to be self-correcting toward a general social mean or median of that group. If one individual deviates in an unpredictable direction from the central ideas and decisions of the overall group, other more conservative individuals will tend to moderate the individual outliers. Another way to understand this difference in prediction is to realize that agents in a bottom-up systems will have similar interactive associations between the agents. Thus, a change in one agent is not likely to affect all the other agents. In fact, the greater number of other agents is more likely to bring you an agreement with the preponderance of the greater group. Of course, bottom-up groups may make risky decisions because, as shown by the *Risky Shift Phenomenon* in social psychology, the danger and responsibility of a risky decision are shared among the group members. Nevertheless, the risky behavior and decisions are predictable, whereas accurately predicting the risky behavior of an individual is more difficult. That individual may choose to repeat their previous behaviors and, in that way, be predictable, but predicting when that person will decide to deviate from past activities and ideas will be quite difficult.

The behaviors in a top-down system are likely to be made by one or a very few individuals, and so they will not have the conservative self-correction of a bottom-up group. The predicted behavior of an individual in a top-down group may be quite stable but is more susceptible to emergence influences and other environmental changes. This difference between the two systems can often be seen in political situations. The decisions and behaviors of dictators are likely to be less predictable than those of a large group of citizens in a bottom-up democracy. Since dictators are a single variable, there are no interconnections with other agents to modify extreme beliefs and behaviors, and in a single variable top-down system, there can be no self-correcting influence. Dictators may also be inclined to change their behaviors or dictums in the face of any perceived threat to their status or their life. Of course, we need to remember that knowing whether a system is bottom-up or top-down is only a general rule of prediction, and history has shown that accurate or poor prediction is possible in either situation.

Prediction in Large- and Small-Scale Environments

Scale refers to the actual or perceived size of any phenomenon. As we develop cognitive models that reflect our exterior environments, we naturally see our environments as composed of many diverse parts which are the stimuli for the development of our cognitive models. Some of these parts of our environment we see as large-scale, whereas others we will see on a small scale, and this has important implications for our predictions of the future. As was previously noted, predicting the future is anticipating the way in which our environment changes over time in terms of its many characteristics such as movement, size, position, and even the very existence of that environment. As a general rule, predictive cognitive models will be more accurate in predicting large-scale phenomena in our environment and less accurate in predicting small-scale phenomena, and this finding has to do with the level of precision associated with large- and small-scale prediction.

Small-scale phenomena as by their very nature are less obvious, therefore less likely to be noticed, and their importance may not be recognized, whereas large-scale phenomena are likely to be recognized because they are larger and more obvious. Therefore, small-scale items are less likely to be included in a predictive cognitive model. If there are many small-scale items, then any particular one is likely to get lost among the many other items. As an example, we can look at the predictions of storms at sea. Certainly, we can predict the general behavior of a hurricane (within some limits) since it is a large-scale event, but trying to predict the formation and dissipation of a particular wave within that hurricane would be impossible because it is a small-scale object within a huge number of other small-scale waves. We can certainly predict that waves will form and disappear and each will be slightly different from the others, but even if we were able to see the many waves in our hurricane, we would hardly possess the precision to predict the formation and life span of a particular wave from the others. We could use statistical techniques to predict the overall behavior of waves within a hurricane, but that is an approach that does not identify our particular wave, and all statistical methods contain and accept a certain degree of error. However, the overall hurricane is a rather large-scale event that can hardly be missed and ignored in our cognitive models and predictions of its motion, wind direction, and strength, could hardly be ignored in a predictive cognitive model of the weather.

Another factor explaining the difference between prediction in a small- and large-scale environment has to do with the fact that large-scale phenomenon is composed of many parts whereas small-scale phenomenon is by nature simpler with fewer elements. As changes occur in a future environment, a large-scale phenomenon will be more robust and will not be affected by changes because any change will need to have its effects on all or most parts of the large-scale phenomenon. While certain parts of a large-scale phenomenon might be sensitive to the change, other parts are likely to be unaffected, and so there will be little or no overall change in that entity. Small-scale entities might have only one or a few elements, and so a new environmental stimulus can more easily change the small-scale entity. If there are fewer elements to change and a significant number of those elements are susceptible to new environmental influences, then the small-scale entity will be easier to change.

A good example of this aspect of this rule is predicting changes in cultures rather than changes in individuals of that culture. With the exception of revolutions which are rare events, cultural change occurs very slowly. Among many others, the Russian and Chinese cultures have for many centuries had top-down authoritarian political cultures whether it was Czars, Emperors, Communist leaders, or seemingly elected leaders, and this has continued in some form to the present day. Revolutions and protests have occurred in these cultures, but the culture has only made very small changes. Predicting significant changes in these cultures composed of many parts (people) is unlikely to be in error because their inherent complexity makes them very stable. Any study of their history documents a very slow rate of change in cultures, and so our predictive cognitive models will be most accurate by assuming no or little changes in that culture. There are always "experts" who will predict catastrophic changes, but they are seldom correct and their erroneous predictions are usually forgotten after a period of time.

Individuals within a culture are small-scale entities and their beliefs, opinions, and behaviors are likely to vary more than the properties of their culture, and therefore individual beliefs and behaviors are less predictable. They are more likely to change in response to an environmental event, personal fortune or misfortune, and even a casual remark from a friend. They still may have core beliefs, but their opinion of environmental events can vary. The prejudice that has existed in American culture initiated by the system of the slavery of African Americans has slowly changed over the past three centuries, but that change has been very slow, and still exists in many forms and is not difficult to predict.

In respect to individual Americans, some still harbor that prejudice, but those individual beliefs can be and are often changed by events or personal encounters, and such personal social changes are likely to be reasonably rapid compared to the slow pace of American cultural change. Predicting the extent of racial prejudice in American culture is much easier and more accurate than predicting that level of prejudice within an individual. The extent and type of racial prejudice among any particular individual would be very difficult to predict with certainty unless we had definitive knowledge of that individual's beliefs, but that is not prediction. That is certainty based on valid knowledge.

As a final thought, we must realize that these rules about the accuracy of predictive cognitive models are only general rules and do not apply in all situations. Our world is too diverse and complex to have rules that are perfectly accurate in all situations. Perfect prediction only exists in mathematical equations, and only if we have selected the correct variables and their quantities. If we are generating predictive cognitive models to help us understand and survive the environment we inhabit, then these rules might be useful in judging the accuracy of those models. Having knowledge (and some humility) about our predictions will be important information to guide how we navigate our universe. However, just as human prediction is by its very nature a flawed human enterprise, any rules or guides about prediction will also not be accurate in individual situations.

Now that I have come to the end of the last chapter and the end of this text, I believe I can describe this text in a single sentence. To understand any complex environment, first, reduce the number of variables in the environment and, second, minimize the number of interactions between them. Perhaps that is a definition of creativity and intelligence.

References

Aboraya, A. (2007). The reliability of psychiatric diagnoses. *Psychiatry (Edgmont), 4*(1), 22–25. Published online, Jan.

Alexander, R. D. (1987). *The biology of moral systems*. Aldine de Gruyter.

Allsopp, K., Read, J., Corcoran, R., & Kinderman, P. (2019). Heterogeneity in psychiatric diagnostic classification. *Psychiatry Research, 279*, 15. https://doi.org/10.1016/j.psychres.2019.07.005

Angner, E. (2016). *A course in behavioral economics* (2nd ed.). Palgrave Macmillan.

Aristotle. (1957). *De Anima (on the soul), Aristotle*. Harvard University Press.

Ash, P. (1949). The reliability of psychiatric diagnoses. *The Journal of Abnormal and Social Psychology, 44*(2), 272–276. https://doi.org/10.1037/h0058417

Badgerow, J. P. (1988). An analysis of function in the formation flight of Canada geese. *The Auk, 105*(4), 749–755. https://www.jstor.org/stable/4087389

Ballatt, J., & Campling, P. (2011). *Intelligent kindness: Reforming the culture of healthcare*. RCPsych Publications.

Barton, S. (1994). Chaos, self-organization, and psychology. *American Psychologist, 49*(1), 5–14.

Basar, E. (Ed.). (1990). *Chaos in brain function*. Springer-Verlag.

Bejan, A. (2016). *The physics of life: The evolution of everything*. St Martins Press.

Cassier, E. (1950). *The problem of knowledge*. Yale University Press.

Chanute, O. (1997). *Progress in flying machines*. Dover.

Clark, A. (2019). Surfing Uncertainty:Prediction, Action, and the Embodied Mind. Oxford University Press.

Clayton, P., & Davies, P. (2006). *The re-emergence of emergence: The emergent hypothesis from science to religion*. Oxford University Press.

Cordier, P., Mendes France, M., Pailhous, J., & Bolon, P. (1994). Entropy as a global variable of the learning process. *Human Movement Science, 13*, 745–763.

Crouch, T. D. (2002). *A dream of wings; Americans and the airplane, 1875–1905*. Norton.

Dawkins, R. (1976). *The selfish gene*. Oxford University Press.

Dennis, W. (1960). Causes of retardation among institutionalized children. *The Journal of Genetic Psychology: Research and Theory on Human Development, 96*, 47–59.

Edelman, G. M. (1992). *Bright air, brilliant fire: On the matter of the mind*. Basic Books.

Freeman, W. (1991). The physiology of perception. *Scientific American, 264*, 78–85.

Friedlander, S. (2007). The Years of Extermination: Nazi Germany and the Jews, 1939-1945. Harper Collins.

Goldberger, L. (1966). Experimental isolation: An overview. *The American Journal of Psychiatry, 122*(7), 774–782.

Goudsmit, A. L. (Ed.). (1989). *Self-organization in psychotherapy*. Springer-Verlag.

R. Leve, *The Complexity of Human Thought*,
https://doi.org/10.1007/978-3-031-09104-9

Harari, Y. (2015). Sapiens: *A brief history of humankind*. Harper Collins.

Holden, A. V. (1986). *Chaos*. Princeton University Press.

Holland, J. (1996). *Hidden order, how adaptation builds complexity*. Addison-Wesley.

Hoyert, M. S. (1992). Order and chaos in fixed interval schedules of reinforcement. *Journal of the Experimental Analysis of Behavior, 57*, 339–363.

Inchingolo, G. M. (1994). Psycho-biological adaptive dynamics in aging populations. *Archives of Gerontology and Geriatrics, 4*, 107–116.

Jablensky, A. (2016). Psychiatric classifications: Validity and utility. *World Psychiatry, 15*(1), 26–31.

Jakab, P., & Young, R. (2000). *The published writings of Wilbur and Orville Wright*. Smithsonian Institution Press.

Jakab, P. L. (1990). *Visions of a flying machine*. Smithsonian Institution Press.

James, W. (1950). *The principles of psychology*. Holt, Rinehart, & Winston.

Jantsch, E. (1980). *The self-organizing universe*. Pergamon Press.

Judsmit, A. L. (Ed.). (1989). *Self-organization in psychotherapy*. Springer-Verlag.

Kauffman, S. A. (1985). Self-organization, selective adaptation and its limits: A new pattern of inference in evolution and development. In J. DePew & B. H. Weber (Eds.), *Evolution at the crossroads*. MIT Press.

Kauffman, S. A. (1986). Developmental logic and its evolution. *BioEssays, 6*, 82.

Kauffman, S. A. (1991). Antichaos and adaptation. *Scientific American., 265*, 78.

Kauffman, S. A. (1993). *The origins of order*. Oxford University Press.

Kauffman, S. A. (1995). *At home in the universe*. Oxford University Press.

Kincanon, E., & Powel, W. (1995). Chaotic analysis in psychology and psychoanalysis. *Journal of Psychology, 129*(5), 495–505.

Koestler, A., & Smythies, J. (1972). *Beyond reductionism: New perspectives in the life sciences*. Hutchinson.

Kogan, L., Saslow, L., Impett, E., Oveis, C., Keltner, D., & Saturn, S. (2017). *Thin-slicing study of the oxytocin receptor (OXTR) gene and the evaluation and expression of the prosocial disposition*. Proceeding of the National Academy of Science of the United States.

Langton, C. (1990). *Adaptation to the edge of chaos*. Presented at the Second Artificial Life Conference, Santa Fe, N.M.

Levav, I., Ran, A., & Turetsky, N. (1984). Diagnostic reliability among psychiatrists: Results of two exercises. *Israel Journal of Psychiatry and Related Sciences, 21*(4), 217–233.

Leve, R. (2004). Informational acquisition and cognitive models. *Complexity, 9*(1), 31–37.

Leve, R. (2006). Cognition, complexity, and the principles of flight. *Complexity, 11*(3), 11–19.

Leve, R. M., & Neese, W. (2011). *Time as a factor in complex multi-interactive problems*. Eighth International Conference on Complex Systems, New England Complex Systems Institute.

Lilienthal, O. (2001). *Bird flight as the basis of aviation*. Markowski International Publishers.

Lissaman, P. B. S., & Shollenberger, C. A. (1970). Formation flight of birds. *Science, 168*(3934), 1003–1005. https://www.jstor.org/stable/1729351

Little, W. A. (1974). The existence of persistent states in the brain. *Mathematical Biosciences, 19*, 101.

Luhmann, N. (1995). *Social systems*. Stanford University Press.

Marshall, A. (2002). *The utility of nature*. Imperial College Press.

Martin, S. J., Funch, R. R., Hanson, P. R., & Yoo, E.-H. (2018). A vast 4,000-year-old spatial pattern of termite mounds. *Current Biology, 28*, 1292–1293. https://doi.org/10.1016/j.cub.2018.09.061

McFarland, M. W. (2001a). *The papers of Wilbur and Orville Wright; volume 1, 1899–1905*. McGraw-Hill.

McFarland, M. W. (2001b). *The papers of Wilbur and Orville Wright; volume 2, 1906–1948*. McGraw-Hill.

Miller, M. (2009). *Complexity: A guided tour*. Oxford University Press.

Morowitz, H. (2002). *The emergence of everything, how the world became complex*. Oxford University Press.

Morrison, F. (1991). *The art of modeling dynamic systems*. Wiley.

Needham, J., Ling, W., & Gwei-Djen, L. (1971). *Science and civilization in China* (Vol. 4). Cambridge University Press.

Nelson, C. A., III, Zeanah, C. H., Fox, N. A., Marshall, P. J., Smyke, A. T., & Guthrie, D. (2007). Cognitive recovery in socially deprived young children: The Bucharest early intervention project. *Science, 318*, 1937–1940. https://doi.org/10.1126/science.1143921

Odum, H. T. (1988). Self-organization, transformity, & information. *Science, 242*, 1132–1139.

Piaget, J. (1954). *The construction of reality in the child*. Basic Books.

Piaget, J. (1969). *The Child's conception of time*. Ballantine Books.

Pirk, C. W. W., Hepburn, H. R., Radloff, S. E., & Tautz, J. (2004). Honeybee combs: Construction through a liquid equilibrium process? *Naturwissenschaften, 91*, 350–353. https://doi.org/10.1007/s00114-004-0539-3

Prigogine, I., & Stangers, I. (1984). *Order out of chaos: Man's new dialogue with nature*. Bantam Books.

Rees, L. (2005). Aushwitz: *A new history*. Mjf Books.

Schmid, G. B. (1991). Chaos theory and schizophrenia: Elementary aspects. *Psychopathology, 24*, 185–198.

Steinhoff, J., (1994). Voices from the Third Reich: An Oral History. De Capo Press.

Thaler, R. (2015). *Misbehaving. The making of behavioral economics*. Norton.

Titmuss, R. M. (1977). *The gift relationship: from human blood to social policy*. Exp. sub. edn. New Press.

Trivers, R. (1971). The evolution of reciprocal altruism. *The Quarterly Review of Biology, 46*(1), 35–57. http://www.jstor.org/stable/2822435?origin=JSTOR-pdf

Vandervert, L. R. (1995). Chaos theory and the evolution of consciousness and mind: A thermodynamic-holographic resolution to the mind body problem. *New Ideas in Psychol., 15*(2), 107–127.

Weinberger, E. D. (1991). Local properties of the NK model, a tuneably rugged energy landscape. *Physical Review A, 44*, 6399.

Werner, E. (1972). Infants around the world: Cross-cultural studies of psychomotor development from birth to two years. *Journal of Cross-Cultural Psychology, 3*(2).

Wolfram, S. (2002). *A new kind of science*. Wolfram Media.

Wright, O. (1998). *How we invented the airplane*. Dover Publications.

Wright, O., & Wright, W. (1953). *The papers of Wilber and Orville Wright volume 1 and 2*, M. W. McFarland (Ed.). McGraw Hill.

Wright, W. (1909). How to glide and soaring flight. *Flight*, 400–417.

Index

R. Leve, *The Complexity of Human Thought*,
https://doi.org/10.1007/978-3-031-09104-9

GPSR Compliance
The European Union's (EU) General Product Safety Regulation (GPSR) is a set of rules that requires consumer products to be safe and our obligations to ensure this.

If you have any concerns about our products, you can contact us on

ProductSafety@springernature.com

In case Publisher is established outside the EU, the EU authorized representative is:

Springer Nature Customer Service Center GmbH
Europaplatz 3
69115 Heidelberg, Germany

www.ingramcontent.com/pod-product-compliance
Lightning Source LLC
Chambersburg PA
CBHW071251140426
43118CB00003B/124
9783031091032